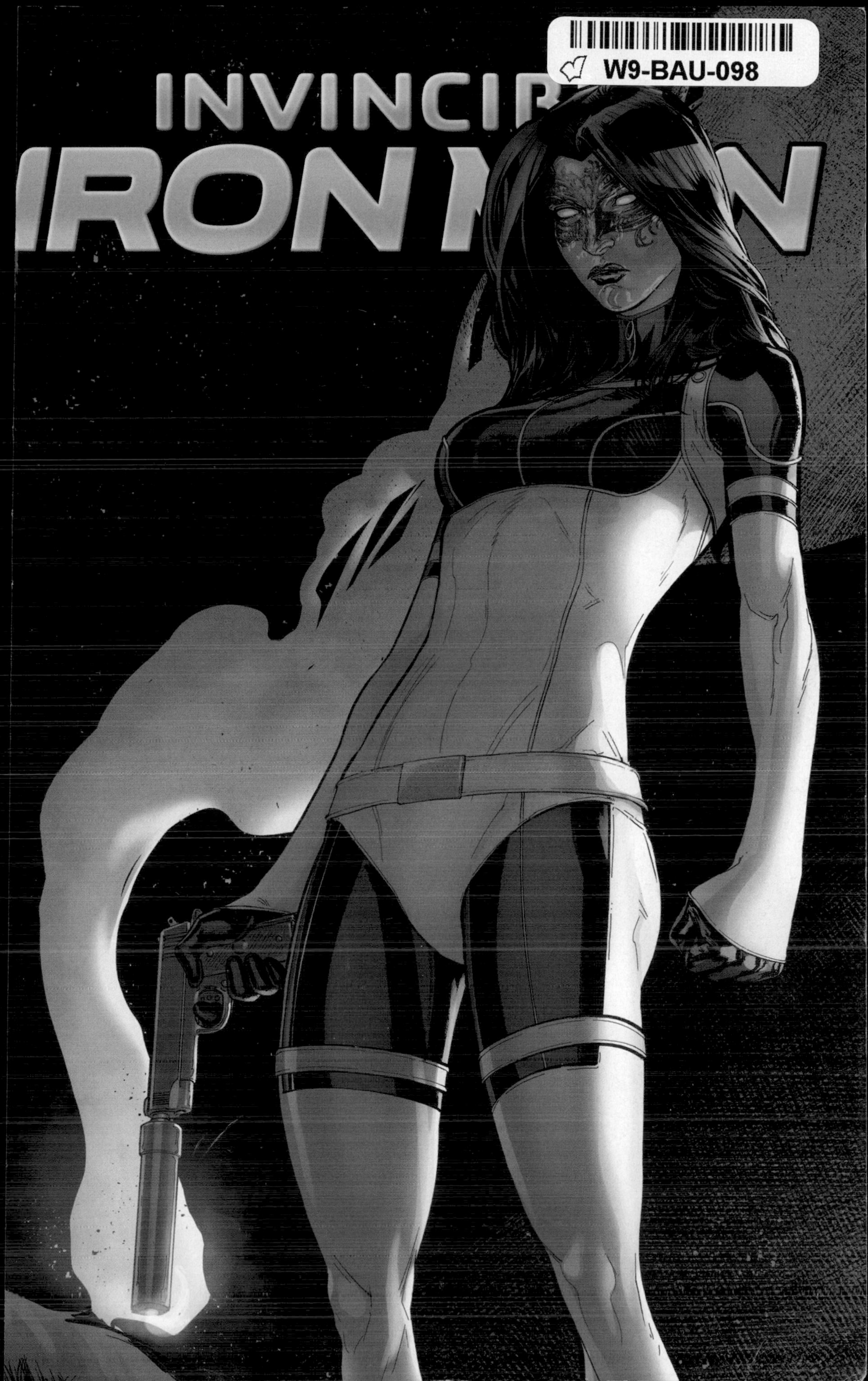
INVINCI
IRON

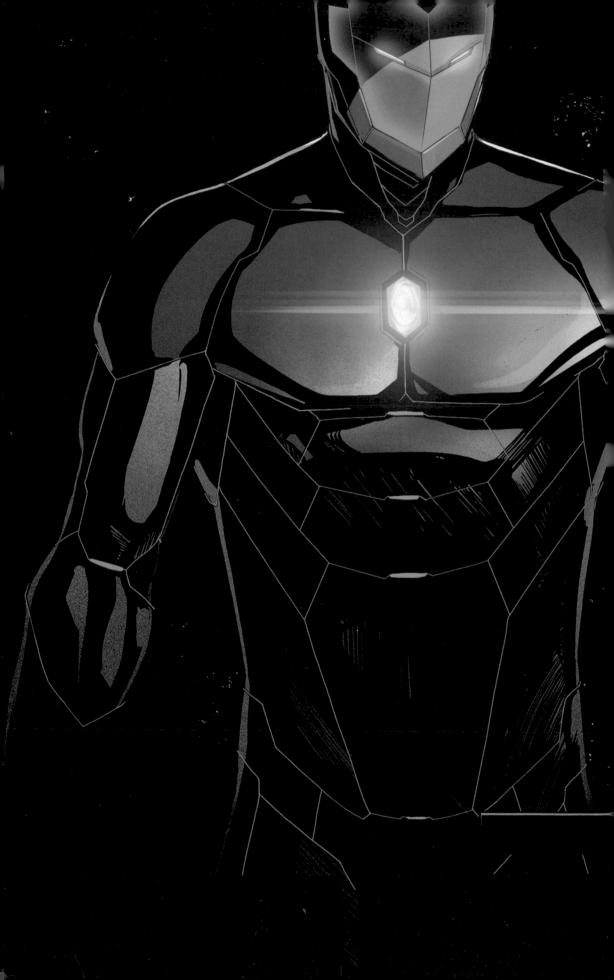

INVINCIBLE
IRON MAN
REBOOT

BRIAN MICHAEL BENDIS
WRITER

DAVID MARQUEZ
ARTIST

JUSTIN PONSOR
COLOR ARTIST

VC'S CLAYTON COWLES
LETTERER

DAVID MARQUEZ
& JUSTIN PONSOR
COVER ART

ALANNA SMITH
ASSISTANT EDITOR

TOM BREVOORT
WITH **KATIE KUBERT**
EDITORS

IRON MAN CREATED BY STAN LEE, LARRY LIEBER, DON HECK & JACK KIRBY

COLLECTION EDITOR: **JENNIFER GRÜNWALD**
ASSOCIATE MANAGING EDITOR: **KATERI WOODY**
ASSOCIATE EDITOR: **SARAH BRUNSTAD**
EDITOR, SPECIAL PROJECTS: **MARK D. BEAZLEY**
VP, PRODUCTION & SPECIAL PROJECTS: **JEFF YOUNGQUIST**
SVP PRINT, SALES & MARKETING: **DAVID GABRIEL**
BOOK DESIGNER: **JAY BOWEN**

EDITOR IN CHIEF: **AXEL ALONSO**
CHIEF CREATIVE OFFICER: **JOE QUESADA**
PUBLISHER: **DAN BUCKLEY**
EXECUTIVE PRODUCER: **ALAN FINE**

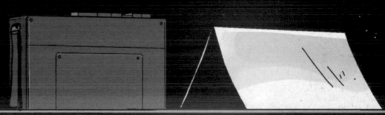

INVINCIBLE IRON MAN VOL. 1: REBOOT. Contains material originally published in magazine form as INVINCIBLE IRON MAN #1-6. First printing 2016. ISBN# 978-0-7851-9940-3. Published by MARVEL WORLDWIDE, INC., a subsidiary of MARVEL ENTERTAINMENT, LLC. OFFICE OF PUBLICATION: 135 West 50th Street, New York, NY 10020. Copyright © 2016 MARVEL No similarity between any of the names, characters, persons, and/or institutions in this magazine with those of any living or dead person or institution is intended, and any such similarity which may exist is purely coincidental. **Printed in the U.S.A.** ALAN FINE, President, Marvel Entertainment; DAN BUCKLEY, President, TV, Publishing & Brand Management; JOE QUESADA, Chief Creative Officer; TOM BREVOORT, SVP of Publishing; DAVID BOGART, SVP of Business Affairs & Operations, Publishing & Partnership; C.B. CEBULSKI, VP of Brand Management & Development, Asia; DAVID GABRIEL, SVP of Sales & Marketing, Publishing; JEFF YOUNGQUIST, VP of Production & Special Projects; DAN CARR, Executive Director of Publishing Technology; ALEX MORALES, Director of Publishing Operations; SUSAN CRESPI, Production Manager; STAN LEE, Chairman Emeritus. For information regarding advertising in Marvel Comics or on Marvel.com, please contact Vit DeBellis, Integrated Sales Manager, at vdebellis@marvel.com. For Marvel subscription inquiries, please call 888-511-5480. **Manufactured between 11/4/2016 and 12/12/2016 by LSC COMMUNICATIONS INC., SALEM, VA, USA.**

#1

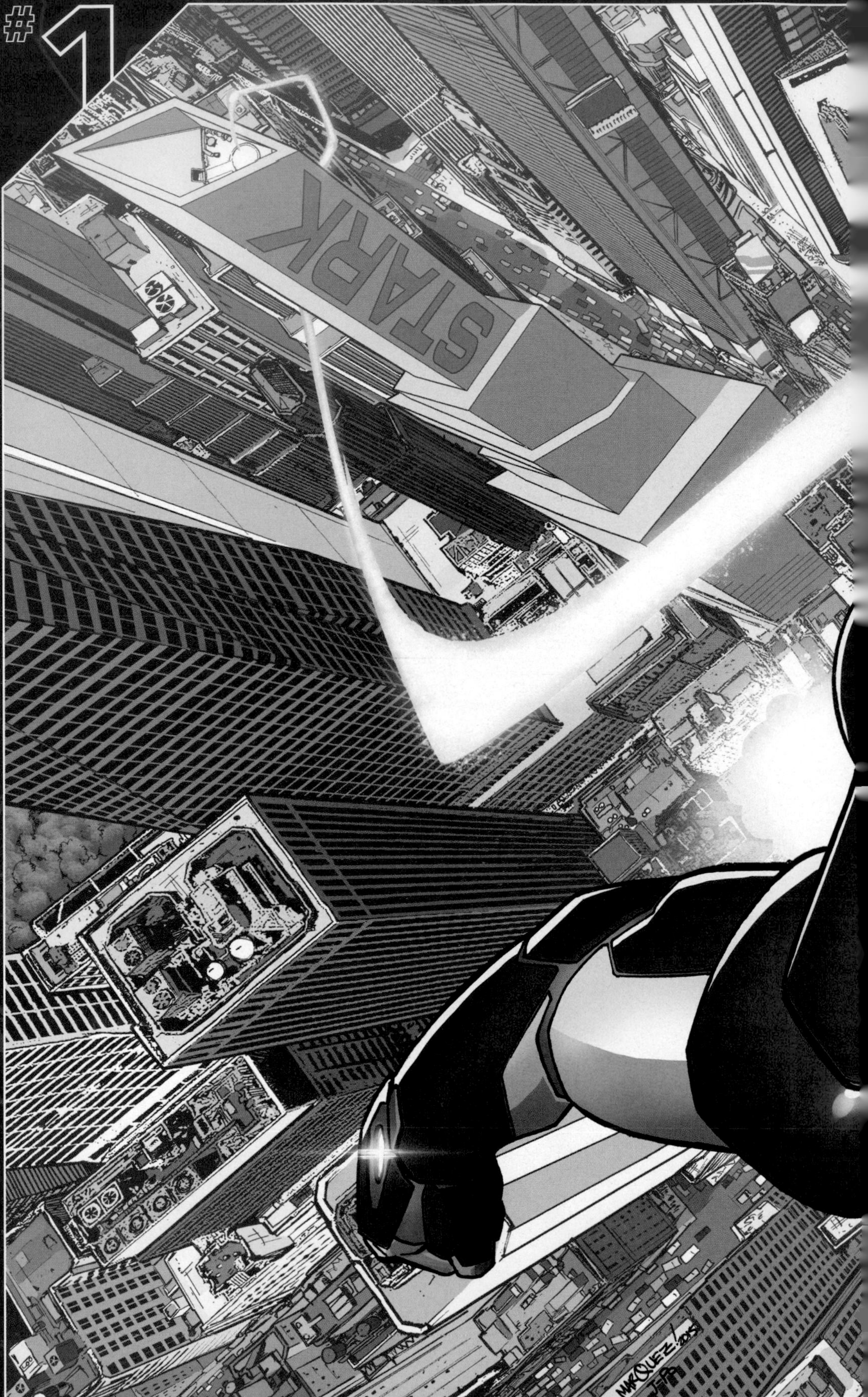
STARK

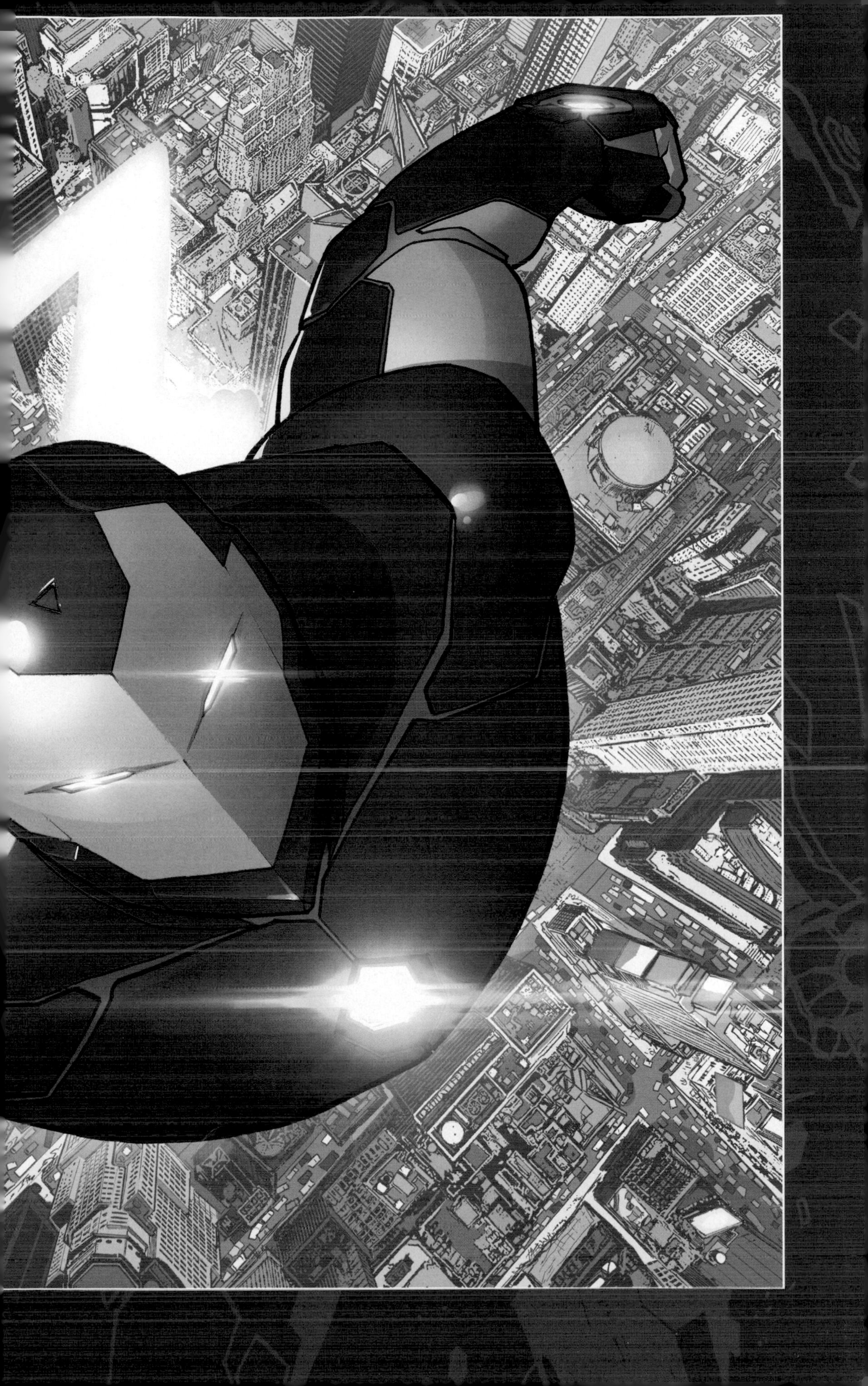

INVINCIBLE IRON MAN

ANOTHER STARK INNOVATION

Billionaire playboy and genius industrialist To...
Stark was kidnapped during a routine weapor
test. His captors attempted to force him :
build a weapon of mass destruction. Instea
he created a powered suit of armor that save
his life. From that day on, he used the suit t
protect the world as the invincible Avenge
IRON MAN

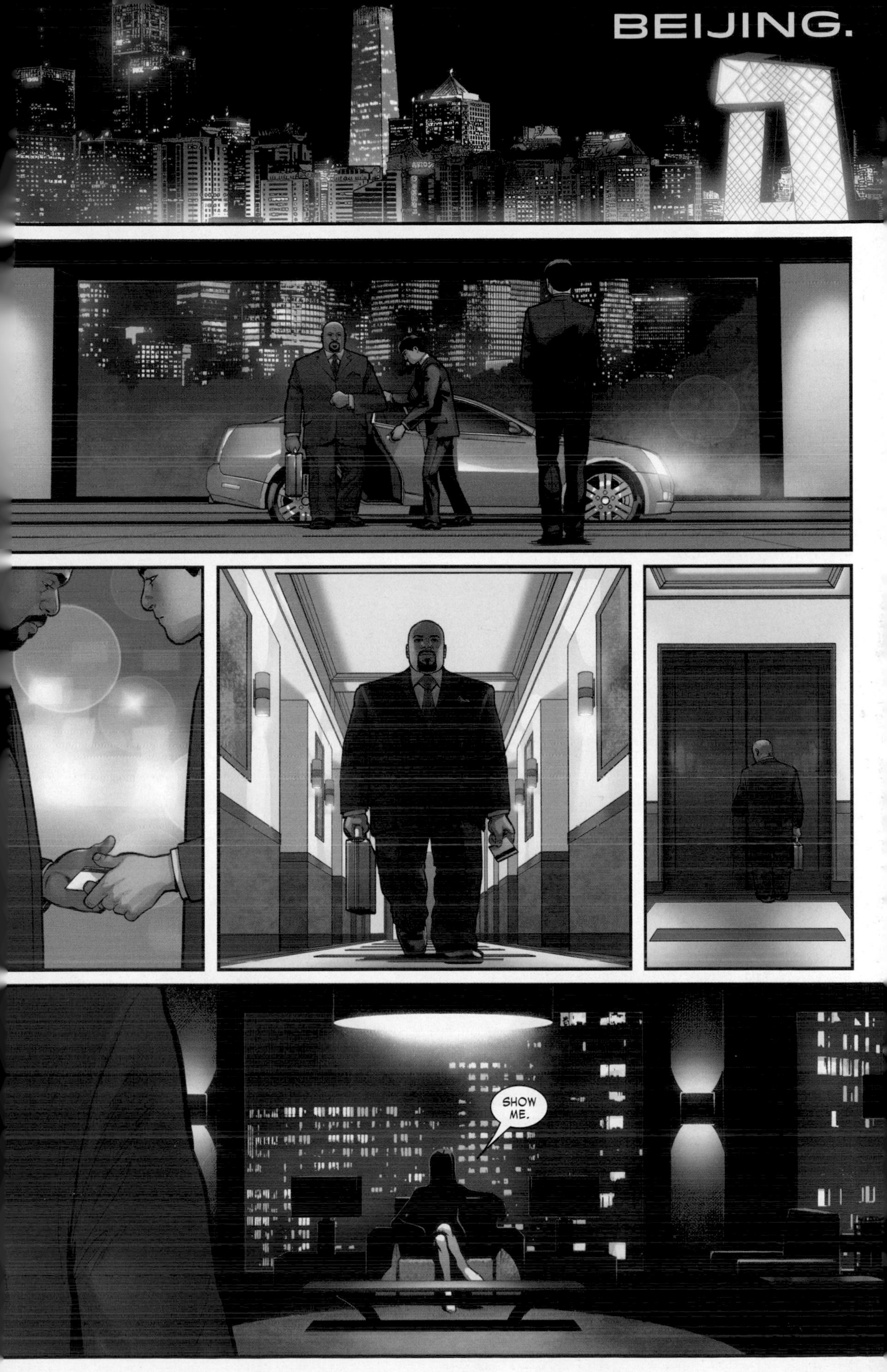
BEIJING.
SHOW ME.

HERE.

THAT'S IT?

ALL OF IT.

WHY DID YOU DO THIS?

WHY?

I WANT TO KNOW.

BECAUSE A.I.M. IS A BUNCH OF WACKADOOS AND I'VE WASTED HALF MY LIFE THERE.

AND I JUST WANT A BUYOUT BIG ENOUGH TO DISAPPEAR...

...IN STYLE.

I DESERVE THAT MUCH.

IS IT REAL?

OH, IT'S REAL.

BECAUSE IF IT'S NOT...

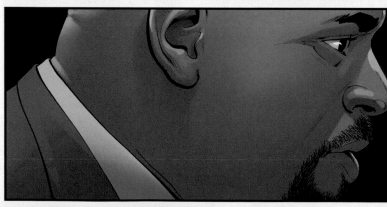

YOU'LL FIND ME AND KILL ME.

YES.

BELIEVE ME, I KNOW.

OPEN IT.

SEE FOR YOURSELF.

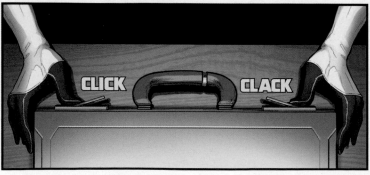

CLICK

CLACK

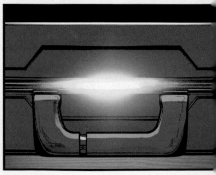

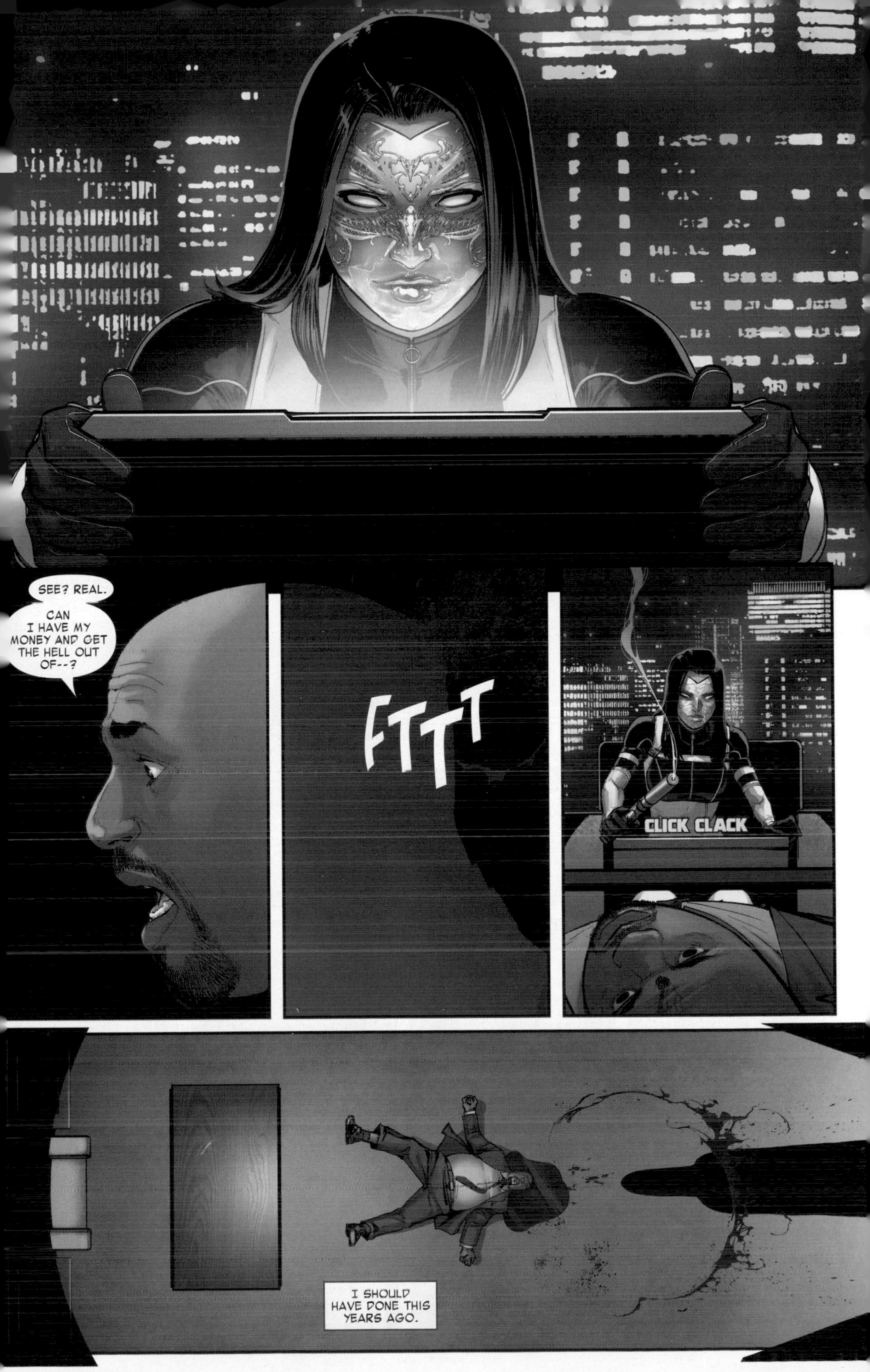
SEE? REAL.
CAN I HAVE MY MONEY AND GET THE HELL OUT OF--?
FTTT
CLICK CLACK
I SHOULD HAVE DONE THIS YEARS AGO.

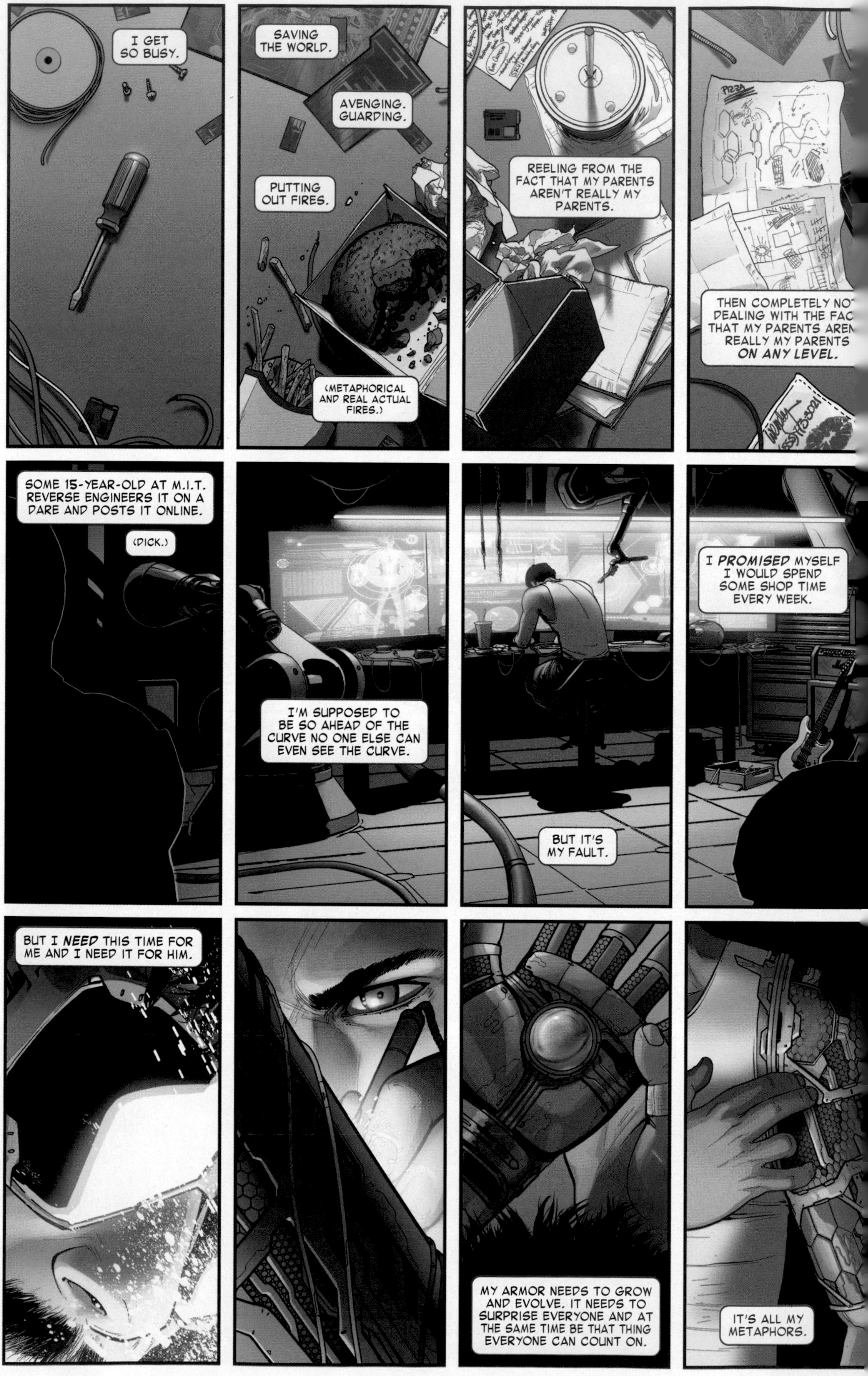
I GET SO BUSY.
SAVING THE WORLD.
AVENGING. GUARDING.
PUTTING OUT FIRES.
(METAPHORICAL AND REAL ACTUAL FIRES.)
REELING FROM THE FACT THAT MY PARENTS AREN'T REALLY MY PARENTS.
THEN COMPLETELY NOT DEALING WITH THE FACT THAT MY PARENTS AREN'T REALLY MY PARENTS ON ANY LEVEL.
SOME 15-YEAR-OLD AT M.I.T. REVERSE ENGINEERS IT ON A DARE AND POSTS IT ONLINE.
(DICK.)
I'M SUPPOSED TO BE SO AHEAD OF THE CURVE NO ONE ELSE CAN EVEN SEE THE CURVE.
BUT IT'S MY FAULT.
I PROMISED MYSELF I WOULD SPEND SOME SHOP TIME EVERY WEEK.
BUT I NEED THIS TIME FOR ME AND I NEED IT FOR HIM.
MY ARMOR NEEDS TO GROW AND EVOLVE. IT NEEDS TO SURPRISE EVERYONE AND AT THE SAME TIME BE THAT THING EVERYONE CAN COUNT ON.
IT'S ALL MY METAPHORS.

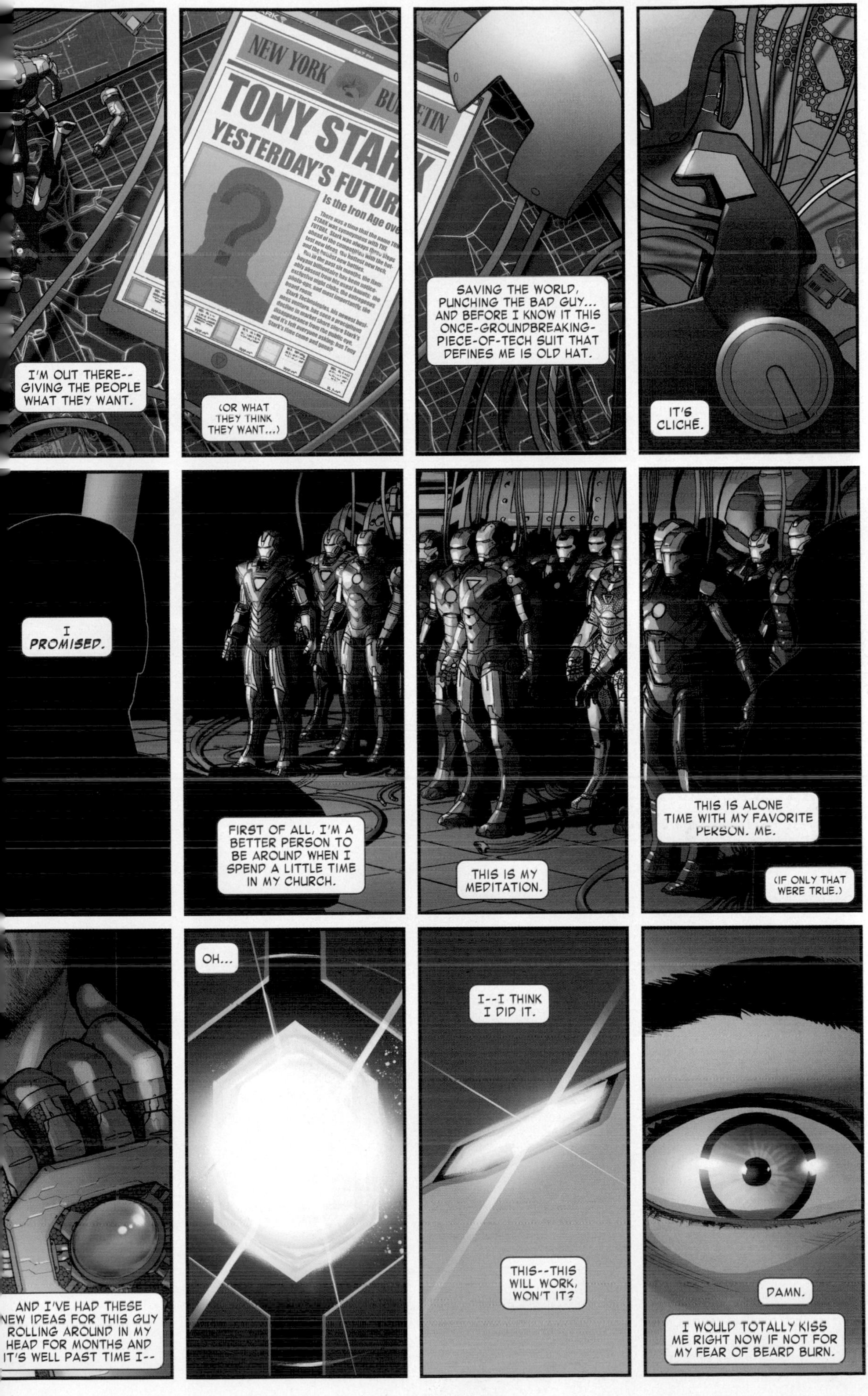
I'M OUT THERE--
GIVING THE PEOPLE
WHAT THEY WANT.
NEW YORK
YESTERDAY'S
(OR WHAT
THEY THINK
THEY WANT...)
SAVING THE WORLD,
PUNCHING THE BAD GUY...
AND BEFORE I KNOW IT THIS
ONCE-GROUNDBREAKING-
PIECE-OF-TECH SUIT THAT
DEFINES ME IS OLD HAT.
IT'S
CLICHÉ.
I
PROMISED.
FIRST OF ALL, I'M A
BETTER PERSON TO
BE AROUND WHEN I
SPEND A LITTLE TIME
IN MY CHURCH.
THIS IS MY
MEDITATION.
THIS IS ALONE
TIME WITH MY FAVORITE
PERSON. ME.
(IF ONLY THAT
WERE TRUE.)
AND I'VE HAD THESE
NEW IDEAS FOR THIS GUY
ROLLING AROUND IN MY
HEAD FOR MONTHS AND
IT'S WELL PAST TIME I--
OH...
I--I THINK
I DID IT.
THIS--THIS
WILL WORK,
WON'T IT?
DAMN.
I WOULD TOTALLY KISS
ME RIGHT NOW IF NOT FOR
MY FEAR OF BEARD BURN.

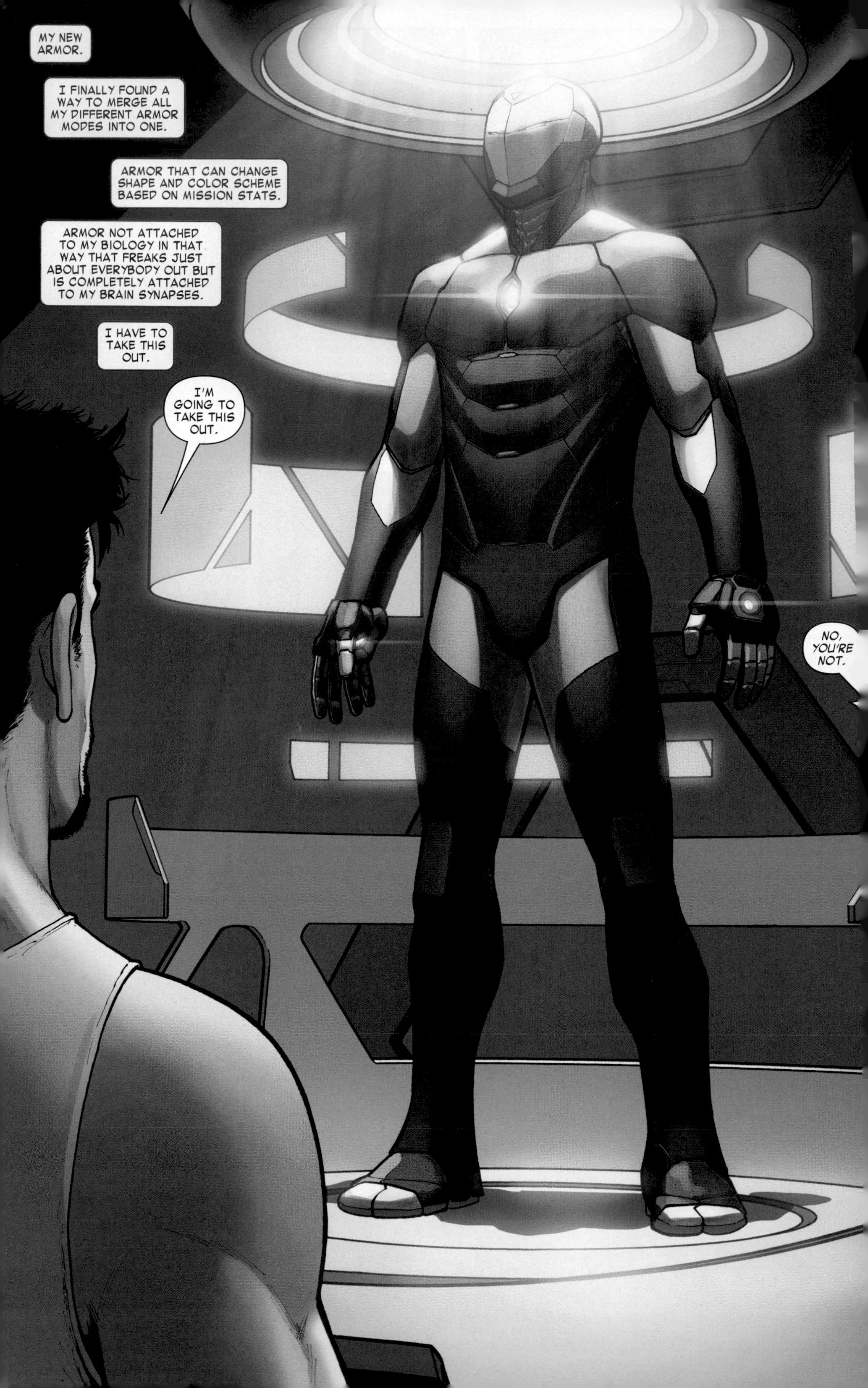
MY NEW ARMOR.
I FINALLY FOUND A WAY TO MERGE ALL MY DIFFERENT ARMOR MODES INTO ONE.
ARMOR THAT CAN CHANGE SHAPE AND COLOR SCHEME BASED ON MISSION STATS.
ARMOR NOT ATTACHED TO MY BIOLOGY IN THAT WAY THAT FREAKS JUST ABOUT EVERYBODY OUT BUT IS COMPLETELY ATTACHED TO MY BRAIN SYNAPSES.
I HAVE TO TAKE THIS OUT.
I'M GOING TO TAKE THIS OUT.
NO, YOU'RE NOT.

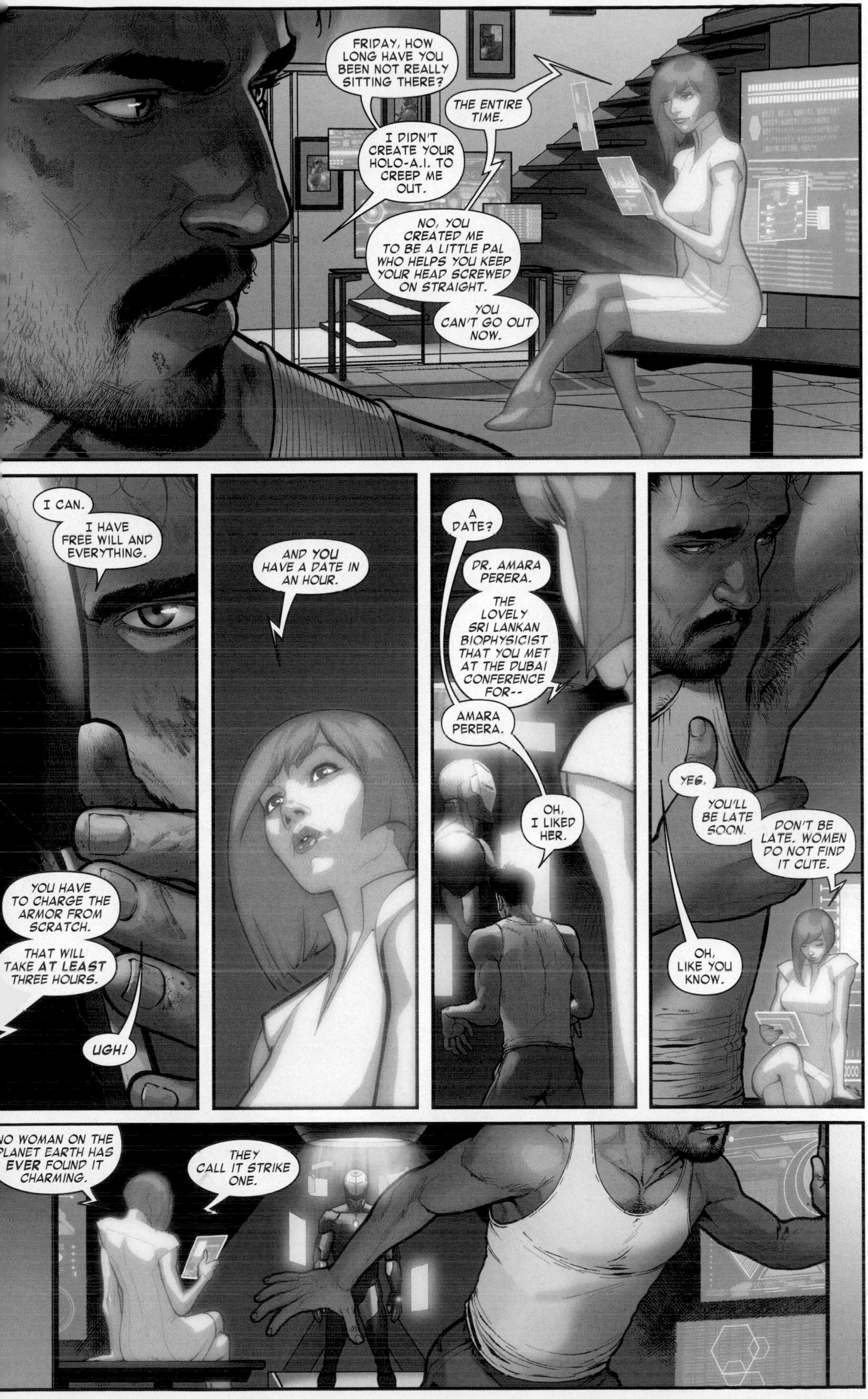
FRIDAY, HOW LONG HAVE YOU BEEN NOT REALLY SITTING THERE?
THE ENTIRE TIME.
I DIDN'T CREATE YOUR HOLO-A.I. TO CREEP ME OUT.
NO, YOU CREATED ME TO BE A LITTLE PAL WHO HELPS YOU KEEP YOUR HEAD SCREWED ON STRAIGHT.
YOU CAN'T GO OUT NOW.
I CAN.
I HAVE FREE WILL AND EVERYTHING.
YOU HAVE TO CHARGE THE ARMOR FROM SCRATCH.
THAT WILL TAKE AT LEAST THREE HOURS.
UGH!
AND YOU HAVE A DATE IN AN HOUR.
A DATE?
DR. AMARA PERERA.
THE LOVELY SRI LANKAN BIOPHYSICIST THAT YOU MET AT THE DUBAI CONFERENCE FOR--
AMARA PERERA.
OH, I LIKED HER.
YES.
YOU'LL BE LATE SOON.
DON'T BE LATE. WOMEN DO NOT FIND IT CUTE.
OH, LIKE YOU KNOW.
NO WOMAN ON THE PLANET EARTH HAS EVER FOUND IT CHARMING.
THEY CALL IT STRIKE ONE.

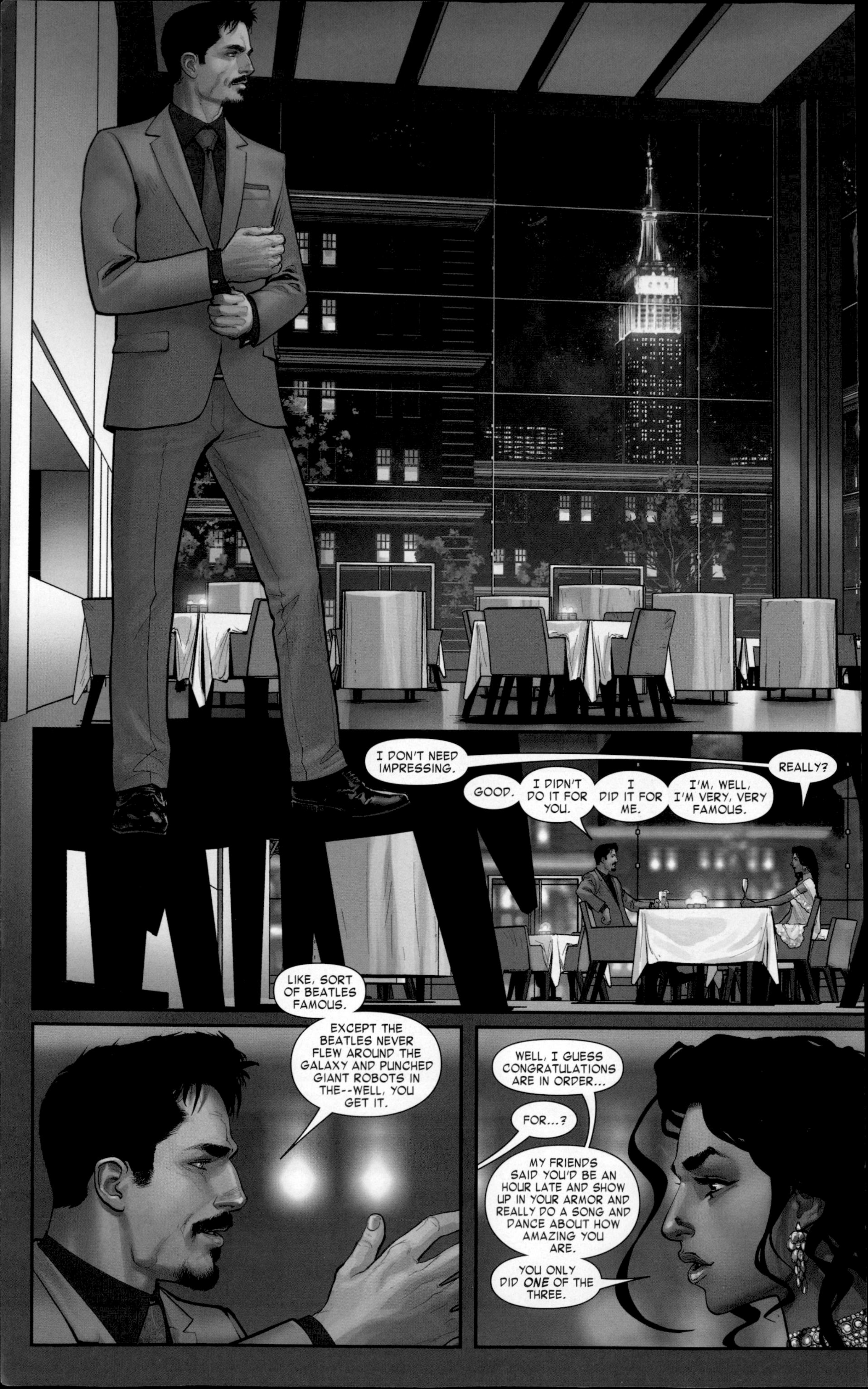
I DON'T NEED IMPRESSING.
GOOD.
I DIDN'T DO IT FOR YOU.
I DID IT FOR ME.
I'M, WELL, I'M VERY, VERY FAMOUS.
REALLY?
LIKE, SORT OF BEATLES FAMOUS.
EXCEPT THE BEATLES NEVER FLEW AROUND THE GALAXY AND PUNCHED GIANT ROBOTS IN THE--WELL, YOU GET IT.
WELL, I GUESS CONGRATULATIONS ARE IN ORDER...
FOR...?
MY FRIENDS SAID YOU'D BE AN HOUR LATE AND SHOW UP IN YOUR ARMOR AND REALLY DO A SONG AND DANCE ABOUT HOW AMAZING YOU ARE.
YOU ONLY DID *ONE* OF THE THREE.

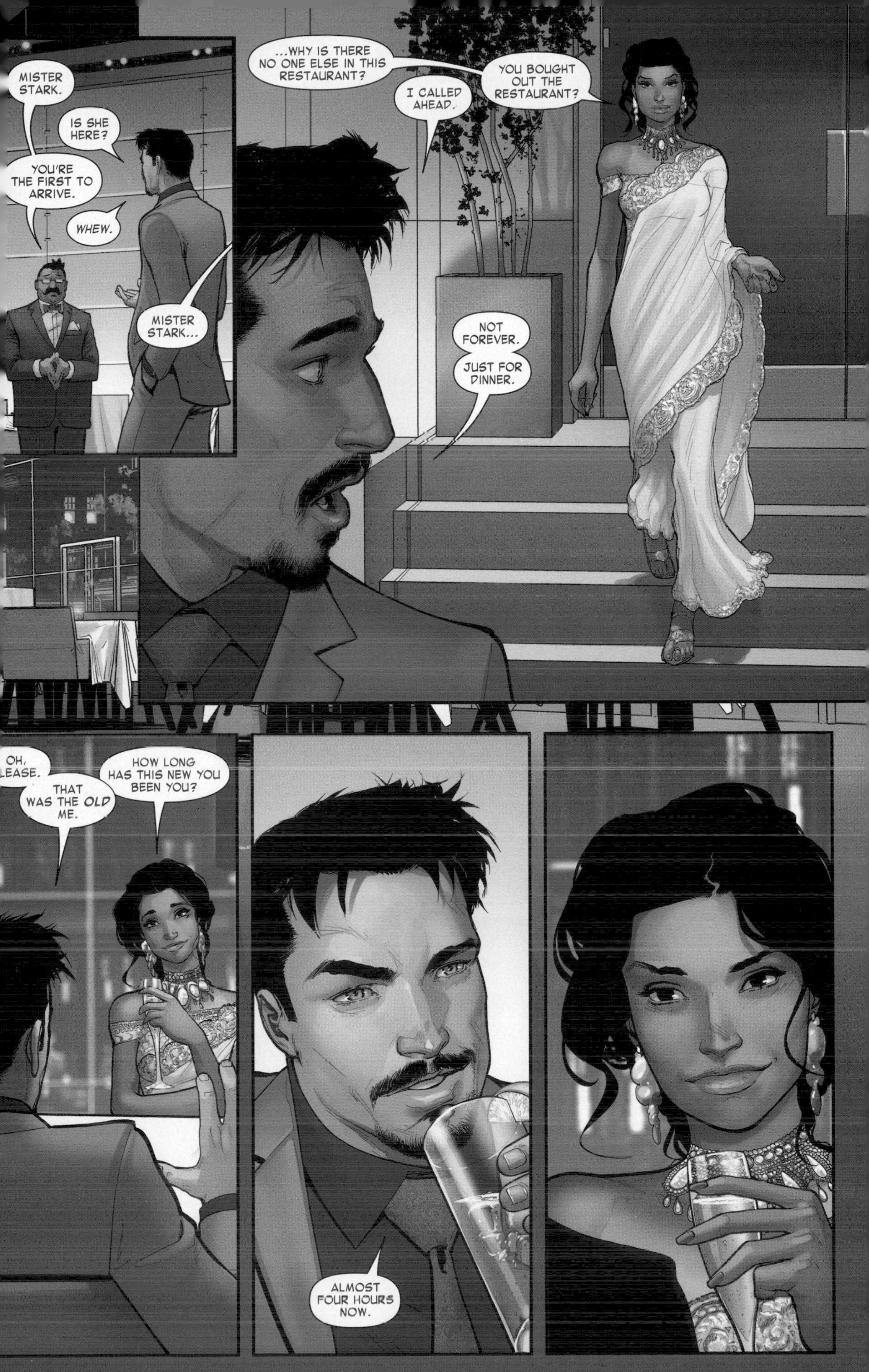
MISTER STARK.
IS SHE HERE?
YOU'RE THE FIRST TO ARRIVE.
WHEW.
MISTER STARK...
...WHY IS THERE NO ONE ELSE IN THIS RESTAURANT?
YOU BOUGHT OUT THE RESTAURANT?
I CALLED AHEAD.
NOT FOREVER.
JUST FOR DINNER.
OH, LEASE.
THAT WAS THE OLD ME.
HOW LONG HAS THIS NEW YOU BEEN YOU?
ALMOST FOUR HOURS NOW.

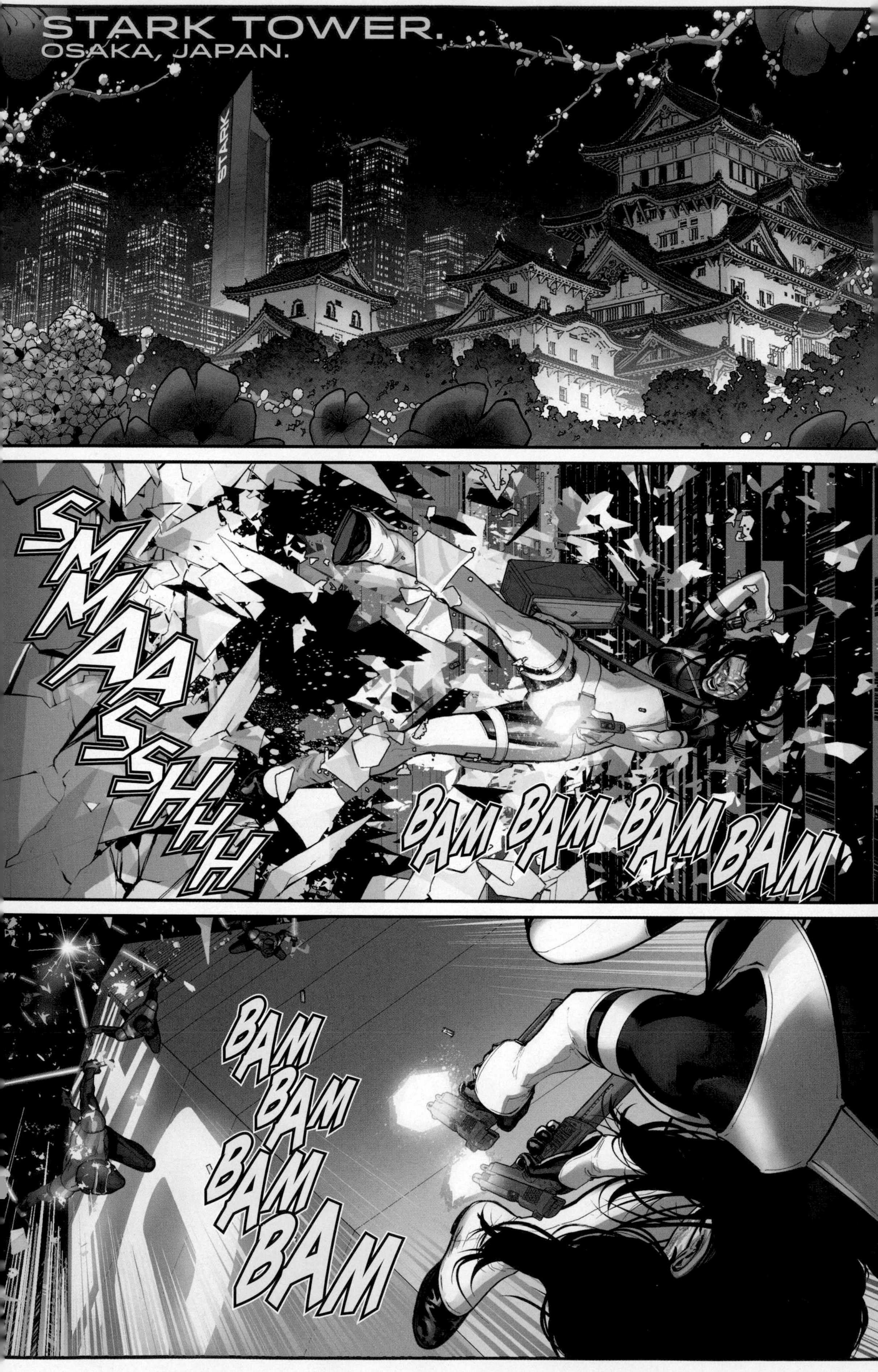
STARK TOWER.
OSAKA, JAPAN.
STARK
SMMAASSHHH
BAM BAM BAM BAM
BAM BAM BAM BAM

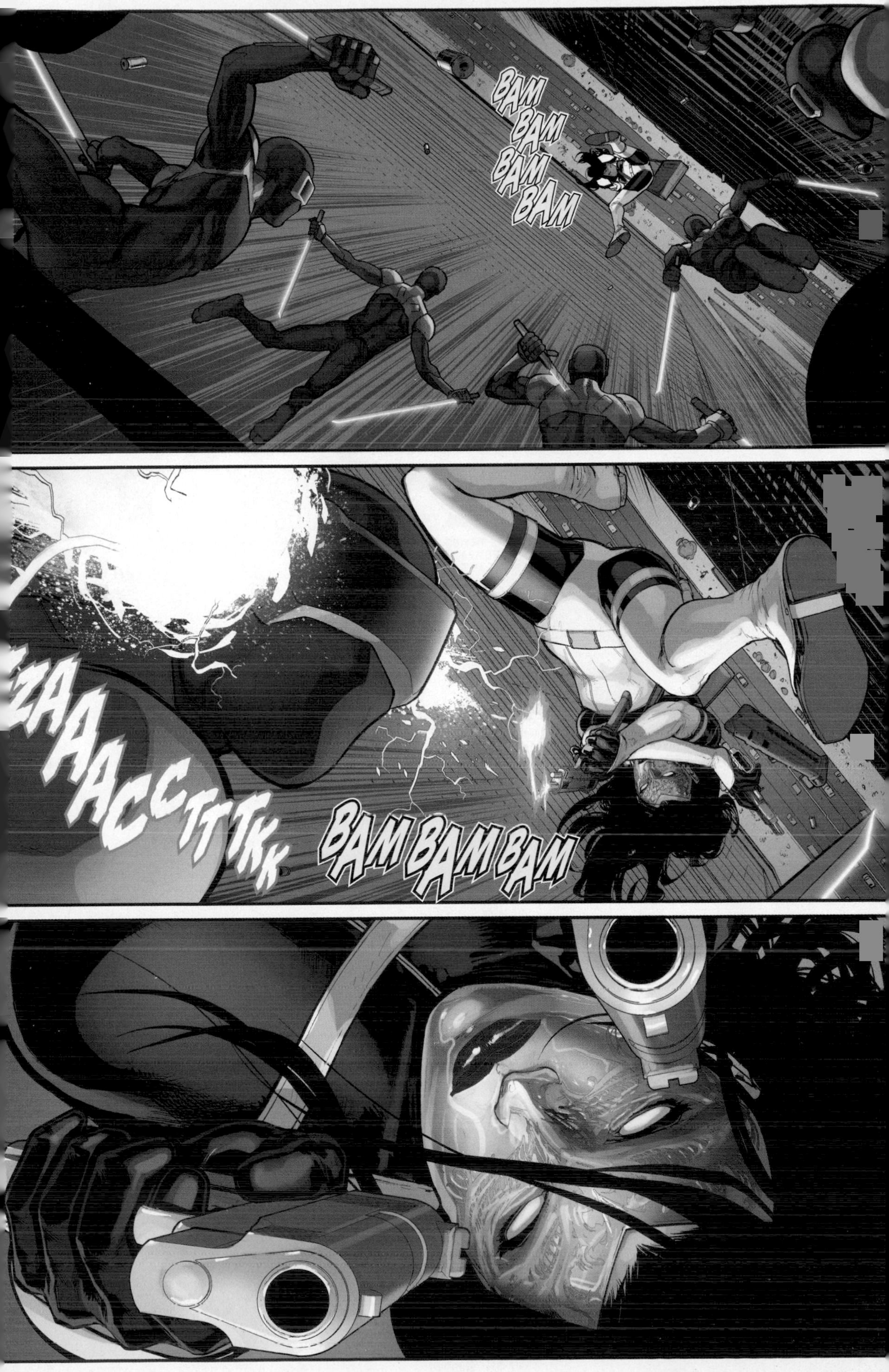
BAM BAM BAM BAM BAM
ZAAACCTTTKK
BAM BAM BAM

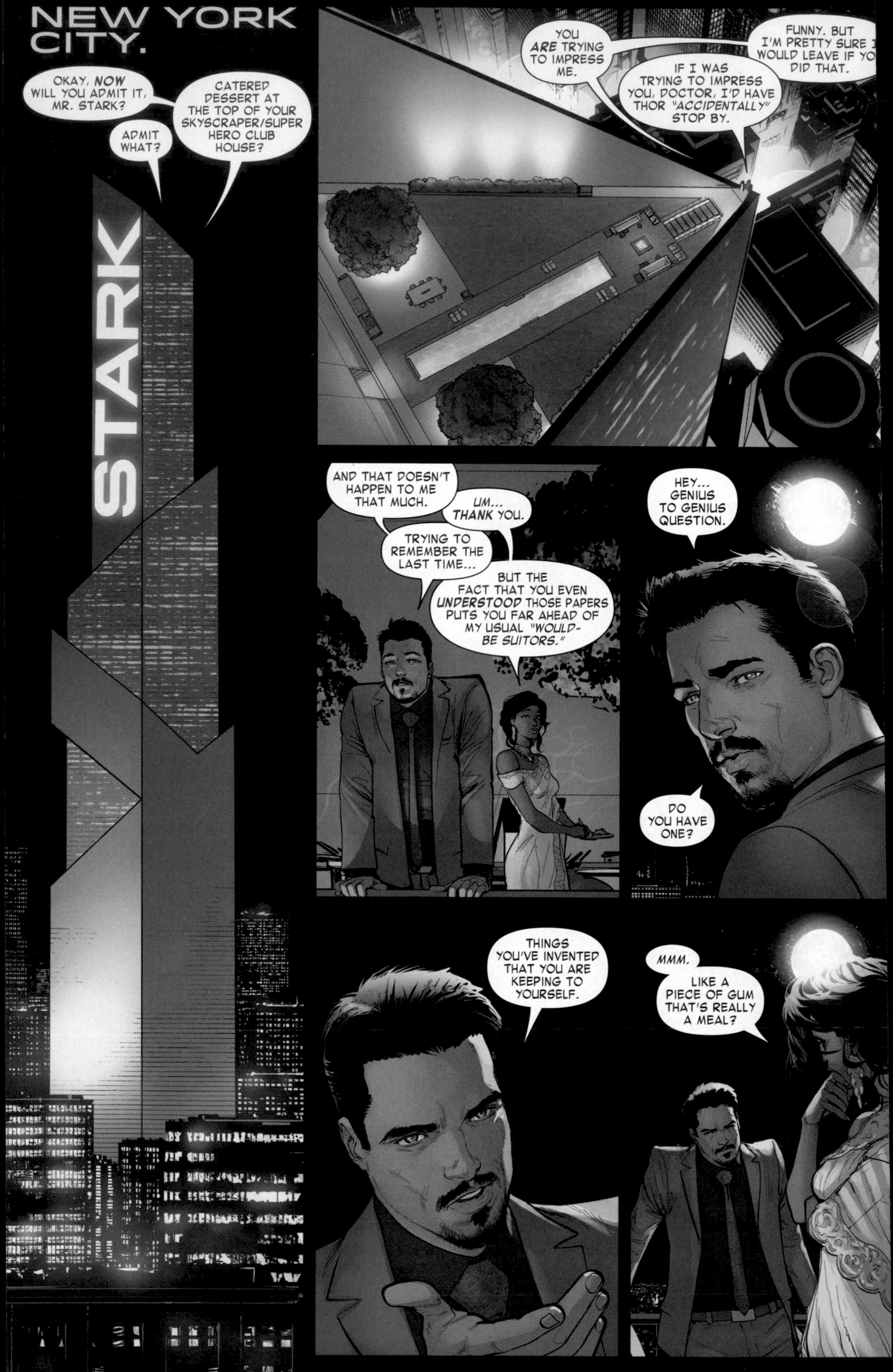

NEW YORK CITY.
OKAY, NOW WILL YOU ADMIT IT, MR. STARK?
ADMIT WHAT?
CATERED DESSERT AT THE TOP OF YOUR SKYSCRAPER/SUPER HERO CLUB HOUSE?
STARK
YOU ARE TRYING TO IMPRESS ME.
IF I WAS TRYING TO IMPRESS YOU, DOCTOR, I'D HAVE THOR "ACCIDENTALLY" STOP BY.
FUNNY. BUT I'M PRETTY SURE I WOULD LEAVE IF YOU DID THAT.
AND THAT DOESN'T HAPPEN TO ME THAT MUCH.
UM... THANK YOU.
TRYING TO REMEMBER THE LAST TIME...
BUT THE FACT THAT YOU EVEN UNDERSTOOD THOSE PAPERS PUTS YOU FAR AHEAD OF MY USUAL "WOULD-BE SUITORS."
HEY... GENIUS TO GENIUS QUESTION.
DO YOU HAVE ONE?
THINGS YOU'VE INVENTED THAT YOU ARE KEEPING TO YOURSELF.
MMM.
LIKE A PIECE OF GUM THAT'S REALLY A MEAL?

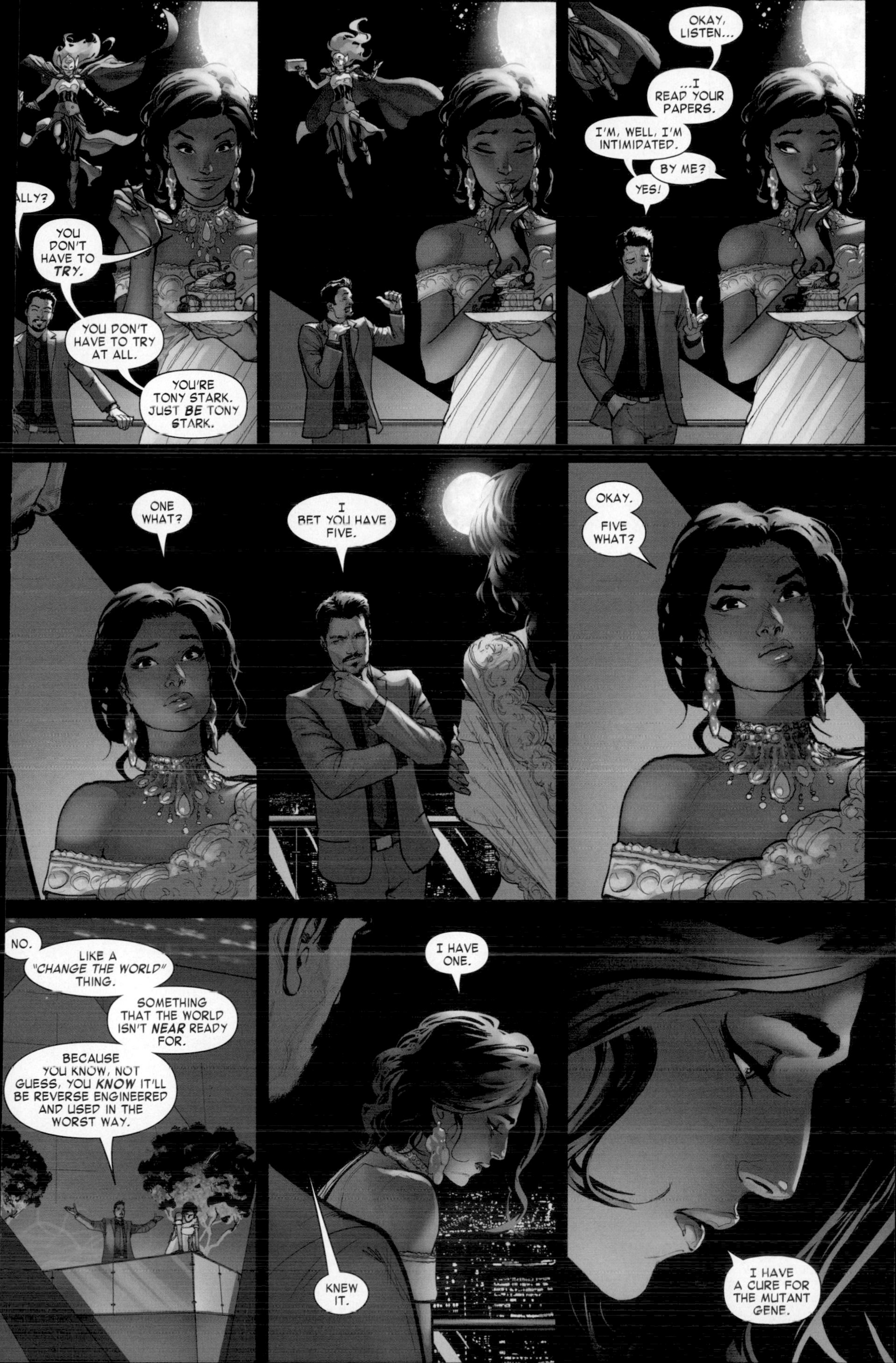
ALLY?
YOU DON'T HAVE TO *TRY.*
YOU DON'T HAVE TO TRY AT ALL.
YOU'RE TONY STARK. JUST *BE* TONY STARK.
OKAY, LISTEN...
...I READ YOUR PAPERS.
I'M, WELL, I'M INTIMIDATED.
BY ME?
YES!
ONE WHAT?
I BET YOU HAVE FIVE.
OKAY.
FIVE WHAT?
NO.
LIKE A *"CHANGE THE WORLD"* THING.
SOMETHING THAT THE WORLD ISN'T *NEAR* READY FOR.
BECAUSE YOU KNOW, NOT GUESS, YOU *KNOW* IT'LL BE REVERSE ENGINEERED AND USED IN THE WORST WAY.
I HAVE ONE.
KNEW IT.
I HAVE A CURE FOR THE MUTANT GENE.

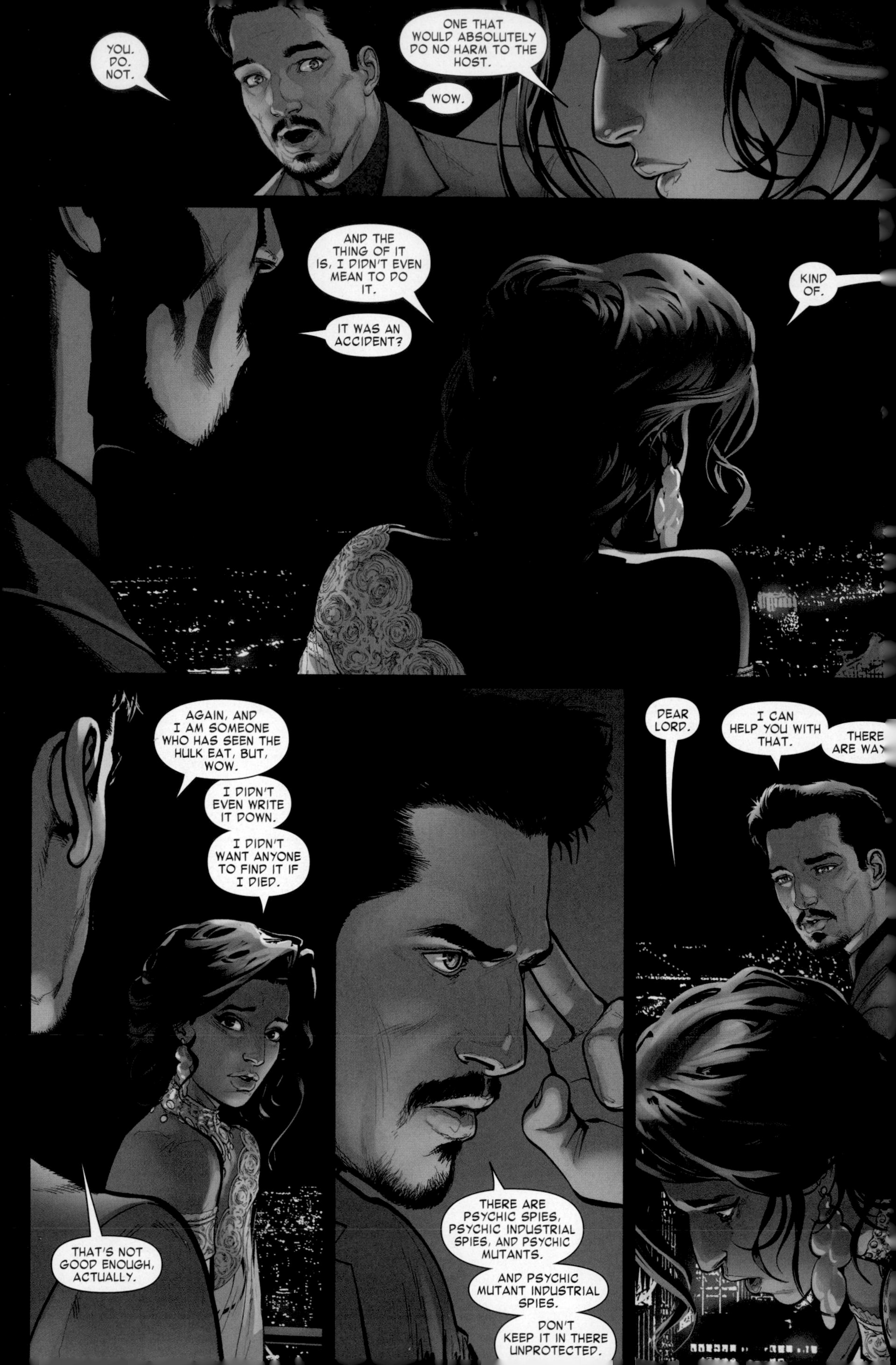
YOU. DO. NOT.
ONE THAT WOULD ABSOLUTELY DO NO HARM TO THE HOST.
WOW.
AND THE THING OF IT IS, I DIDN'T EVEN MEAN TO DO IT.
IT WAS AN ACCIDENT?
KIND OF.
AGAIN, AND I AM SOMEONE WHO HAS SEEN THE HULK EAT, BUT, WOW.
I DIDN'T EVEN WRITE IT DOWN.
I DIDN'T WANT ANYONE TO FIND IT IF I DIED.
THAT'S NOT GOOD ENOUGH, ACTUALLY.
THERE ARE PSYCHIC SPIES, PSYCHIC INDUSTRIAL SPIES, AND PSYCHIC MUTANTS.
AND PSYCHIC MUTANT INDUSTRIAL SPIES.
DON'T KEEP IT IN THERE UNPROTECTED.
DEAR LORD.
I CAN HELP YOU WITH THAT.
THERE ARE WAY

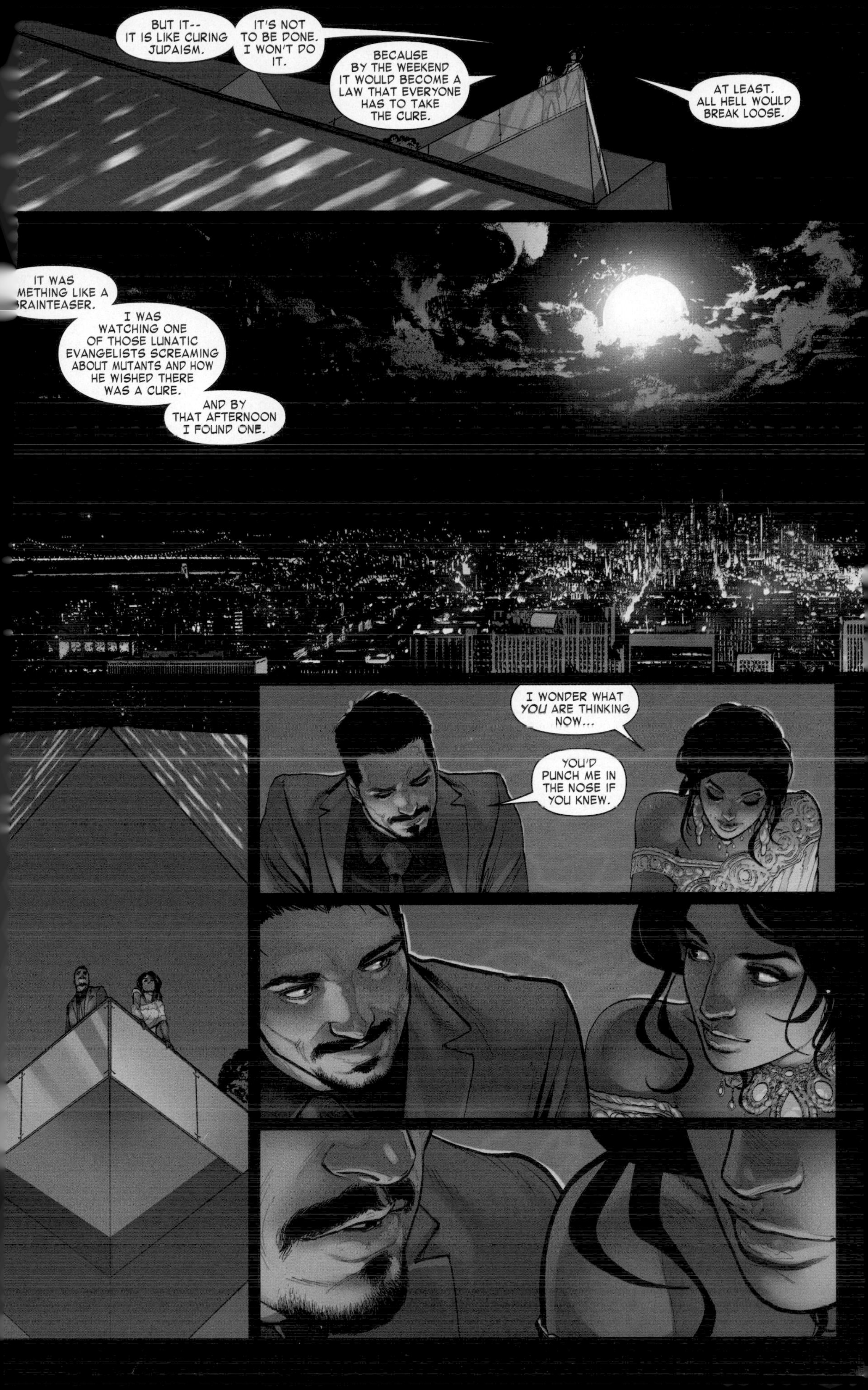
BUT IT-- IT IS LIKE CURING JUDAISM.
IT'S NOT TO BE DONE. I WON'T DO IT.
BECAUSE BY THE WEEKEND IT WOULD BECOME A LAW THAT EVERYONE HAS TO TAKE THE CURE.
AT LEAST. ALL HELL WOULD BREAK LOOSE.
IT WAS METHING LIKE A RAINTEASER.
I WAS WATCHING ONE OF THOSE LUNATIC EVANGELISTS SCREAMING ABOUT MUTANTS AND HOW HE WISHED THERE WAS A CURE.
AND BY THAT AFTERNOON I FOUND ONE.
I WONDER WHAT *YOU* ARE THINKING NOW...
YOU'D PUNCH ME IN THE NOSE IF YOU KNEW.

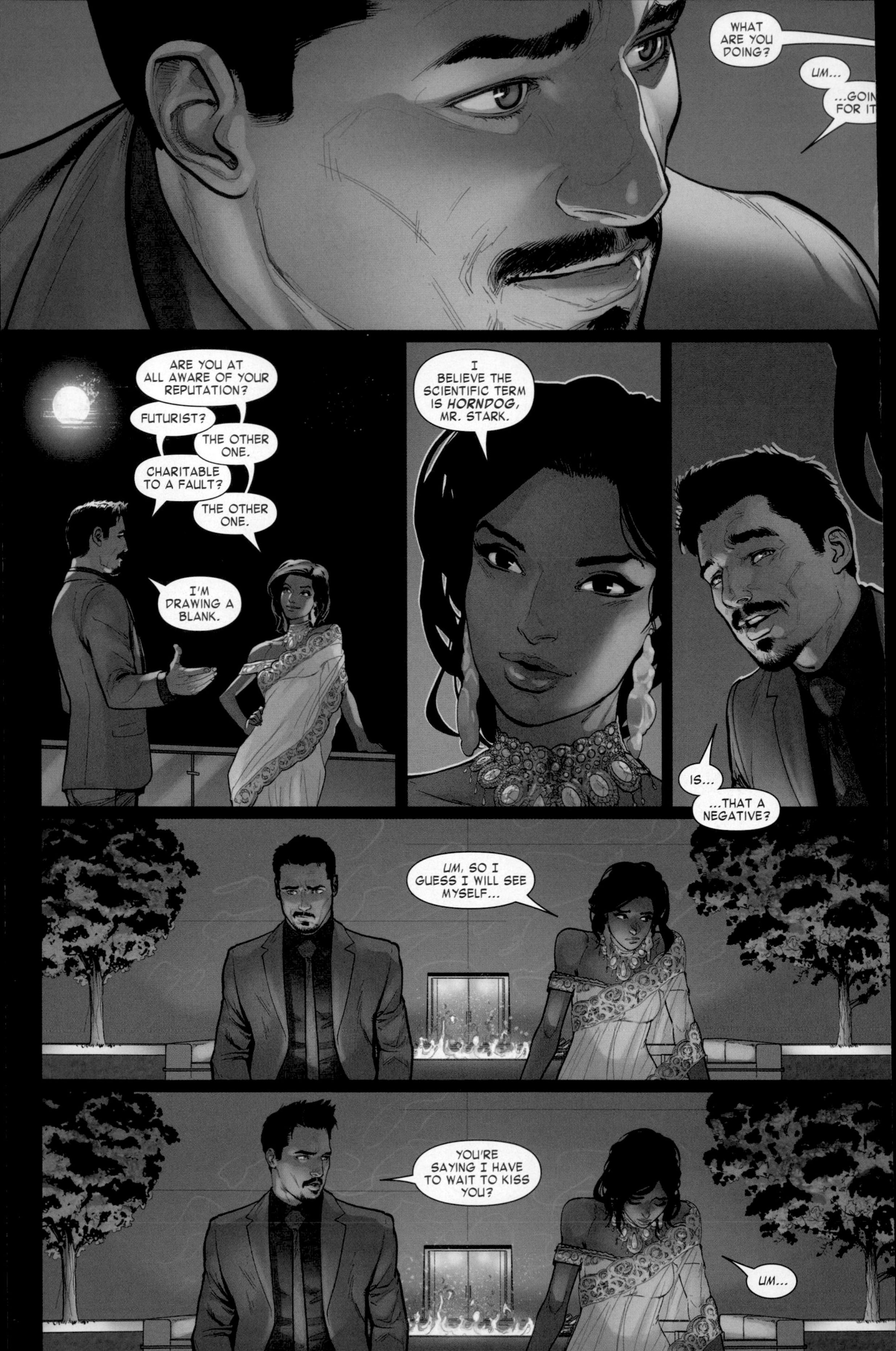
WHAT ARE YOU DOING?
UM...
...GOIN FOR IT
ARE YOU AT ALL AWARE OF YOUR REPUTATION?
FUTURIST?
THE OTHER ONE.
CHARITABLE TO A FAULT?
THE OTHER ONE.
I'M DRAWING A BLANK.
I BELIEVE THE SCIENTIFIC TERM IS HORNDOG, MR. STARK.
IS...
...THAT A NEGATIVE?
UM, SO I GUESS I WILL SEE MYSELF...
YOU'RE SAYING I HAVE TO WAIT TO KISS YOU?
UM...

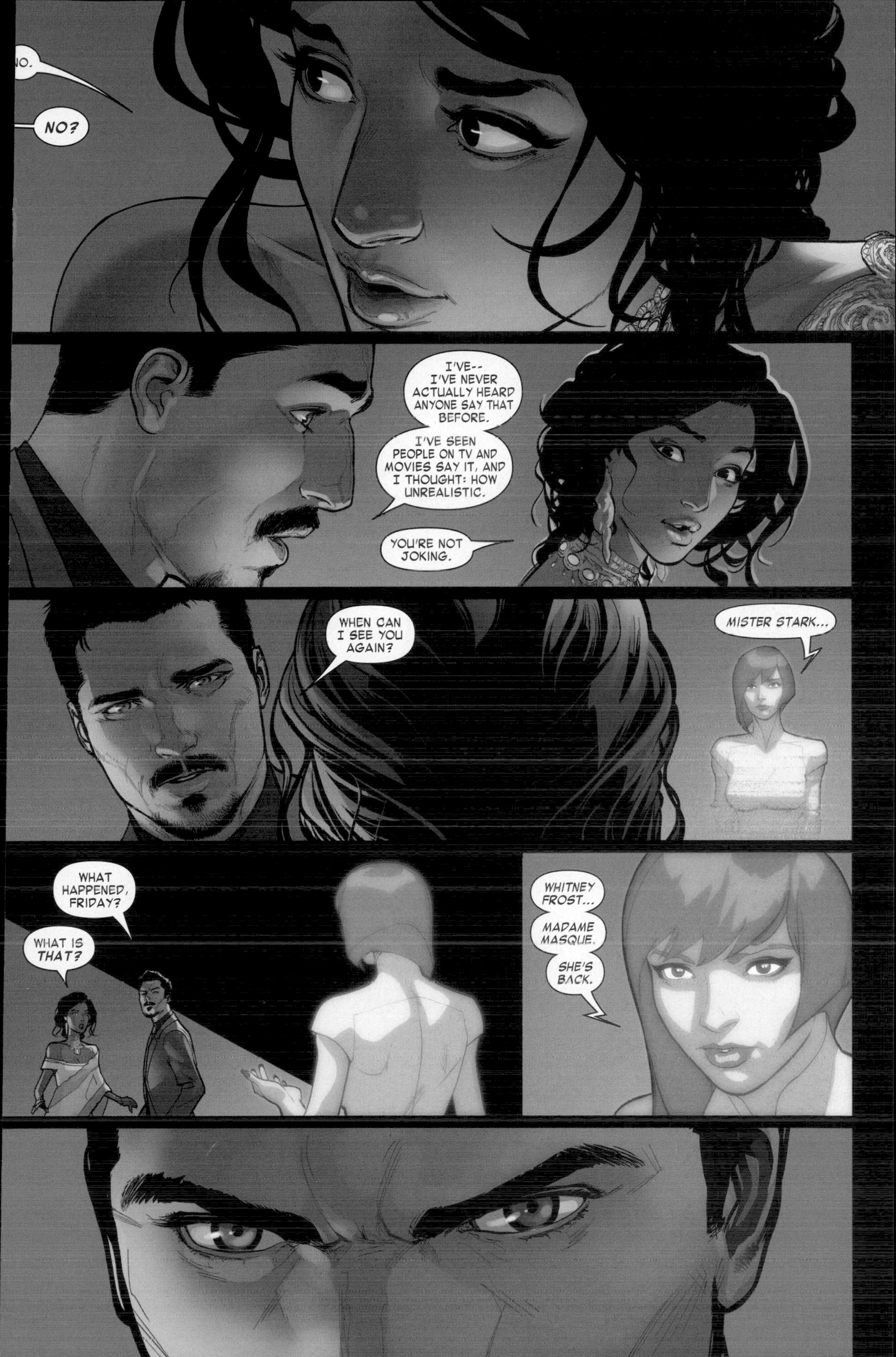
NO.
NO?
I'VE-- I'VE NEVER ACTUALLY HEARD ANYONE SAY THAT BEFORE.
I'VE SEEN PEOPLE ON TV AND MOVIES SAY IT, AND I THOUGHT: HOW UNREALISTIC.
YOU'RE NOT JOKING.
WHEN CAN I SEE YOU AGAIN?
MISTER STARK...
WHAT HAPPENED, FRIDAY?
WHAT IS THAT?
WHITNEY FROST...
MADAME MASQUE.
SHE'S BACK.

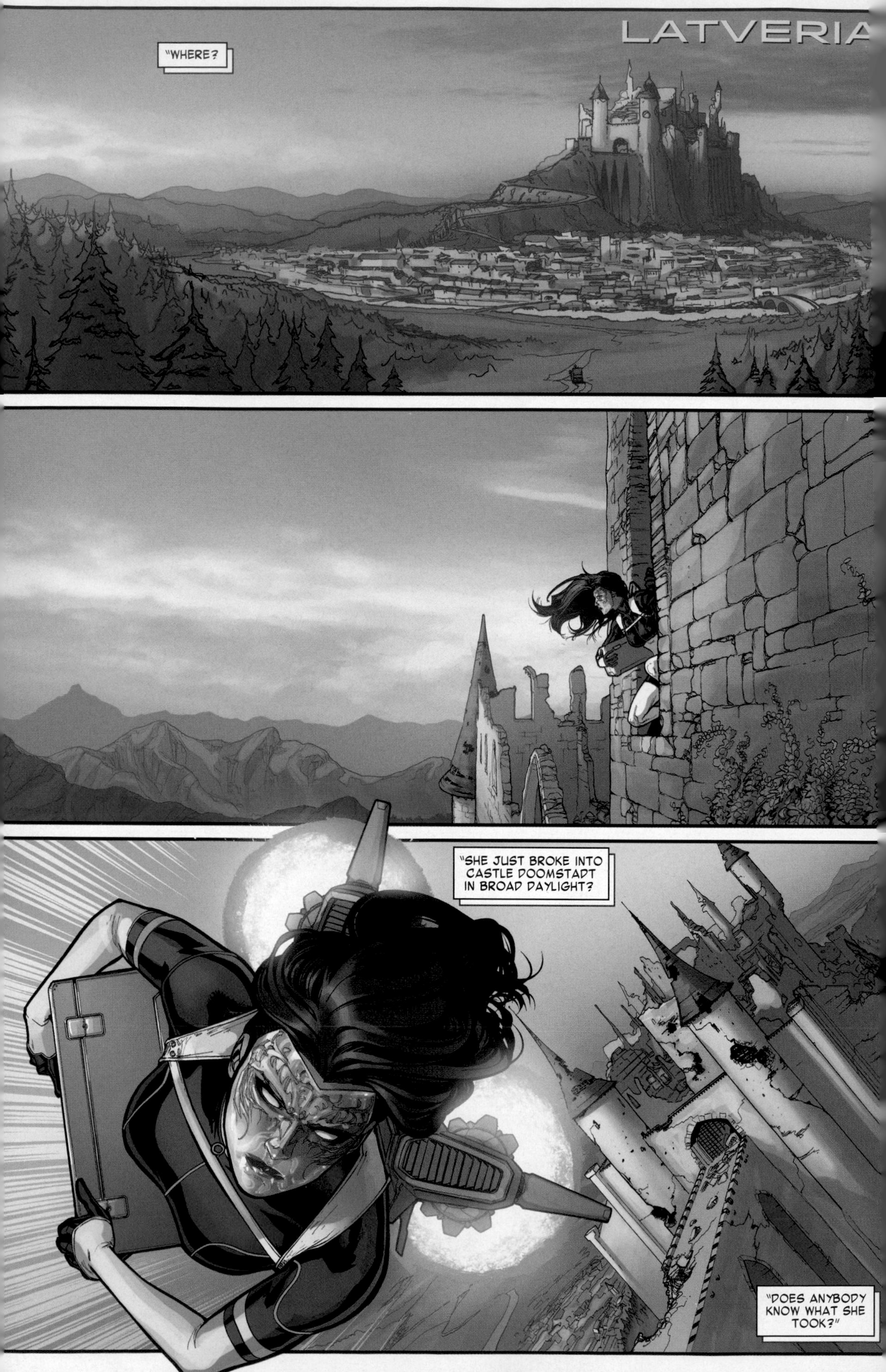
LATVERIA
"WHERE?
"SHE JUST BROKE INTO CASTLE DOOMSTADT IN BROAD DAYLIGHT?
"DOES ANYBODY KNOW WHAT SHE TOOK?"

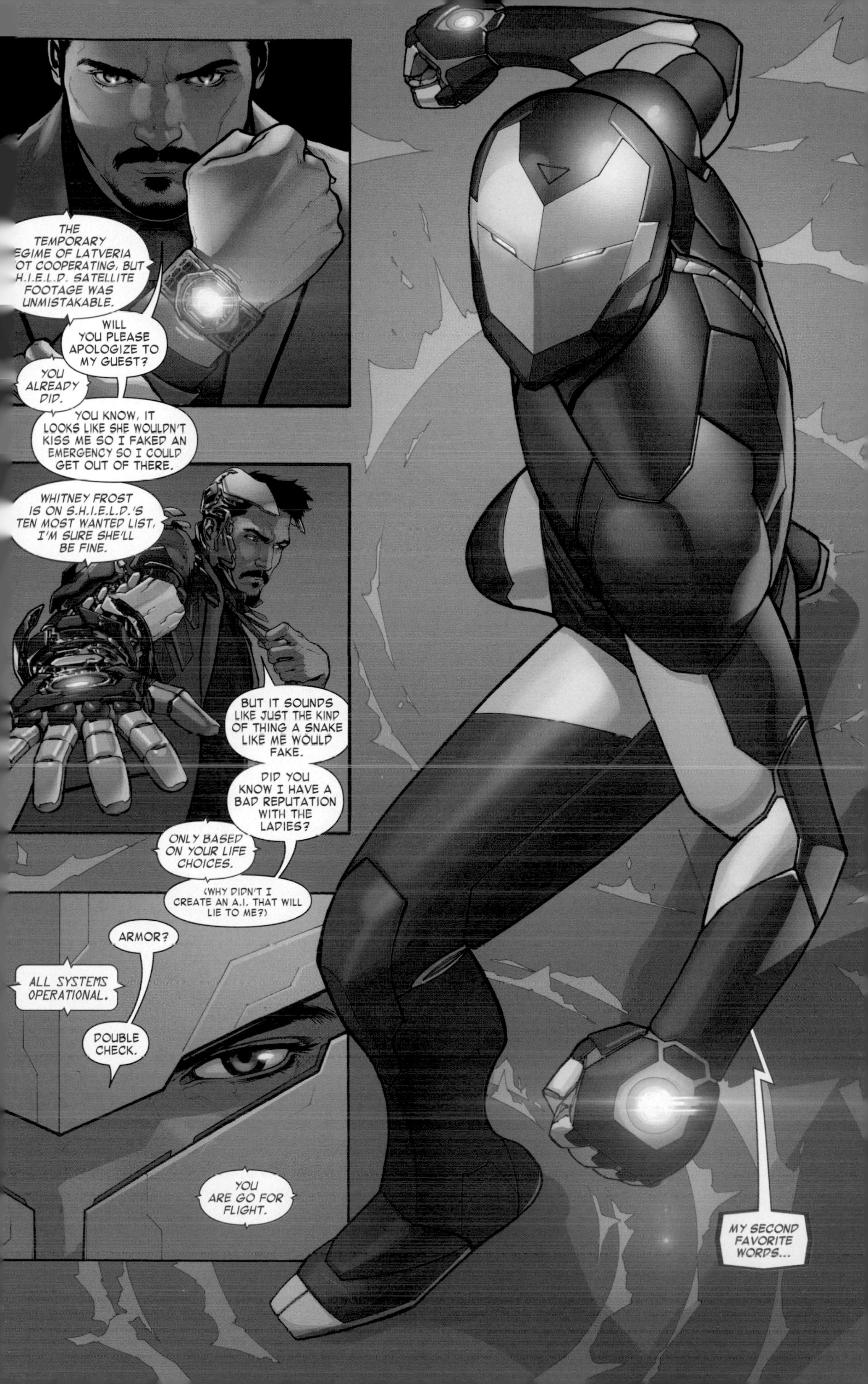
THE TEMPORARY EGIME OF LATVERIA OT COOPERATING, BUT H.I.E.L.D. SATELLITE FOOTAGE WAS UNMISTAKABLE.
WILL YOU PLEASE APOLOGIZE TO MY GUEST?
YOU ALREADY DID.
YOU KNOW, IT LOOKS LIKE SHE WOULDN'T KISS ME SO I FAKED AN EMERGENCY SO I COULD GET OUT OF THERE.
WHITNEY FROST IS ON S.H.I.E.L.D.'S TEN MOST WANTED LIST, I'M SURE SHE'LL BE FINE.
BUT IT SOUNDS LIKE JUST THE KIND OF THING A SNAKE LIKE ME WOULD FAKE.
DID YOU KNOW I HAVE A BAD REPUTATION WITH THE LADIES?
ONLY BASED ON YOUR LIFE CHOICES.
(WHY DIDN'T I CREATE AN A.I. THAT WILL LIE TO ME?)
ARMOR?
ALL SYSTEMS OPERATIONAL.
DOUBLE CHECK.
YOU ARE GO FOR FLIGHT.
MY SECOND FAVORITE WORDS...

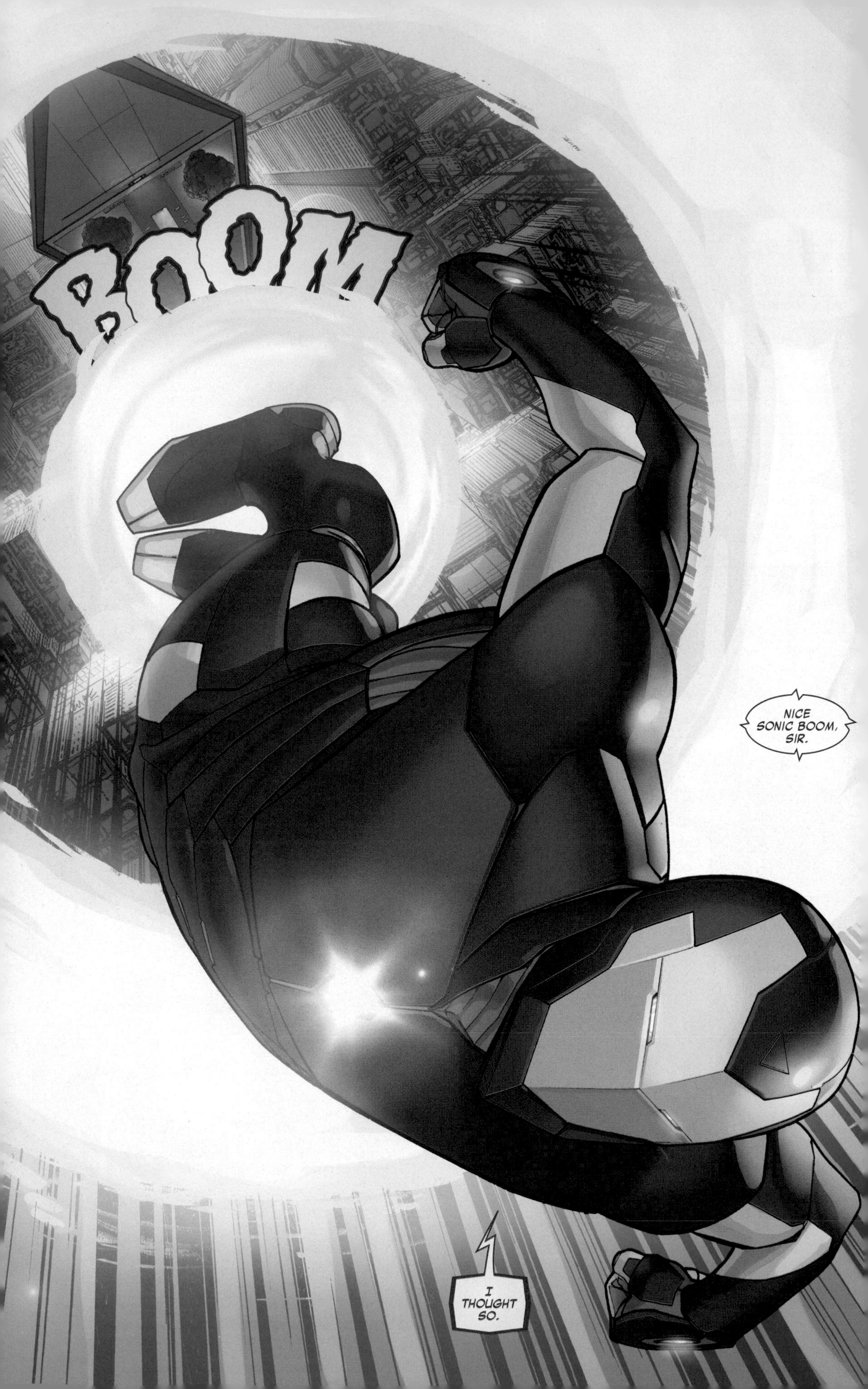
BOOM
NICE SONIC BOOM, SIR.
I THOUGHT SO.

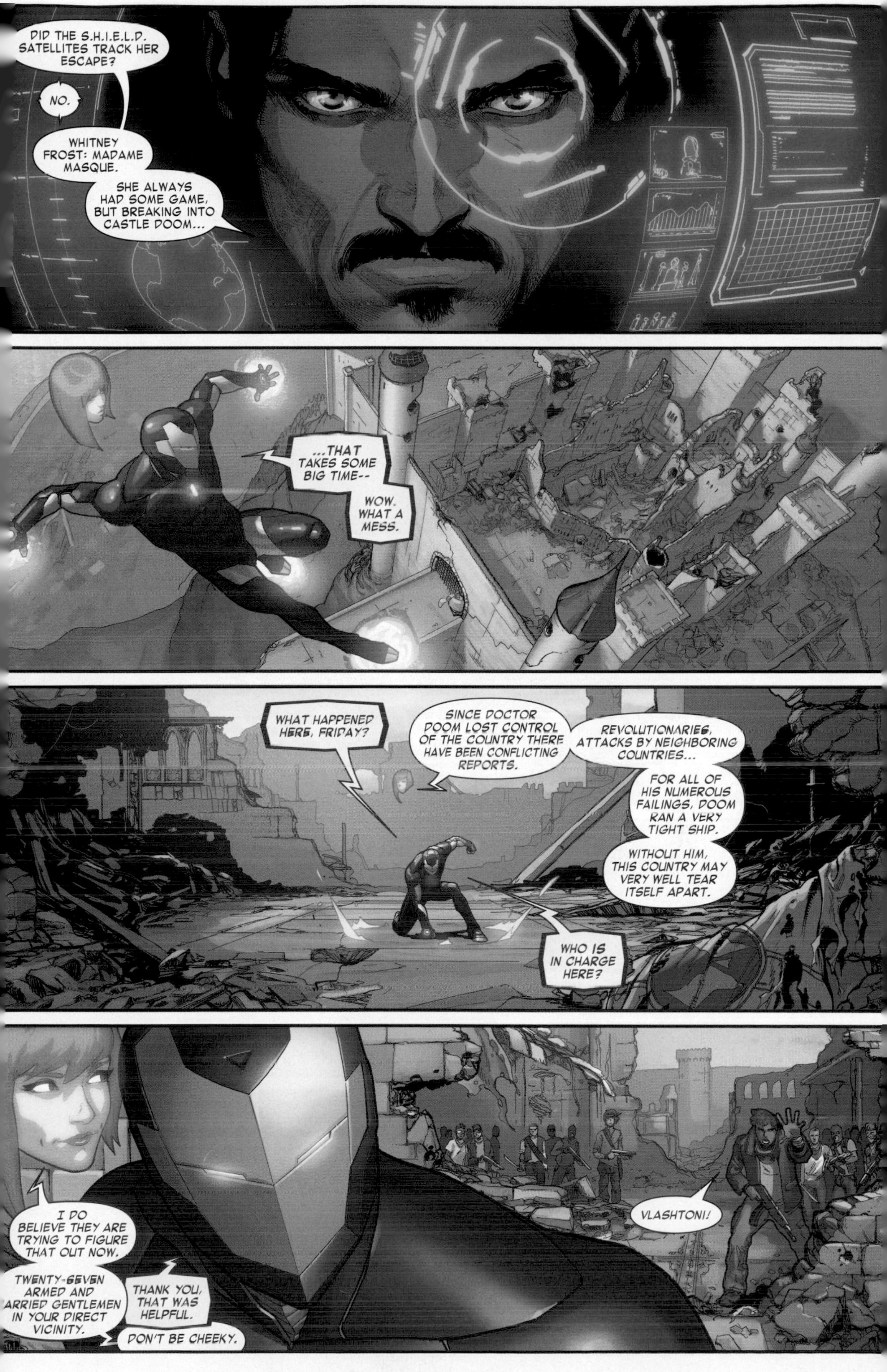
DID THE S.H.I.E.L.D. SATELLITES TRACK HER ESCAPE?
NO.
WHITNEY FROST: MADAME MASQUE.
SHE ALWAYS HAD SOME GAME, BUT BREAKING INTO CASTLE DOOM...
...THAT TAKES SOME BIG TIME--
WOW. WHAT A MESS.
WHAT HAPPENED HERE, FRIDAY?
SINCE DOCTOR DOOM LOST CONTROL OF THE COUNTRY THERE HAVE BEEN CONFLICTING REPORTS.
REVOLUTIONARIES, ATTACKS BY NEIGHBORING COUNTRIES...
FOR ALL OF HIS NUMEROUS FAILINGS, DOOM RAN A VERY TIGHT SHIP.
WITHOUT HIM, THIS COUNTRY MAY VERY WELL TEAR ITSELF APART.
WHO IS IN CHARGE HERE?
I DO BELIEVE THEY ARE TRYING TO FIGURE THAT OUT NOW.
VLASHTONI!
TWENTY-SEVEN ARMED AND ARRIED GENTLEMEN IN YOUR DIRECT VICINITY.
THANK YOU, THAT WAS HELPFUL.
DON'T BE CHEEKY.

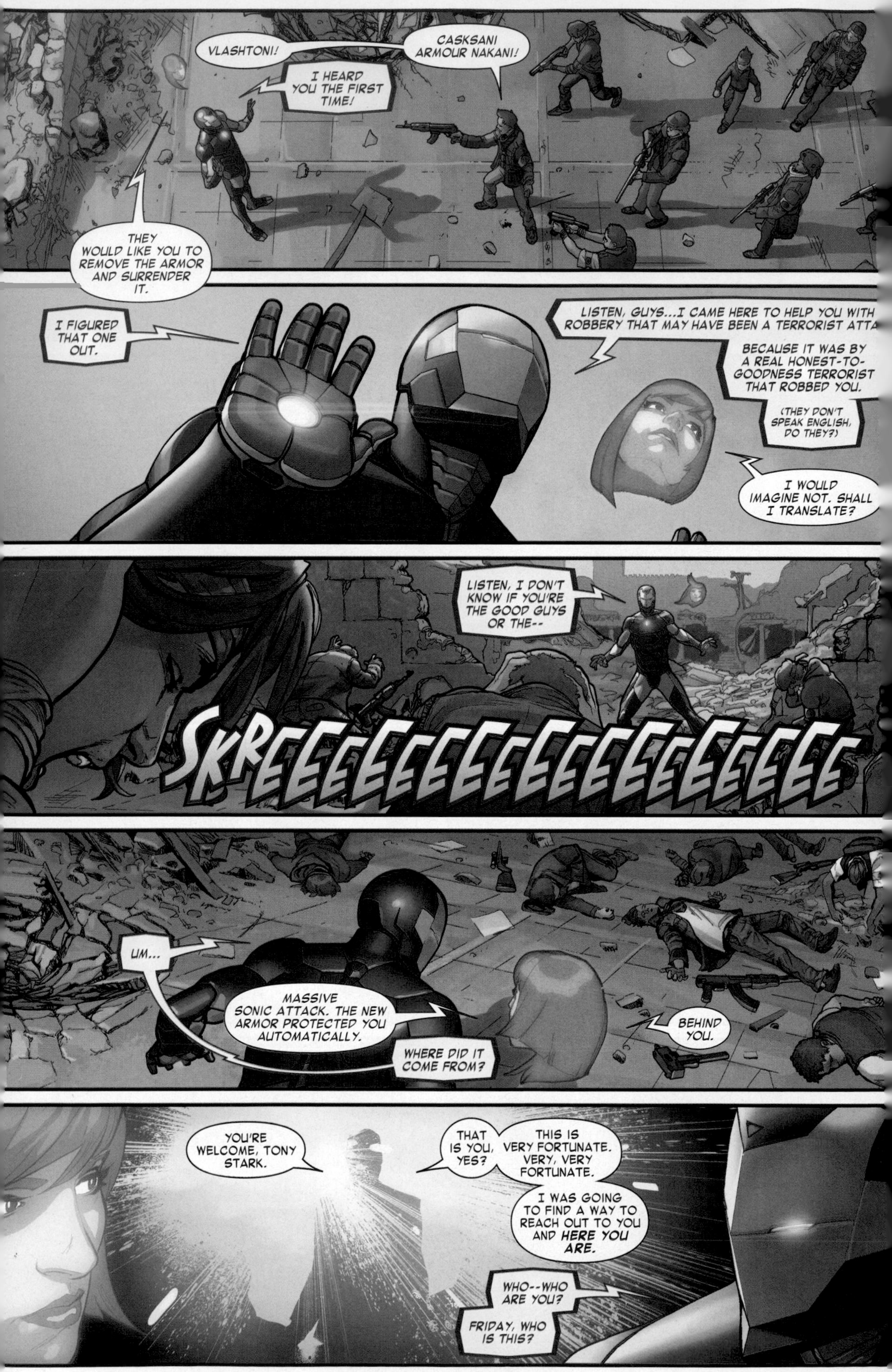
VLASHTONI!
CASKSANI ARMOUR NAKANI!
I HEARD YOU THE FIRST TIME!
THEY WOULD LIKE YOU TO REMOVE THE ARMOR AND SURRENDER IT.
I FIGURED THAT ONE OUT.
LISTEN, GUYS...I CAME HERE TO HELP YOU WITH ROBBERY THAT MAY HAVE BEEN A TERRORIST ATTA
BECAUSE IT WAS BY A REAL HONEST-TO-GOODNESS TERRORIST THAT ROBBED YOU.
(THEY DON'T SPEAK ENGLISH, DO THEY?)
I WOULD IMAGINE NOT. SHALL I TRANSLATE?
LISTEN, I DON'T KNOW IF YOU'RE THE GOOD GUYS OR THE--
SKREEEEEEEEEEEEEEEEEEEE
UM...
MASSIVE SONIC ATTACK. THE NEW ARMOR PROTECTED YOU AUTOMATICALLY.
WHERE DID IT COME FROM?
BEHIND YOU.
YOU'RE WELCOME, TONY STARK.
THAT IS YOU, YES?
THIS IS VERY FORTUNATE. VERY, VERY FORTUNATE.
I WAS GOING TO FIND A WAY TO REACH OUT TO YOU AND **HERE YOU ARE.**
WHO--WHO ARE YOU?
FRIDAY, WHO IS THIS?

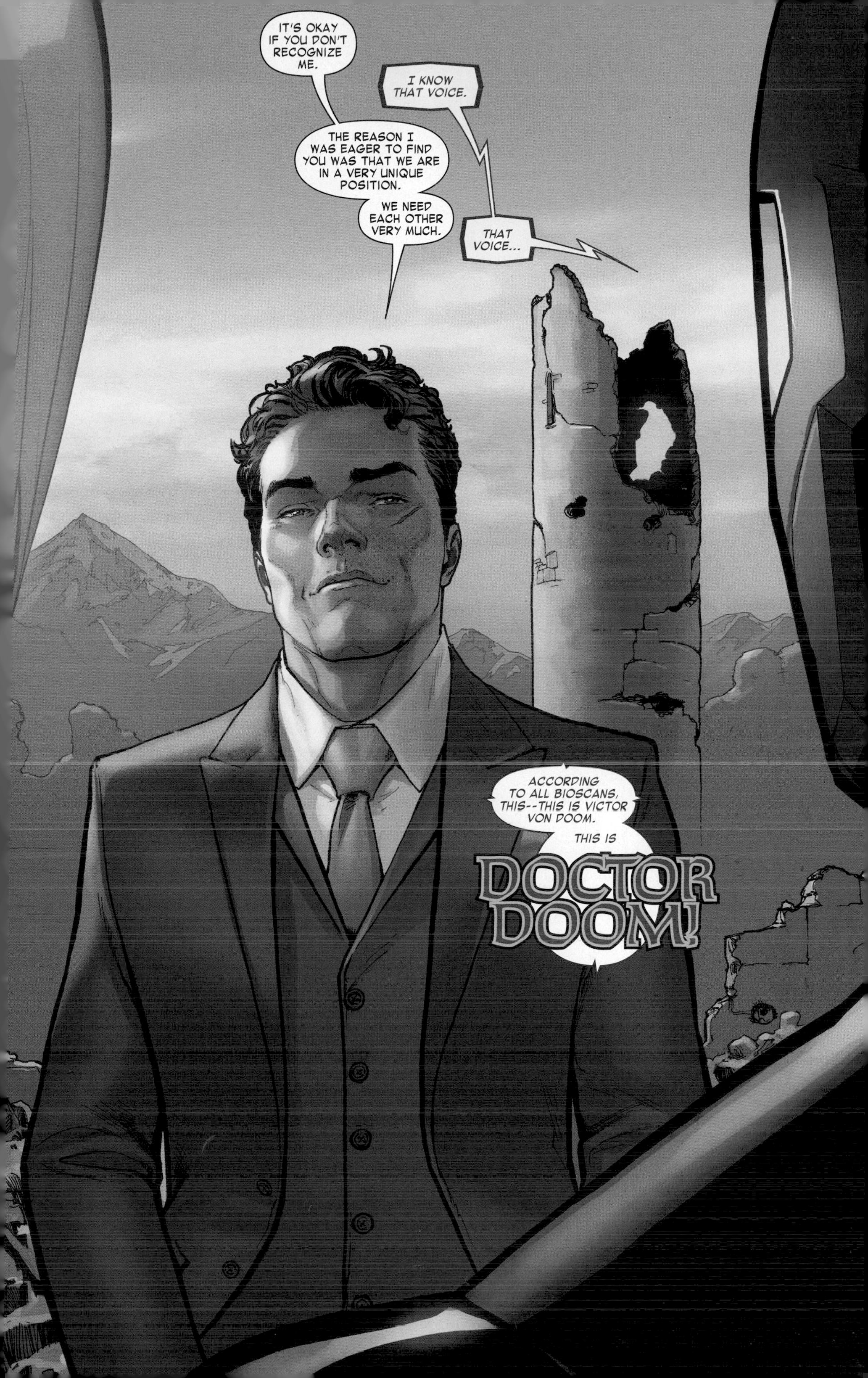
IT'S OKAY IF YOU DON'T RECOGNIZE ME.
I KNOW THAT VOICE.
THE REASON I WAS EAGER TO FIND YOU WAS THAT WE ARE IN A VERY UNIQUE POSITION.
WE NEED EACH OTHER VERY MUCH.
THAT VOICE...
ACCORDING TO ALL BIOSCANS, THIS--THIS IS VICTOR VON DOOM.
THIS IS
DOCTOR DOOM!

#2

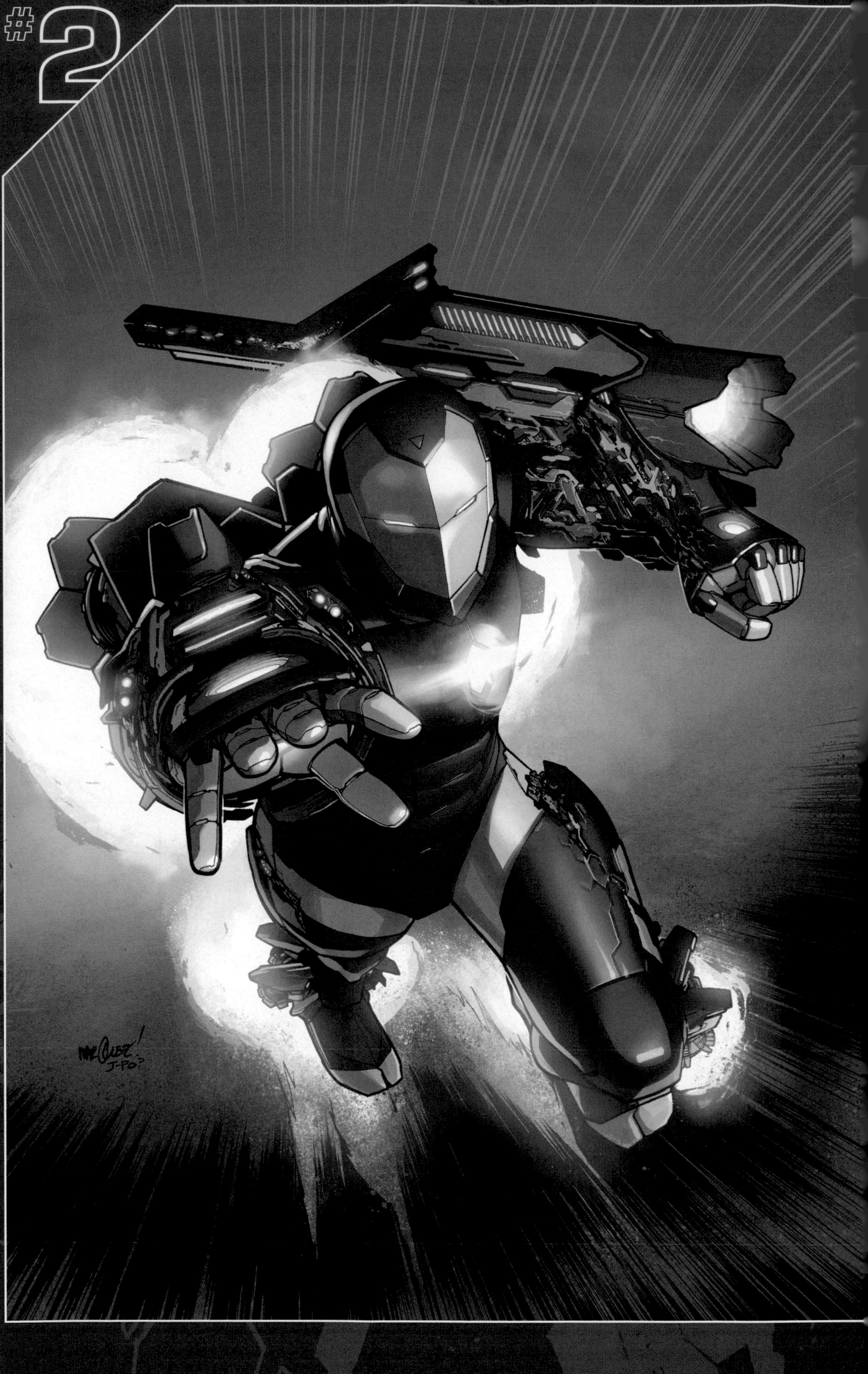

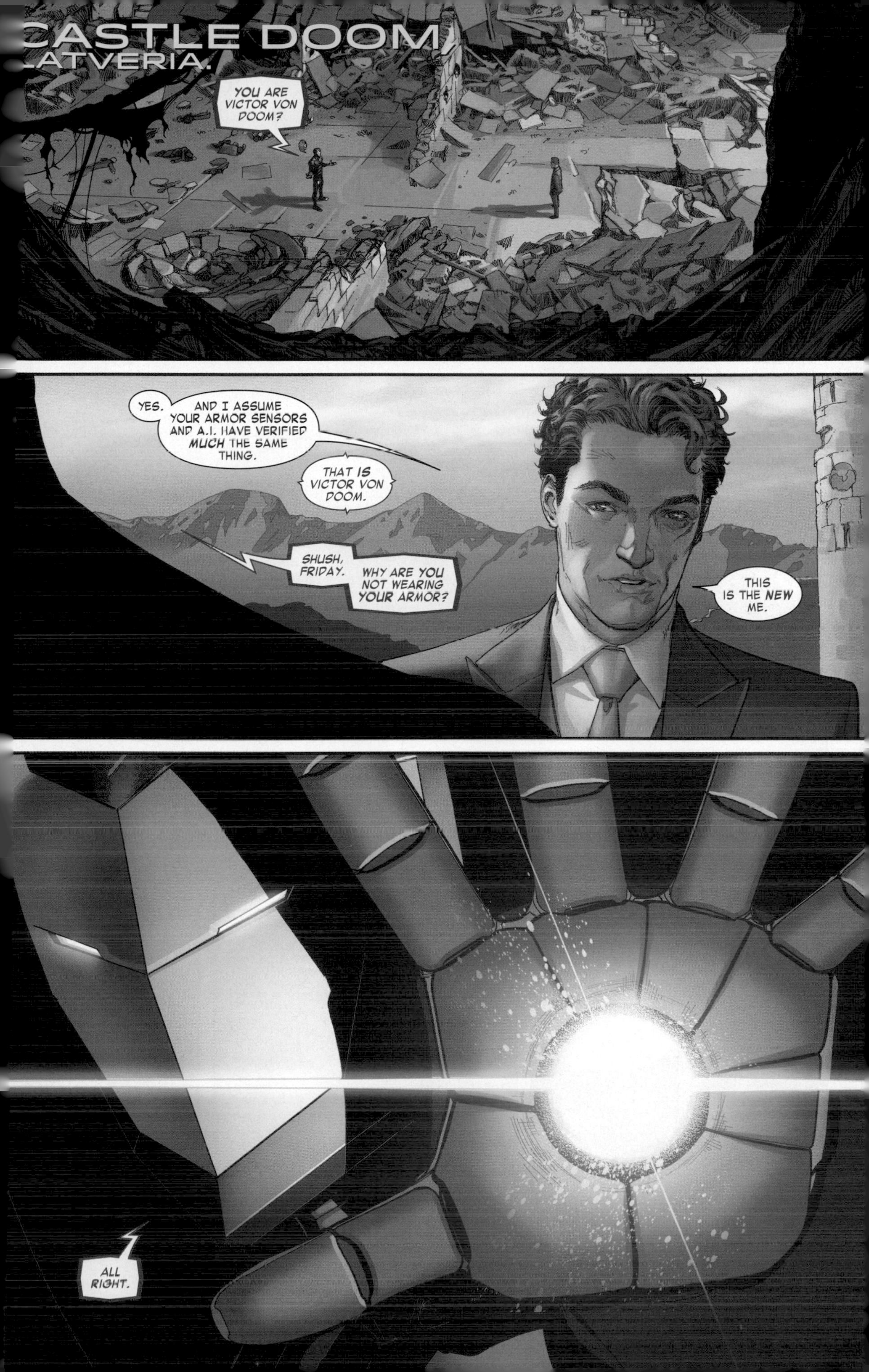
CASTLE DOOM,
LATVERIA.
YOU ARE VICTOR VON DOOM?
YES.
AND I ASSUME YOUR ARMOR SENSORS AND A.I. HAVE VERIFIED MUCH THE SAME THING.
THAT IS VICTOR VON DOOM.
SHUSH, FRIDAY.
WHY ARE YOU NOT WEARING YOUR ARMOR?
THIS IS THE NEW ME.
ALL RIGHT.

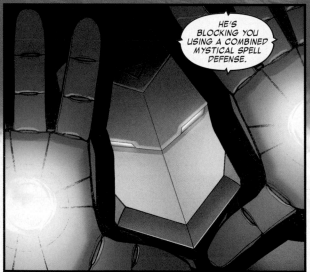

HE'S BLOCKING YOU USING A COMBINED MYSTICAL SPELL DEFENSE.

ARE YOU FINISHED?

HE REALLY IS VICTOR VON DOOM.

I'M NOT SURE WHAT TO DO HERE, FRIDAY...

VICTOR VON DOOM, THE MOST DANGEROUS MAN ON THE PLANET, IS JUST STANDING HERE SMILING AT ME.

IF YOU DON'T BELIEVE ME...

...YOU AND I ONCE TIME-TRAVELED BACK TO THE DAYS OF KING ARTHUR AND HAD QUITE A ROUSING ADVENTURE.

I ALWAYS LOOK BACK ON THAT QUITE FONDLY.

YOU TRIED TO MURDER ME AND LEAVE ME THERE.

FABOOM

FABOOM

YOU'RE THE DOCTOR DOOM?

YES.

I THOUGHT YOUR FACE WAS SCARRED BEYOND ANYTHING ANY HUMAN COULD STAND LOOKING AT.

IT WAS. I'M BETTER.

I SAID I LOOKED BACK ON IT FONDLY, I DIDN'T SAY YOU DID.

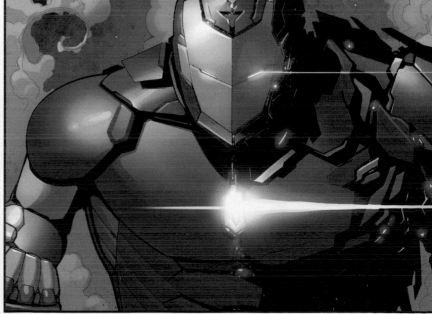

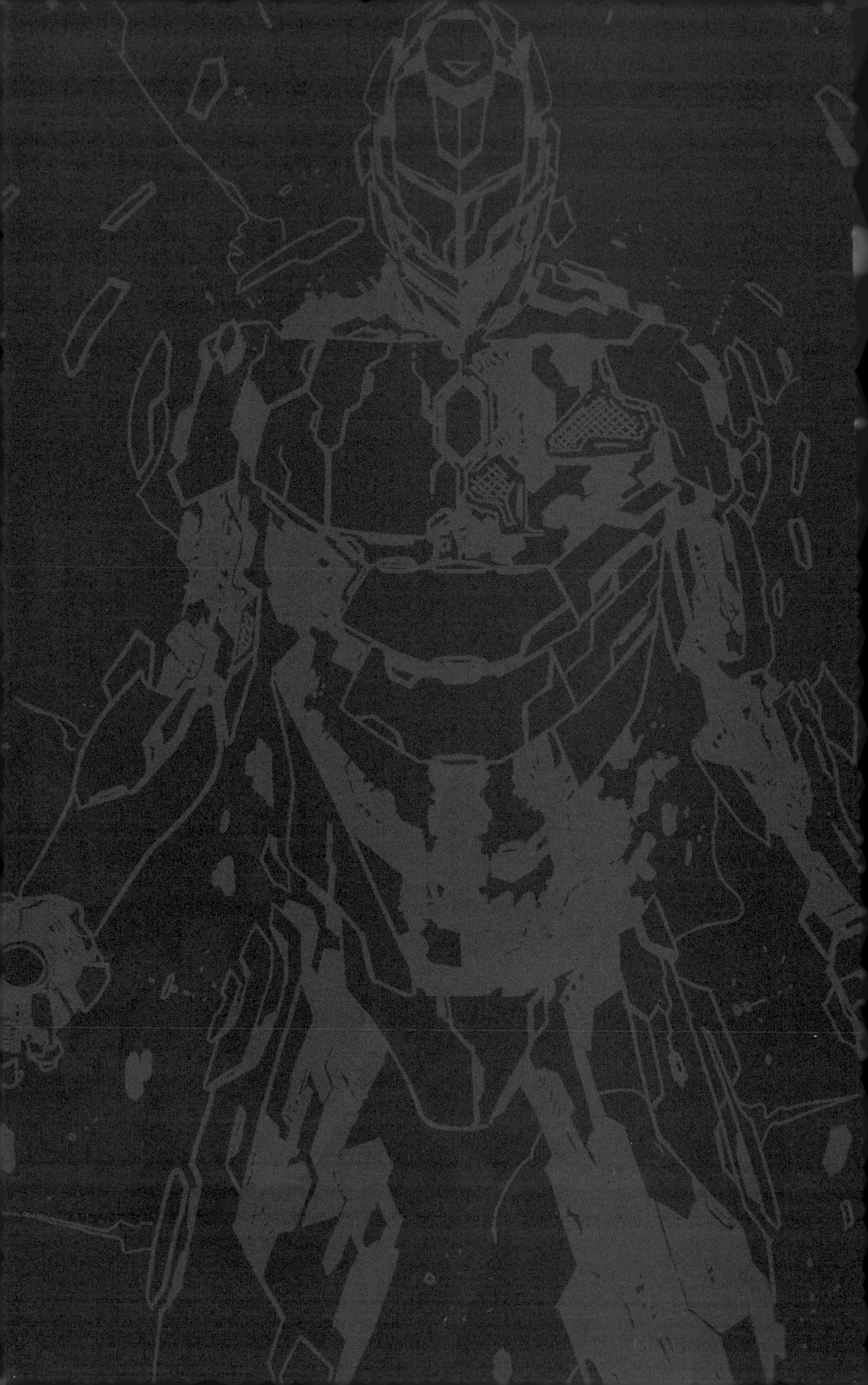

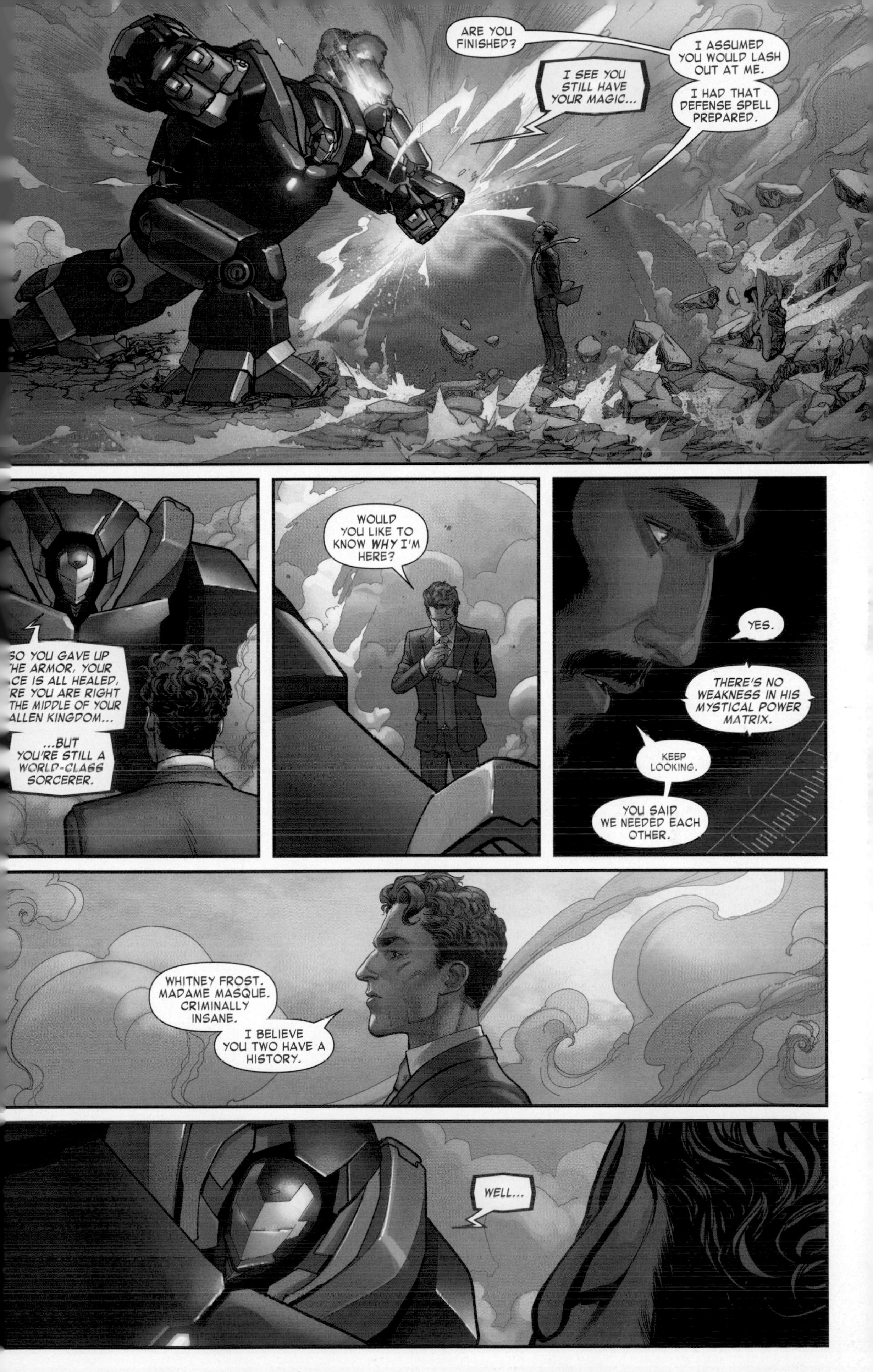

ARE YOU FINISHED?
I SEE YOU STILL HAVE YOUR MAGIC...
I ASSUMED YOU WOULD LASH OUT AT ME.
I HAD THAT DEFENSE SPELL PREPARED.
SO YOU GAVE UP THE ARMOR, YOUR ACE IS ALL HEALED, RE YOU ARE RIGHT THE MIDDLE OF YOUR ALLEN KINGDOM...
...BUT YOU'RE STILL A WORLD-CLASS SORCERER.
WOULD YOU LIKE TO KNOW WHY I'M HERE?
YES.
THERE'S NO WEAKNESS IN HIS MYSTICAL POWER MATRIX.
KEEP LOOKING.
YOU SAID WE NEEDED EACH OTHER.
WHITNEY FROST. MADAME MASQUE. CRIMINALLY INSANE.
I BELIEVE YOU TWO HAVE A HISTORY.
WELL...

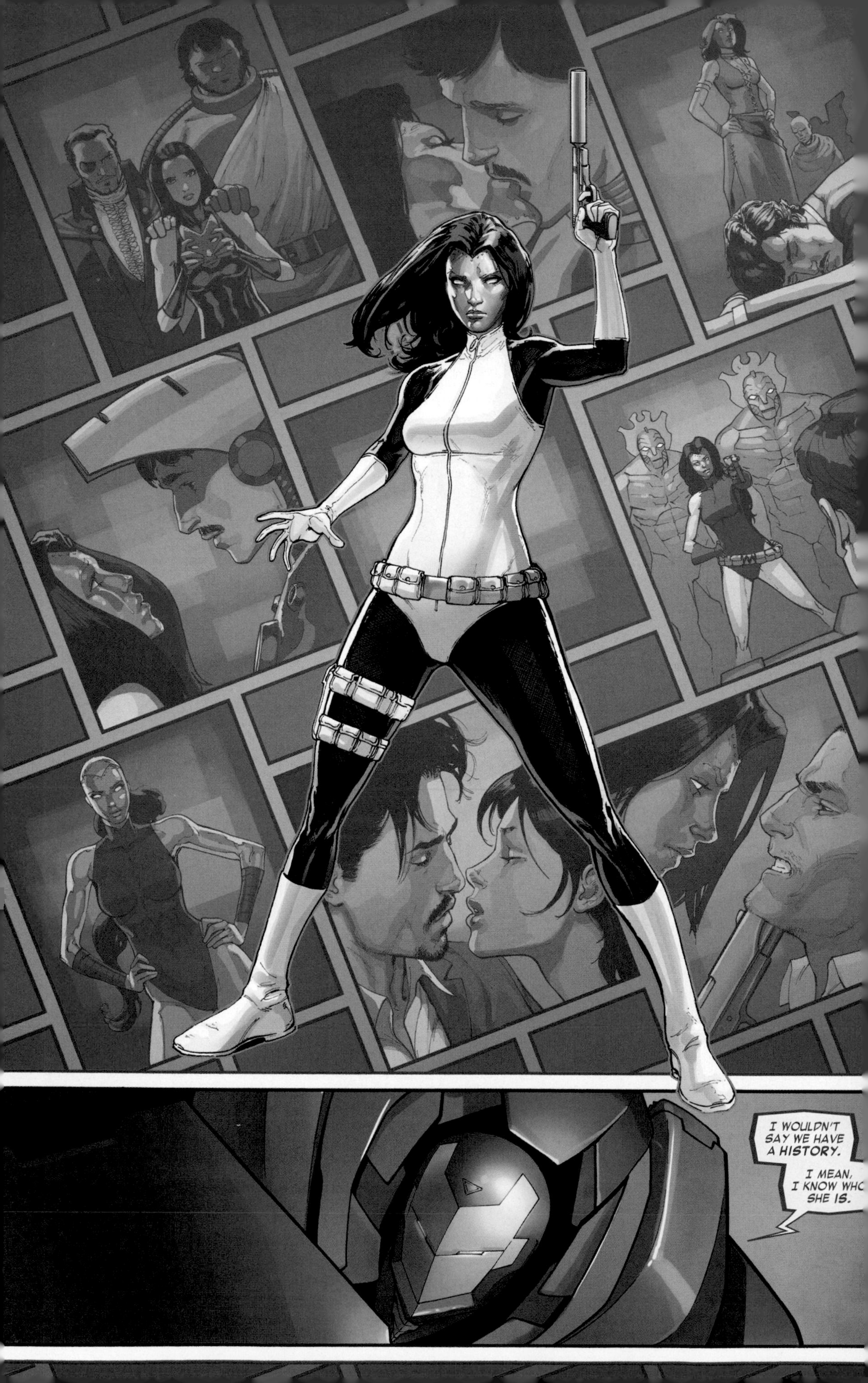
I WOULDN'T SAY WE HAVE A HISTORY.
I MEAN, I KNOW WHO SHE IS.

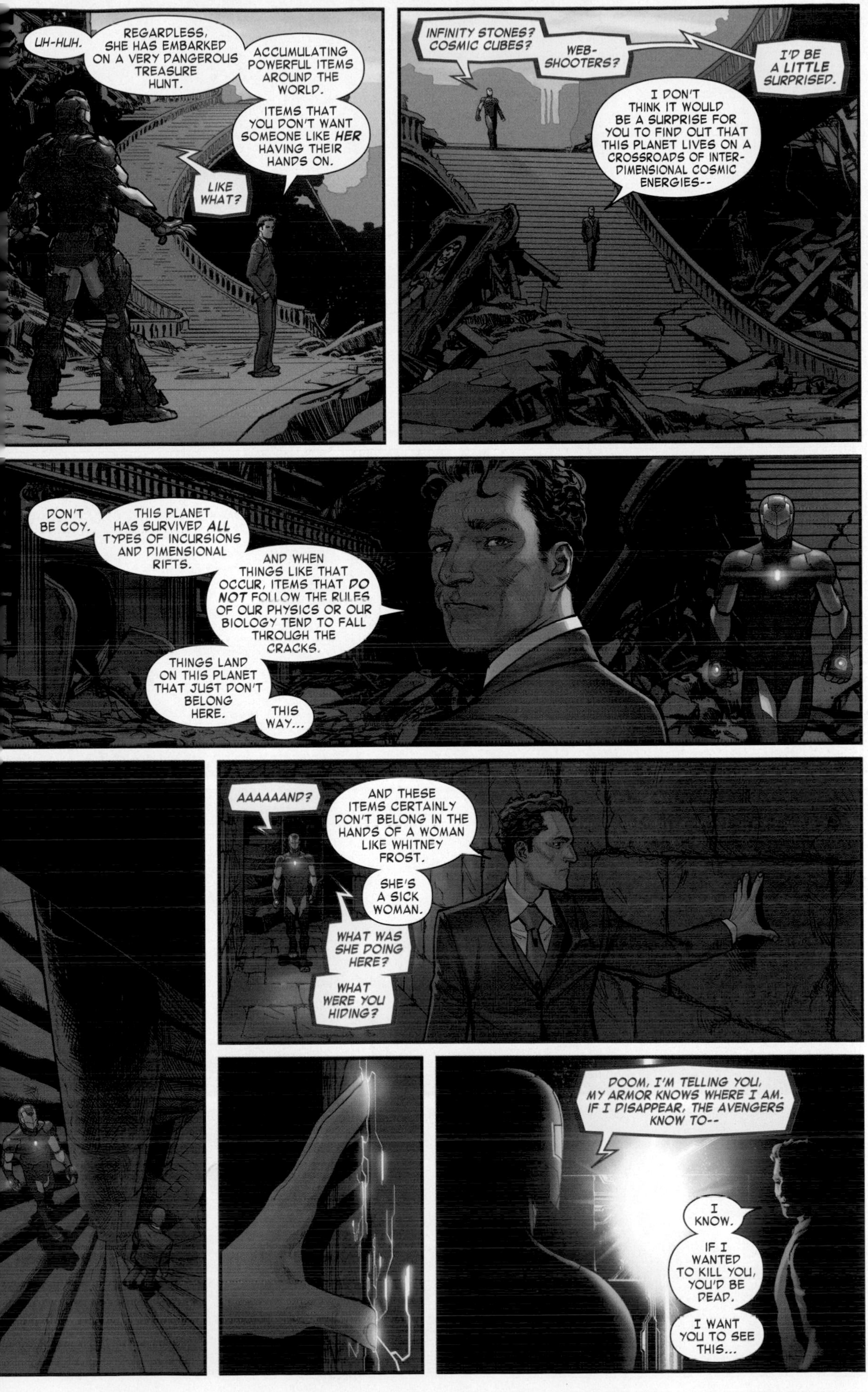
UH-HUH.
REGARDLESS, SHE HAS EMBARKED ON A VERY DANGEROUS TREASURE HUNT.
ACCUMULATING POWERFUL ITEMS AROUND THE WORLD.
ITEMS THAT YOU DON'T WANT SOMEONE LIKE HER HAVING THEIR HANDS ON.
LIKE WHAT?
INFINITY STONES? COSMIC CUBES?
WEB-SHOOTERS?
I'D BE A LITTLE SURPRISED.
I DON'T THINK IT WOULD BE A SURPRISE FOR YOU TO FIND OUT THAT THIS PLANET LIVES ON A CROSSROADS OF INTER-DIMENSIONAL COSMIC ENERGIES--
DON'T BE COY.
THIS PLANET HAS SURVIVED ALL TYPES OF INCURSIONS AND DIMENSIONAL RIFTS.
AND WHEN THINGS LIKE THAT OCCUR, ITEMS THAT DO NOT FOLLOW THE RULES OF OUR PHYSICS OR OUR BIOLOGY TEND TO FALL THROUGH THE CRACKS.
THINGS LAND ON THIS PLANET THAT JUST DON'T BELONG HERE.
THIS WAY...
AAAAAAND?
AND THESE ITEMS CERTAINLY DON'T BELONG IN THE HANDS OF A WOMAN LIKE WHITNEY FROST.
SHE'S A SICK WOMAN.
WHAT WAS SHE DOING HERE?
WHAT WERE YOU HIDING?
DOOM, I'M TELLING YOU, MY ARMOR KNOWS WHERE I AM. IF I DISAPPEAR, THE AVENGERS KNOW TO--
I KNOW.
IF I WANTED TO KILL YOU, YOU'D BE DEAD.
I WANT YOU TO SEE THIS...

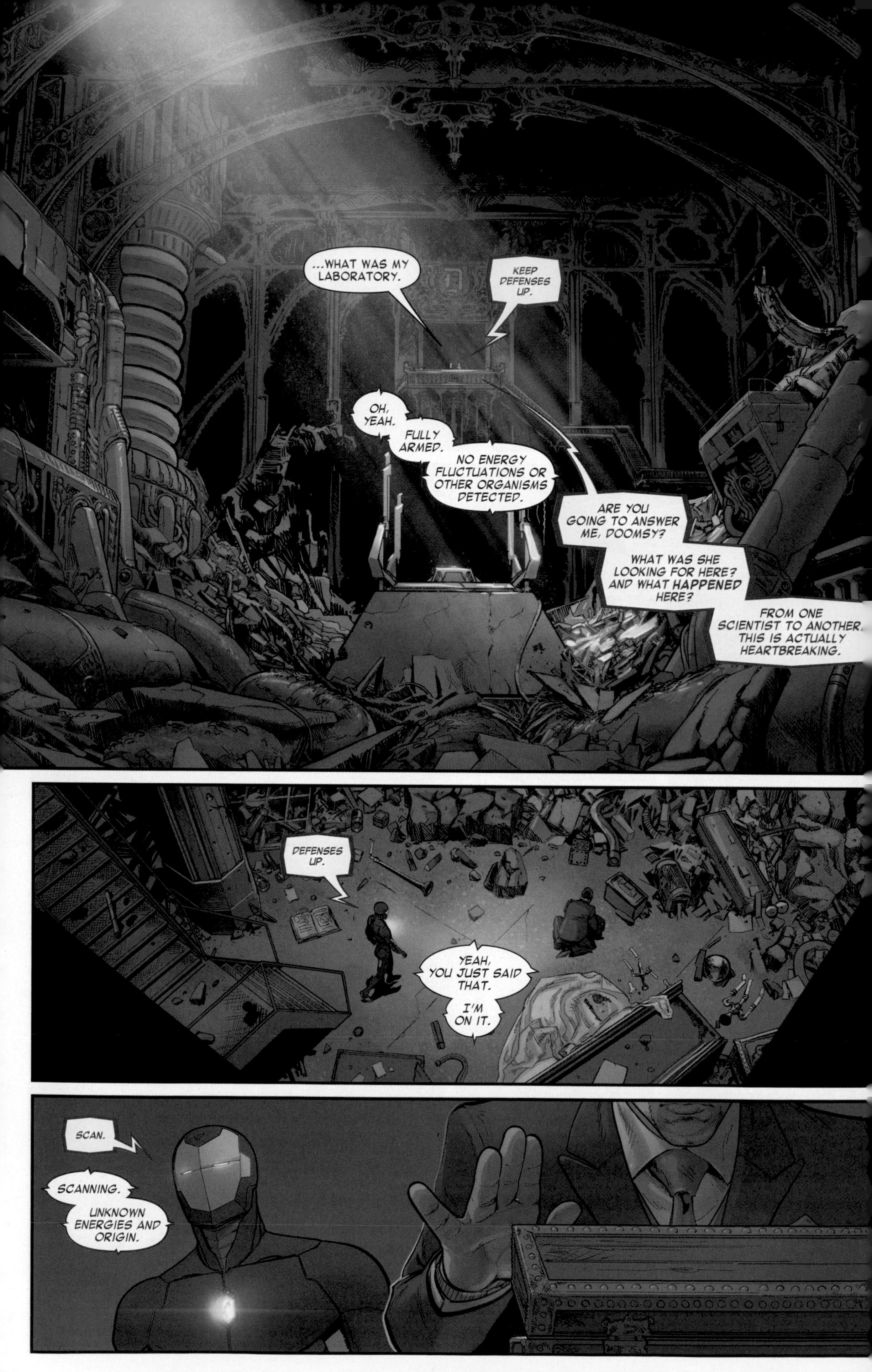
...WHAT WAS MY LABORATORY.
KEEP DEFENSES UP.
OH, YEAH.
FULLY ARMED.
NO ENERGY FLUCTUATIONS OR OTHER ORGANISMS DETECTED.
ARE YOU GOING TO ANSWER ME, DOOMSY?
WHAT WAS SHE LOOKING FOR HERE? AND WHAT HAPPENED HERE?
FROM ONE SCIENTIST TO ANOTHER, THIS IS ACTUALLY HEARTBREAKING.
DEFENSES UP.
YEAH, YOU JUST SAID THAT.
I'M ON IT.
SCAN.
SCANNING.
UNKNOWN ENERGIES AND ORIGIN.

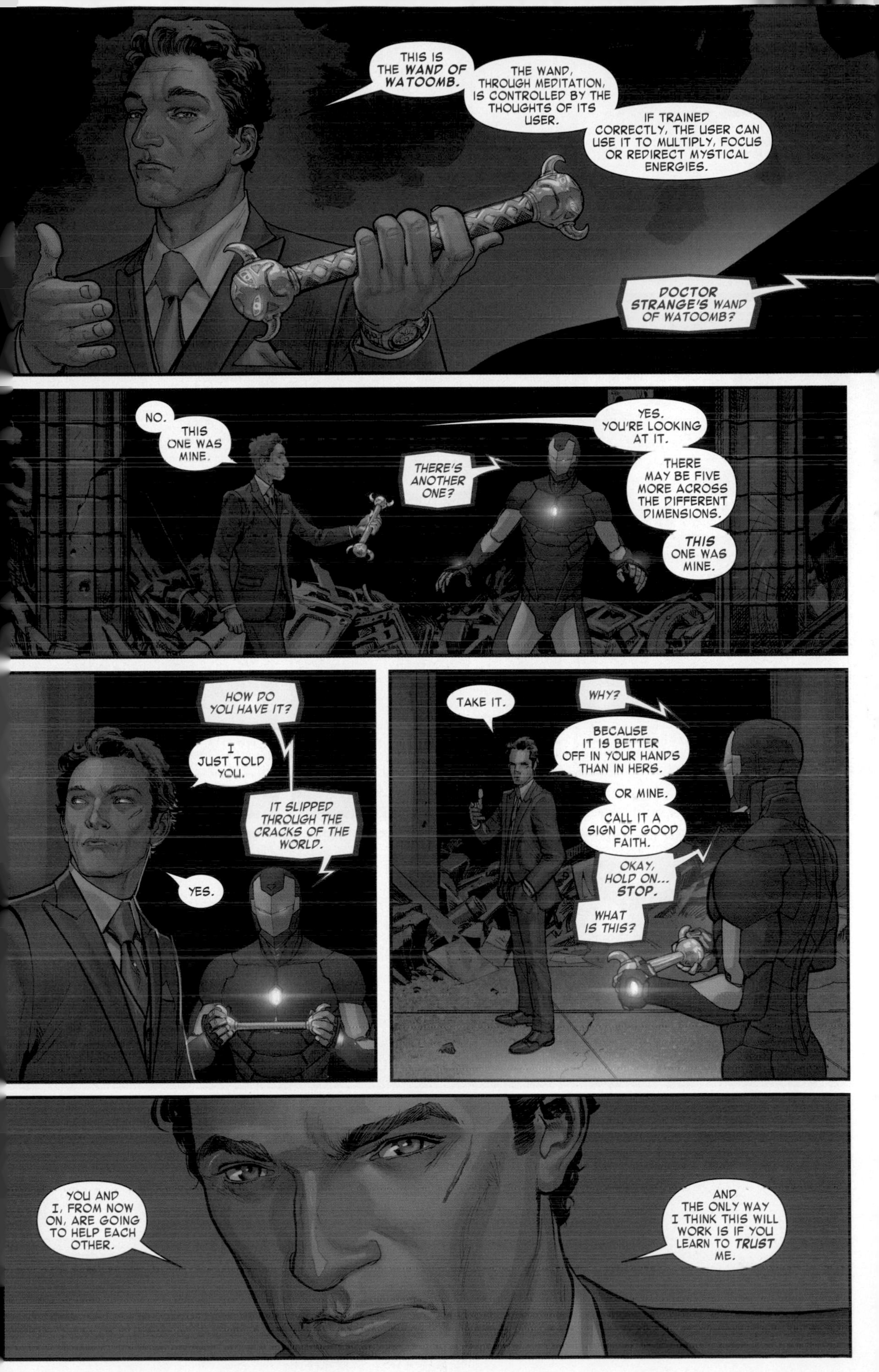
THIS IS THE WAND OF WATOOMB.
THE WAND, THROUGH MEDITATION, IS CONTROLLED BY THE THOUGHTS OF ITS USER.
IF TRAINED CORRECTLY, THE USER CAN USE IT TO MULTIPLY, FOCUS OR REDIRECT MYSTICAL ENERGIES.
DOCTOR STRANGE'S WAND OF WATOOMB?
NO.
THIS ONE WAS MINE.
THERE'S ANOTHER ONE?
YES. YOU'RE LOOKING AT IT.
THERE MAY BE FIVE MORE ACROSS THE DIFFERENT DIMENSIONS.
THIS ONE WAS MINE.
HOW DO YOU HAVE IT?
I JUST TOLD YOU.
IT SLIPPED THROUGH THE CRACKS OF THE WORLD.
YES.
TAKE IT.
WHY?
BECAUSE IT IS BETTER OFF IN YOUR HANDS THAN IN HERS.
OR MINE.
CALL IT A SIGN OF GOOD FAITH.
OKAY, HOLD ON... STOP.
WHAT IS THIS?
YOU AND I, FROM NOW ON, ARE GOING TO HELP EACH OTHER.
AND THE ONLY WAY I THINK THIS WILL WORK IS IF YOU LEARN TO TRUST ME.

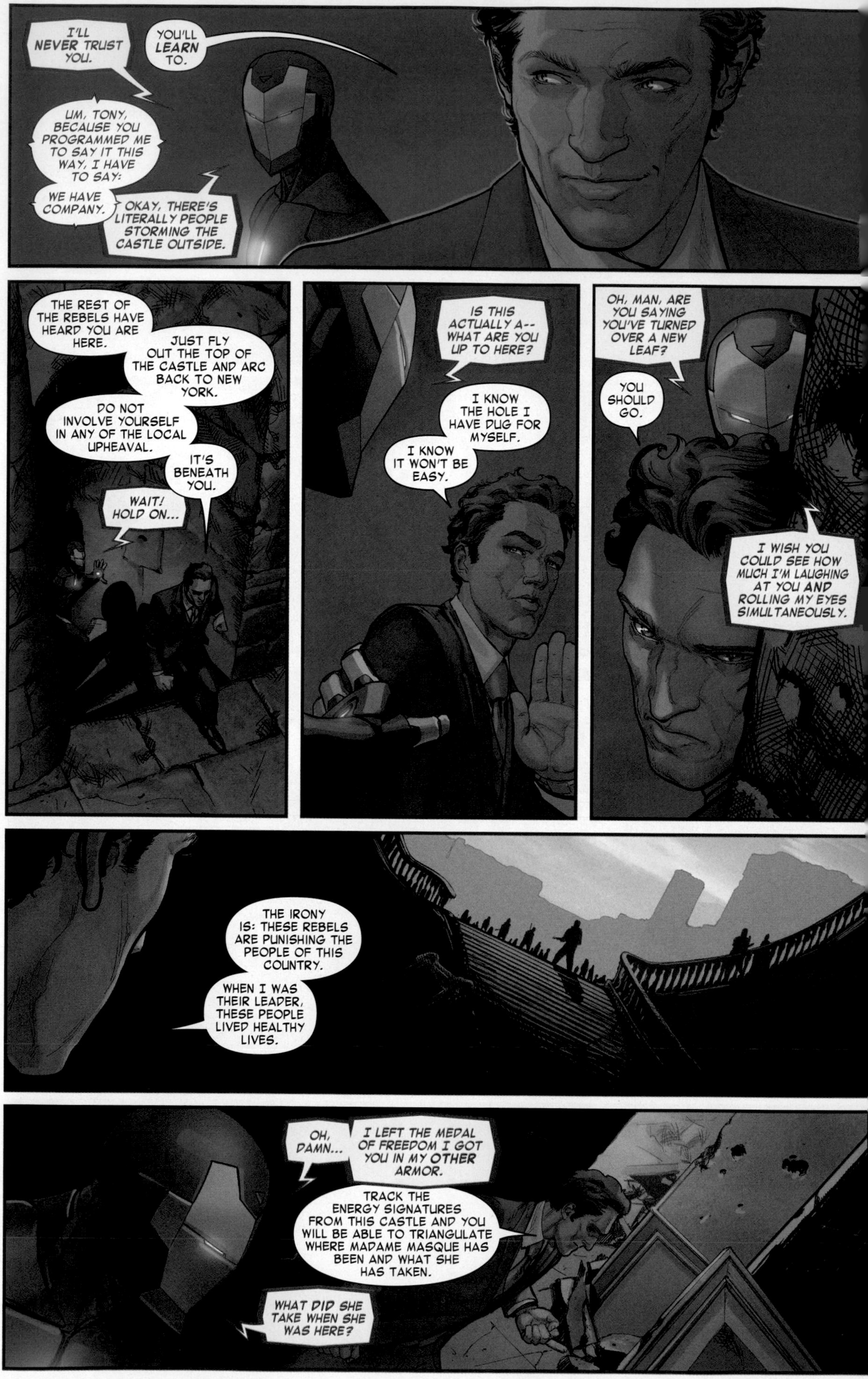
I'LL NEVER TRUST YOU.
YOU'LL LEARN TO.
UM, TONY, BECAUSE YOU PROGRAMMED ME TO SAY IT THIS WAY, I HAVE TO SAY:
WE HAVE COMPANY.
OKAY, THERE'S LITERALLY PEOPLE STORMING THE CASTLE OUTSIDE.
THE REST OF THE REBELS HAVE HEARD YOU ARE HERE.
JUST FLY OUT THE TOP OF THE CASTLE AND ARC BACK TO NEW YORK.
DO NOT INVOLVE YOURSELF IN ANY OF THE LOCAL UPHEAVAL.
IT'S BENEATH YOU.
WAIT! HOLD ON...
IS THIS ACTUALLY A-- WHAT ARE YOU UP TO HERE?
I KNOW THE HOLE I HAVE DUG FOR MYSELF.
I KNOW IT WON'T BE EASY.
OH, MAN, ARE YOU SAYING YOU'VE TURNED OVER A NEW LEAF?
YOU SHOULD GO.
I WISH YOU COULD SEE HOW MUCH I'M LAUGHING AT YOU AND ROLLING MY EYES SIMULTANEOUSLY.
THE IRONY IS: THESE REBELS ARE PUNISHING THE PEOPLE OF THIS COUNTRY.
WHEN I WAS THEIR LEADER, THESE PEOPLE LIVED HEALTHY LIVES.
OH, DAMN...
I LEFT THE MEDAL OF FREEDOM I GOT YOU IN MY OTHER ARMOR.
TRACK THE ENERGY SIGNATURES FROM THIS CASTLE AND YOU WILL BE ABLE TO TRIANGULATE WHERE MADAME MASQUE HAS BEEN AND WHAT SHE HAS TAKEN.
WHAT DID SHE TAKE WHEN SHE WAS HERE?

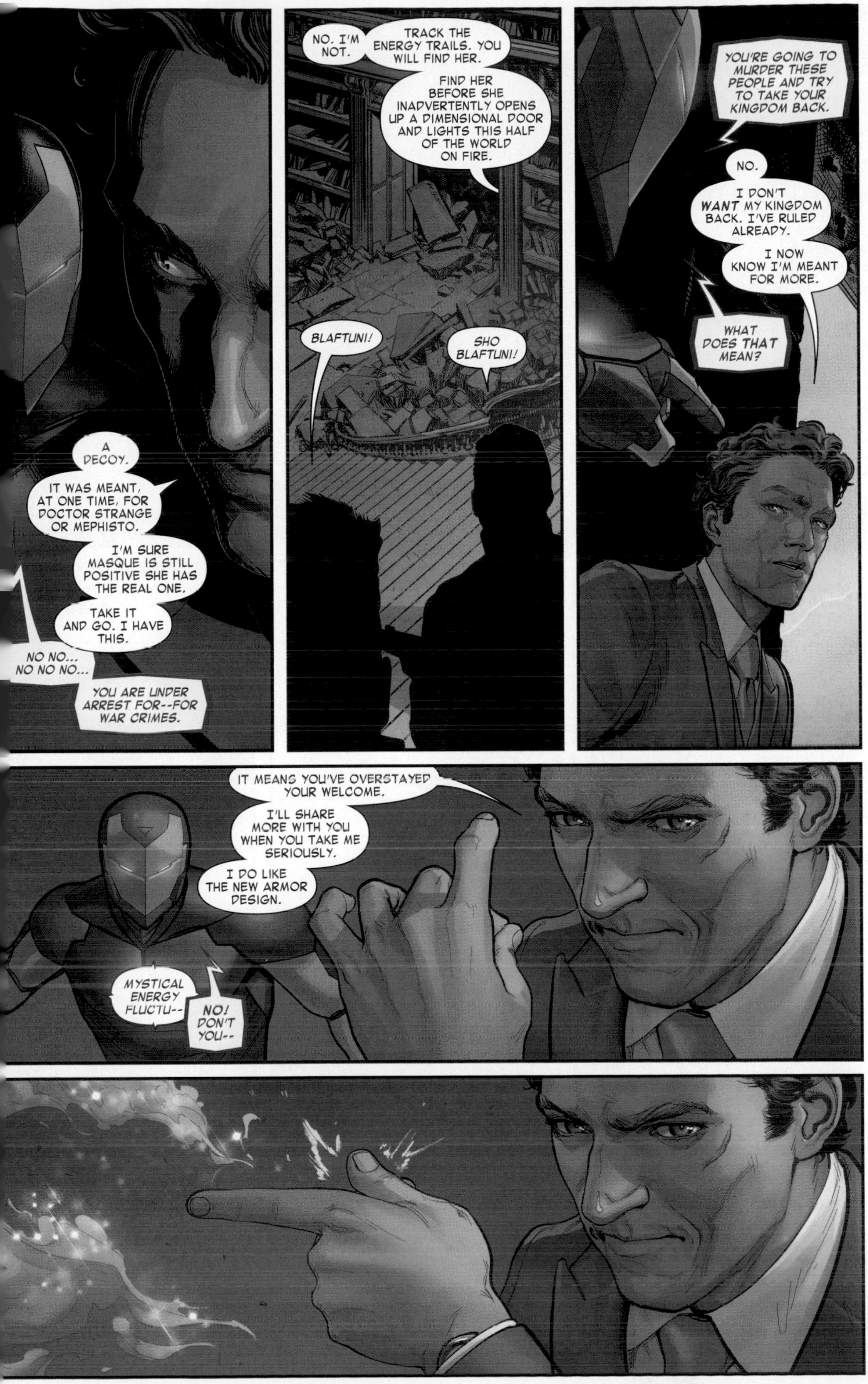
A DECOY.
IT WAS MEANT, AT ONE TIME, FOR DOCTOR STRANGE OR MEPHISTO.
I'M SURE MASQUE IS STILL POSITIVE SHE HAS THE REAL ONE.
TAKE IT AND GO. I HAVE THIS.
NO NO... NO NO NO...
YOU ARE UNDER ARREST FOR--FOR WAR CRIMES.
NO. I'M NOT.
TRACK THE ENERGY TRAILS. YOU WILL FIND HER.
FIND HER BEFORE SHE INADVERTENTLY OPENS UP A DIMENSIONAL DOOR AND LIGHTS THIS HALF OF THE WORLD ON FIRE.
BLAFTUNI!
SHO BLAFTUNI!
YOU'RE GOING TO MURDER THESE PEOPLE AND TRY TO TAKE YOUR KINGDOM BACK.
NO.
I DON'T WANT MY KINGDOM BACK. I'VE RULED ALREADY.
I NOW KNOW I'M MEANT FOR MORE.
WHAT DOES THAT MEAN?
IT MEANS YOU'VE OVERSTAYED YOUR WELCOME.
I'LL SHARE MORE WITH YOU WHEN YOU TAKE ME SERIOUSLY.
I DO LIKE THE NEW ARMOR DESIGN.
MYSTICAL ENERGY FLUCTU--
NO! DON'T YOU--

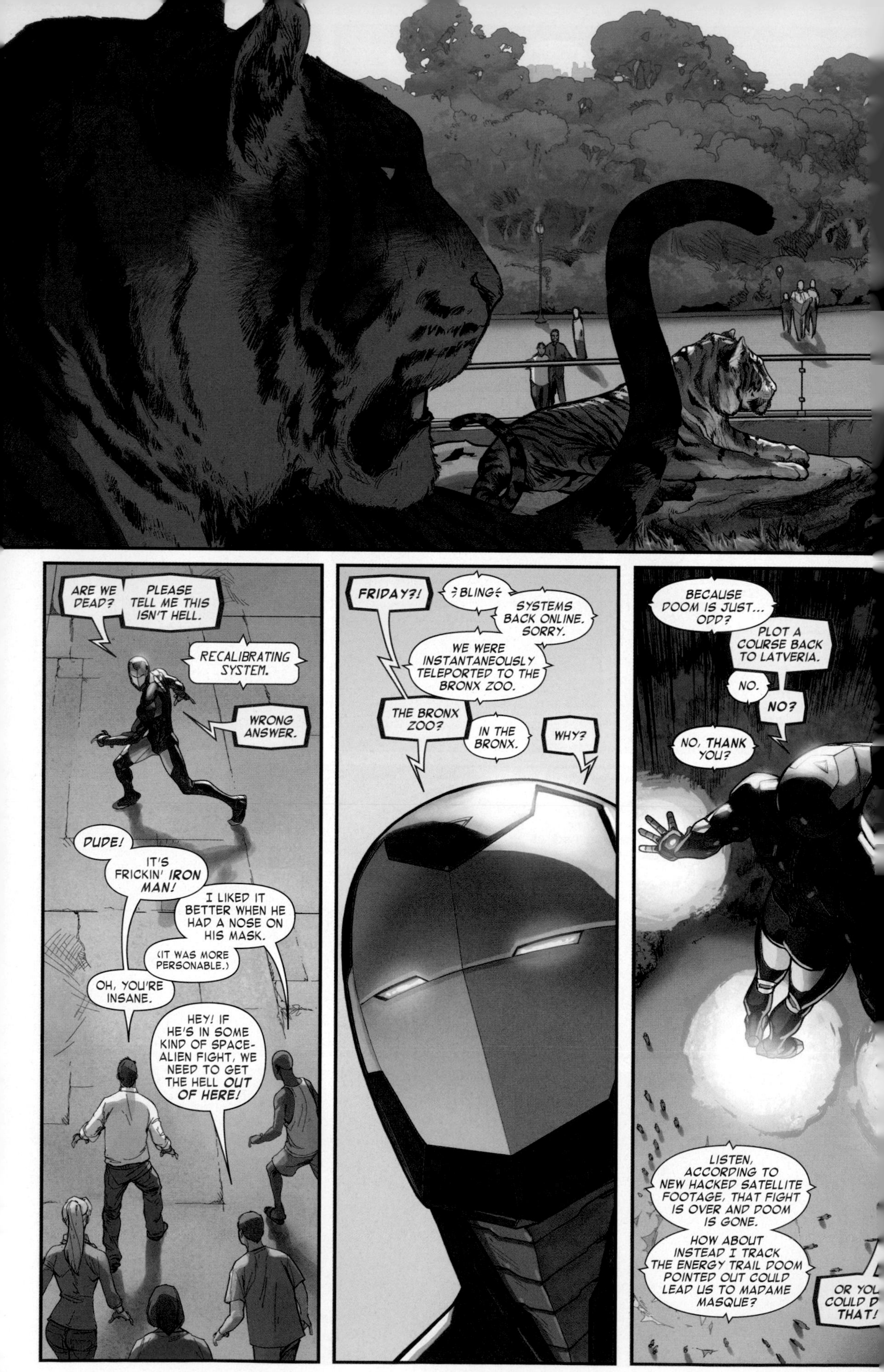
ARE WE DEAD?
PLEASE TELL ME THIS ISN'T HELL.
RECALIBRATING SYSTEM.
WRONG ANSWER.
DUDE!
IT'S FRICKIN' IRON MAN!
I LIKED IT BETTER WHEN HE HAD A NOSE ON HIS MASK.
(IT WAS MORE PERSONABLE.)
OH, YOU'RE INSANE.
HEY! IF HE'S IN SOME KIND OF SPACE-ALIEN FIGHT, WE NEED TO GET THE HELL OUT OF HERE!
FRIDAY?!
BLING
SYSTEMS BACK ONLINE. SORRY.
WE WERE INSTANTANEOUSLY TELEPORTED TO THE BRONX ZOO.
THE BRONX ZOO?
IN THE BRONX.
WHY?
BECAUSE DOOM IS JUST... ODD?
PLOT A COURSE BACK TO LATVERIA.
NO.
NO?
NO, THANK YOU?
LISTEN, ACCORDING TO NEW HACKED SATELLITE FOOTAGE, THAT FIGHT IS OVER AND DOOM IS GONE.
HOW ABOUT INSTEAD I TRACK THE ENERGY TRAIL DOOM POINTED OUT COULD LEAD US TO MADAME MASQUE?
OR YO COULD D THAT!

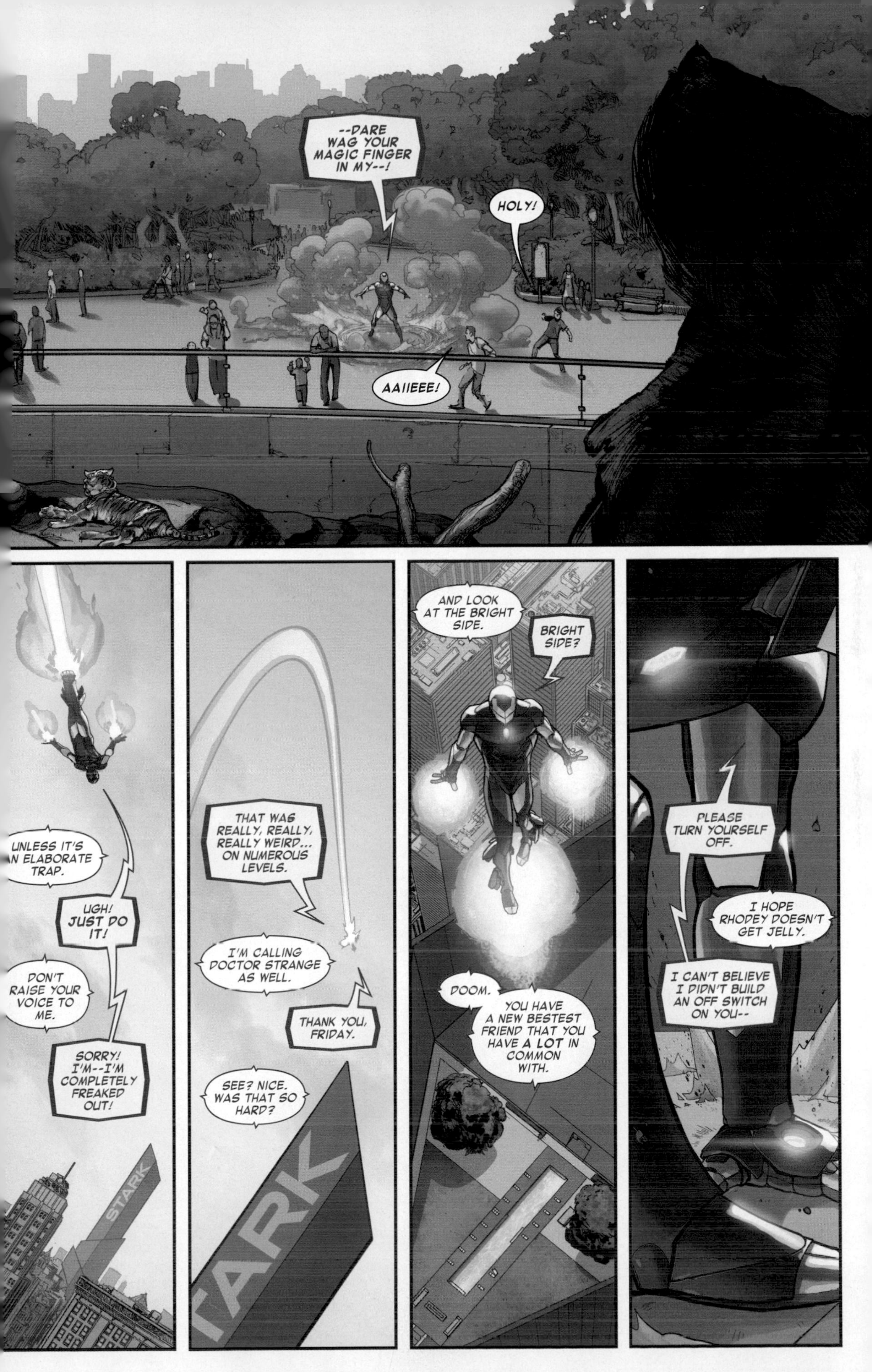
--DARE WAG YOUR MAGIC FINGER IN MY--!
HOLY!
AAIIEEE!
UNLESS IT'S AN ELABORATE TRAP.
UGH! JUST DO IT!
DON'T RAISE YOUR VOICE TO ME.
SORRY! I'M--I'M COMPLETELY FREAKED OUT!
STARK
THAT WAS REALLY, REALLY, REALLY WEIRD... ON NUMEROUS LEVELS.
I'M CALLING DOCTOR STRANGE AS WELL.
THANK YOU, FRIDAY.
SEE? NICE. WAS THAT SO HARD?
STARK
AND LOOK AT THE BRIGHT SIDE.
BRIGHT SIDE?
DOOM.
YOU HAVE A NEW BESTEST FRIEND THAT YOU HAVE A LOT IN COMMON WITH.
PLEASE TURN YOURSELF OFF.
I HOPE RHODEY DOESN'T GET JELLY.
I CAN'T BELIEVE I DIDN'T BUILD AN OFF SWITCH ON YOU--

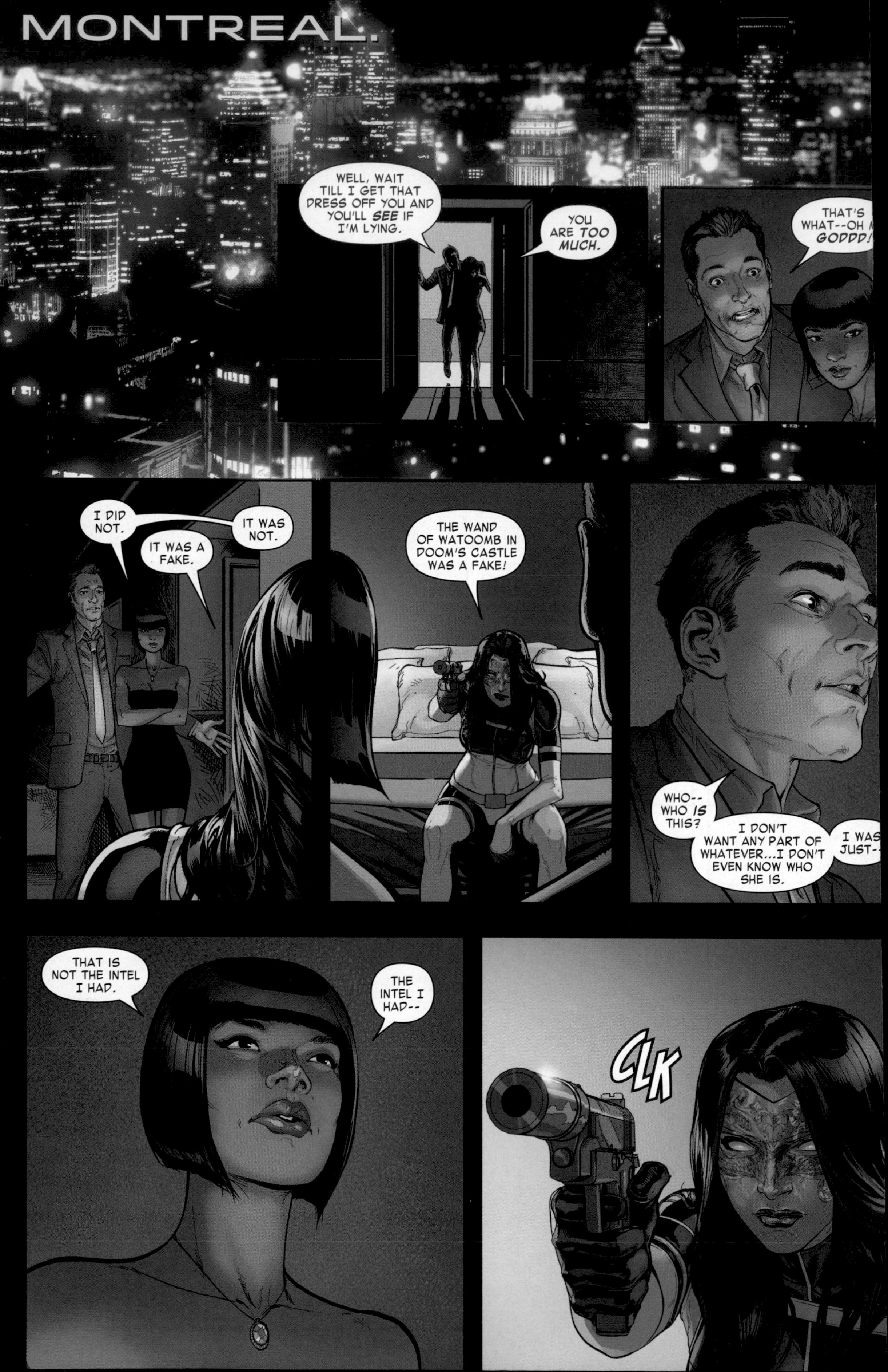
MONTREAL.
WELL, WAIT TILL I GET THAT DRESS OFF YOU AND YOU'LL *SEE* IF I'M LYING.
YOU ARE *TOO MUCH.*
THAT'S WHAT--OH M *GODDD!*
I DID NOT.
IT WAS NOT.
IT WAS A FAKE.
THE WAND OF WATOOMB IN DOOM'S CASTLE WAS A FAKE!
WHO-- WHO *IS* THIS?
I DON'T WANT ANY PART OF WHATEVER...I DON'T EVEN KNOW WHO SHE IS.
I WAS JUST-
THAT IS NOT THE INTEL I HAD.
THE INTEL I HAD--
CLK

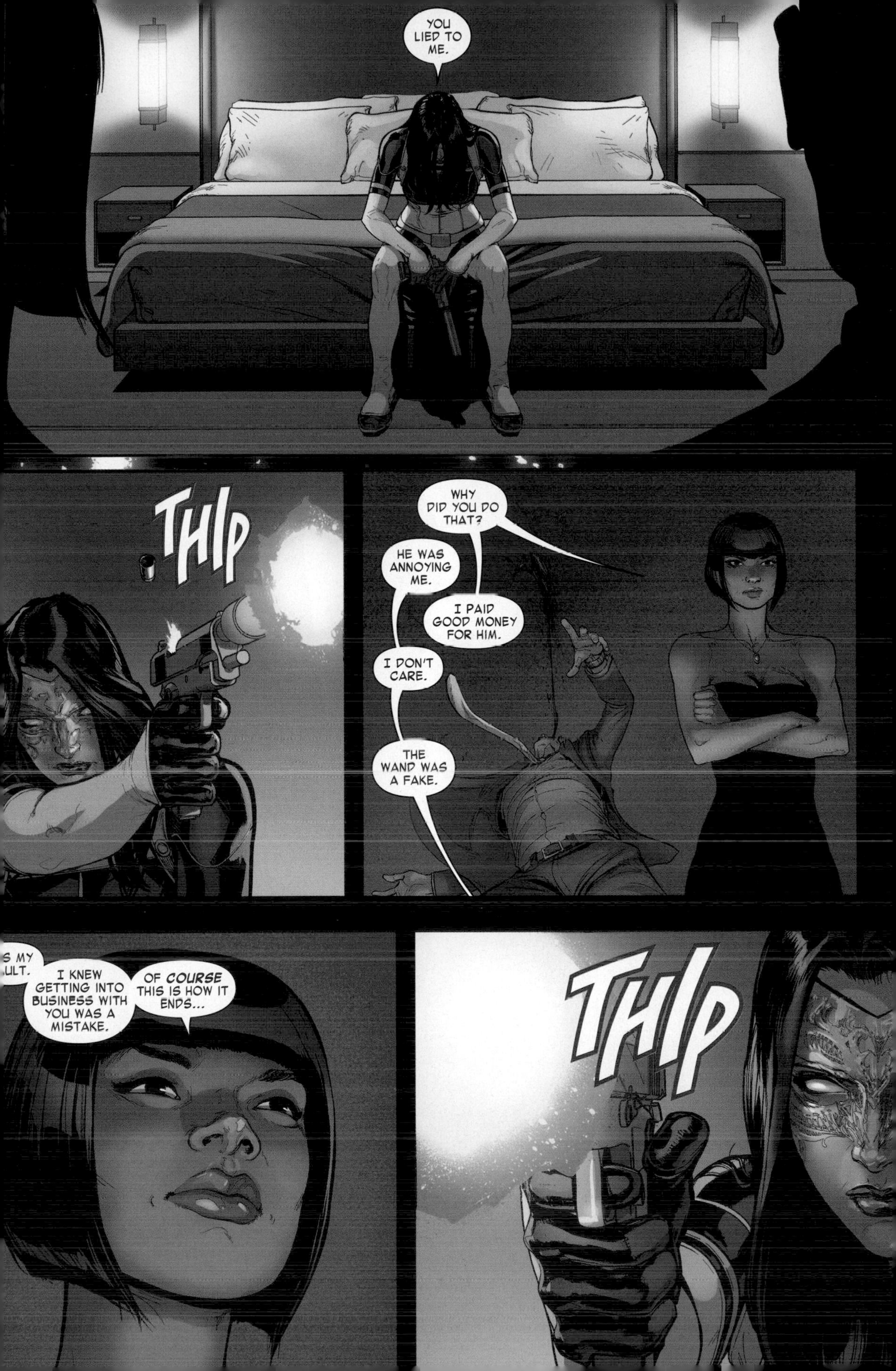
YOU LIED TO ME.
THIP
WHY DID YOU DO THAT?
HE WAS ANNOYING ME.
I PAID GOOD MONEY FOR HIM.
I DON'T CARE.
THE WAND WAS A FAKE.
I KNEW GETTING INTO BUSINESS WITH YOU WAS A MISTAKE.
OF COURSE THIS IS HOW IT ENDS...
THIP

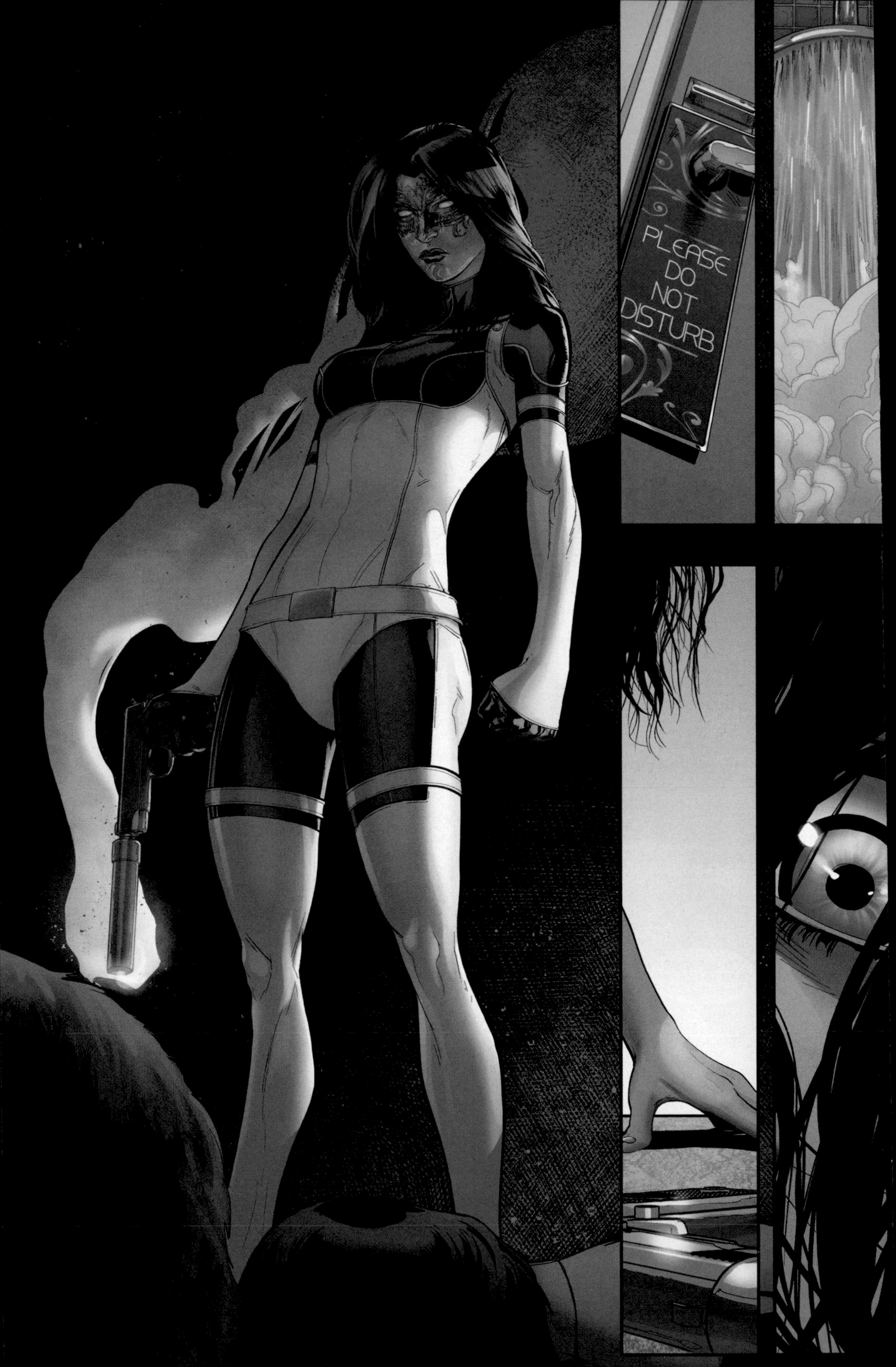
PLEASE
DO
NOT
DISTURB

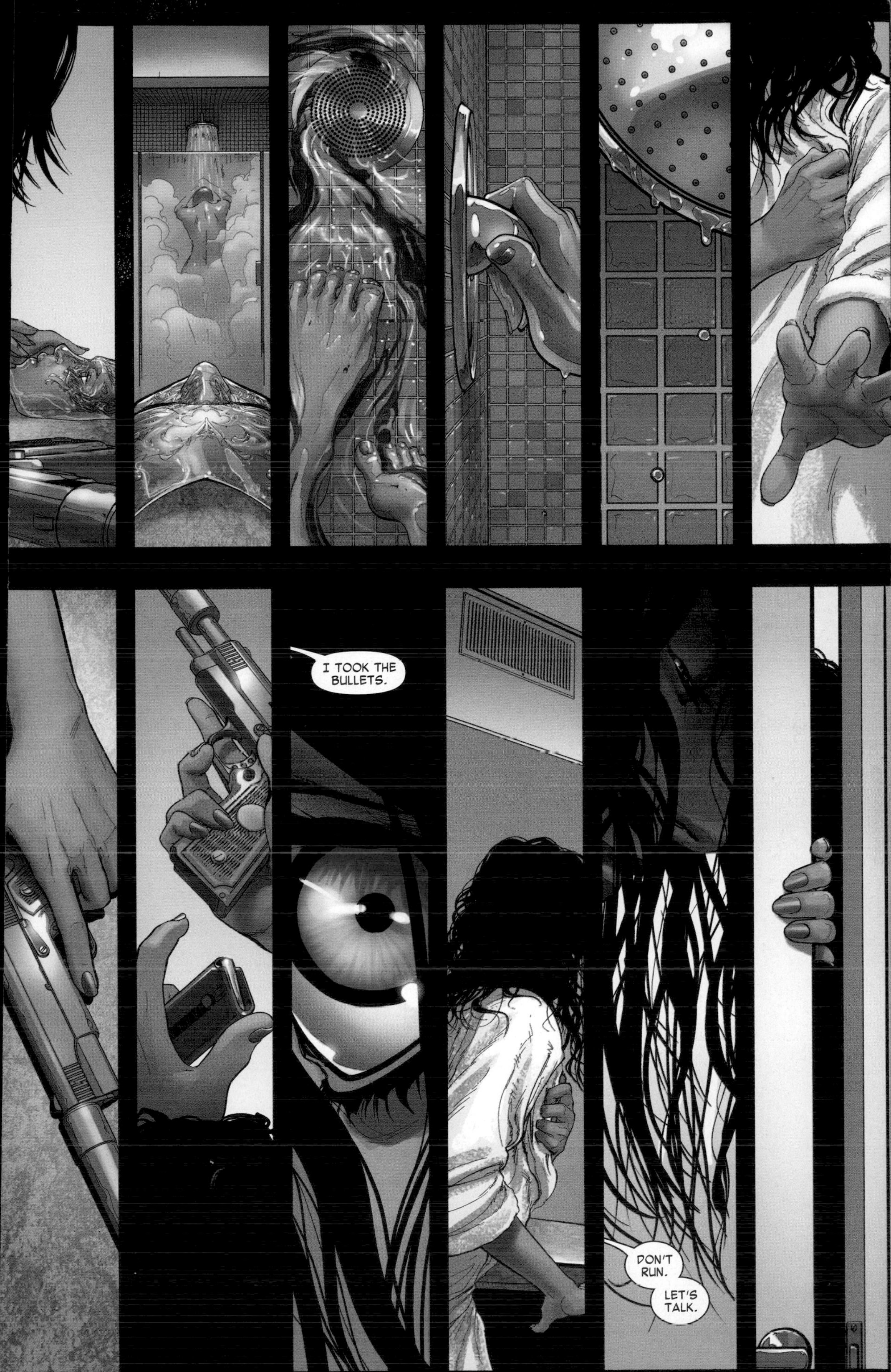
I TOOK THE BULLETS.
DON'T RUN.
LET'S TALK.

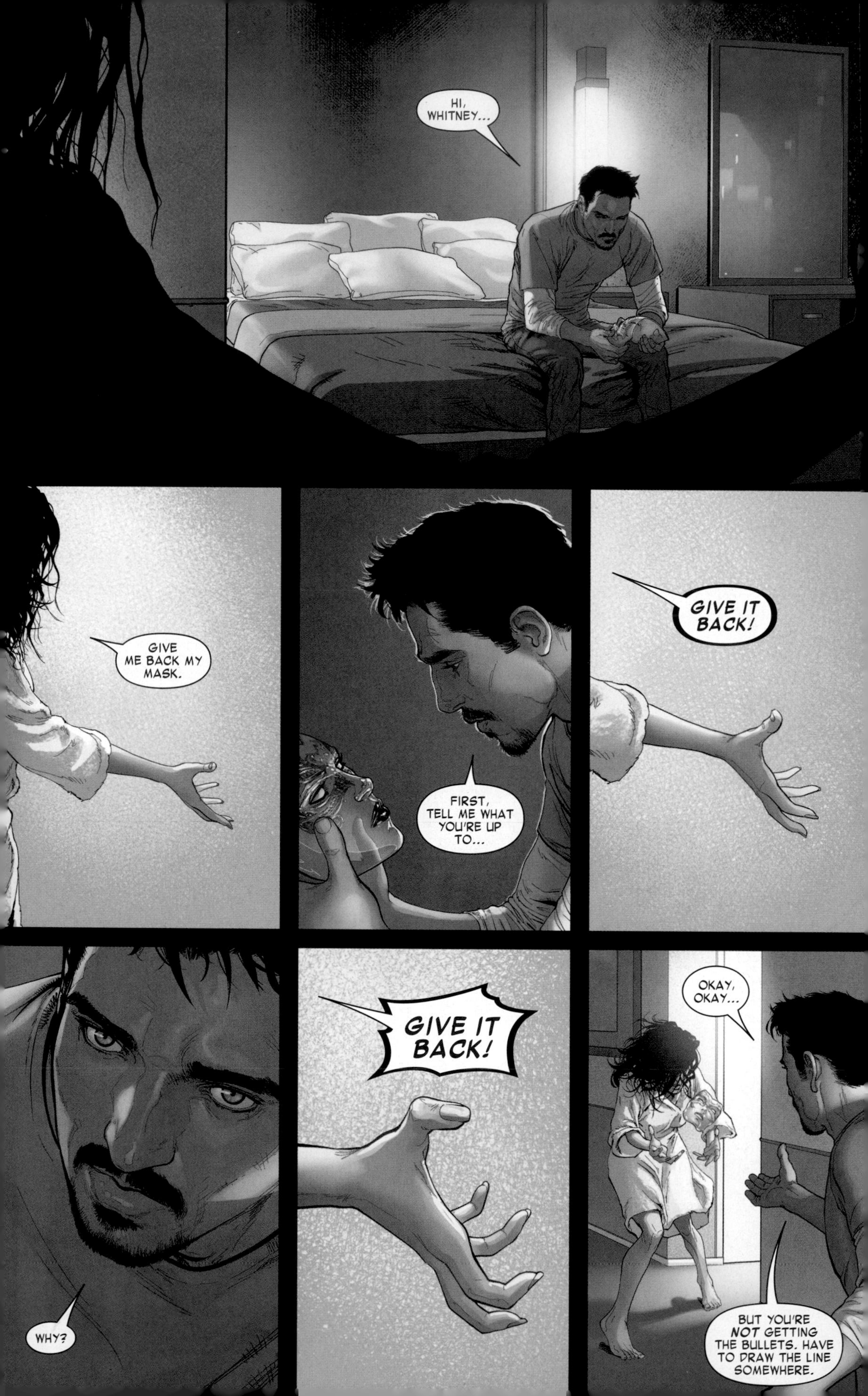
HI, WHITNEY...
GIVE ME BACK MY MASK.
FIRST, TELL ME WHAT YOU'RE UP TO...
GIVE IT BACK!
WHY?
GIVE IT BACK!
OKAY, OKAY...
BUT YOU'RE *NOT* GETTING THE BULLETS. HAVE TO DRAW THE LINE SOMEWHERE.

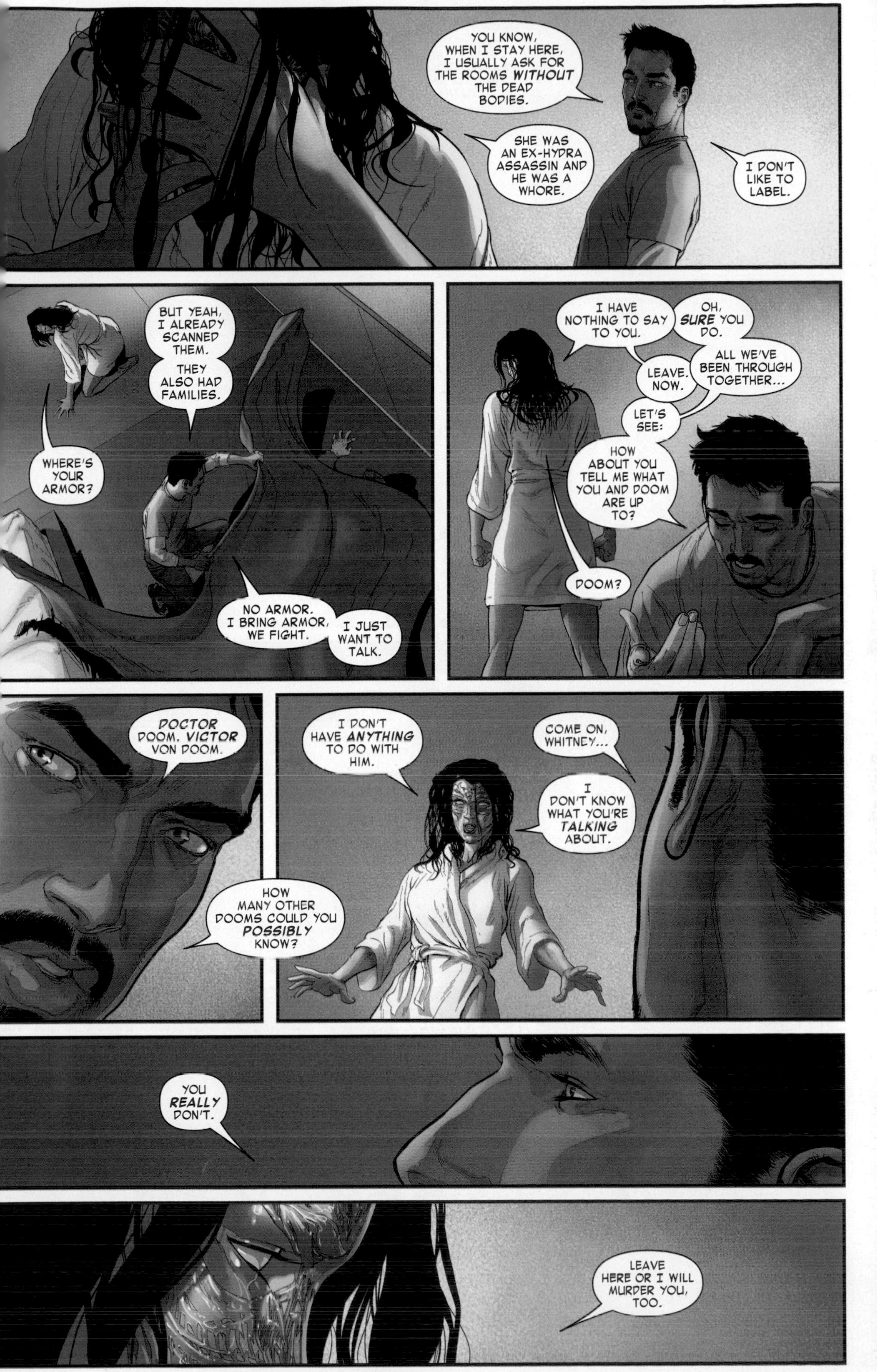
YOU KNOW, WHEN I STAY HERE, I USUALLY ASK FOR THE ROOMS WITHOUT THE DEAD BODIES.
SHE WAS AN EX-HYDRA ASSASSIN AND HE WAS A WHORE.
I DON'T LIKE TO LABEL.
BUT YEAH, I ALREADY SCANNED THEM.
THEY ALSO HAD FAMILIES.
WHERE'S YOUR ARMOR?
NO ARMOR. I BRING ARMOR, WE FIGHT.
I JUST WANT TO TALK.
I HAVE NOTHING TO SAY TO YOU.
OH, SURE YOU DO.
LEAVE. NOW.
ALL WE'VE BEEN THROUGH TOGETHER...
LET'S SEE:
HOW ABOUT YOU TELL ME WHAT YOU AND DOOM ARE UP TO?
DOOM?
DOCTOR DOOM. VICTOR VON DOOM.
HOW MANY OTHER DOOMS COULD YOU POSSIBLY KNOW?
I DON'T HAVE ANYTHING TO DO WITH HIM.
COME ON, WHITNEY...
I DON'T KNOW WHAT YOU'RE TALKING ABOUT.
YOU REALLY DON'T.
LEAVE HERE OR I WILL MURDER YOU, TOO.

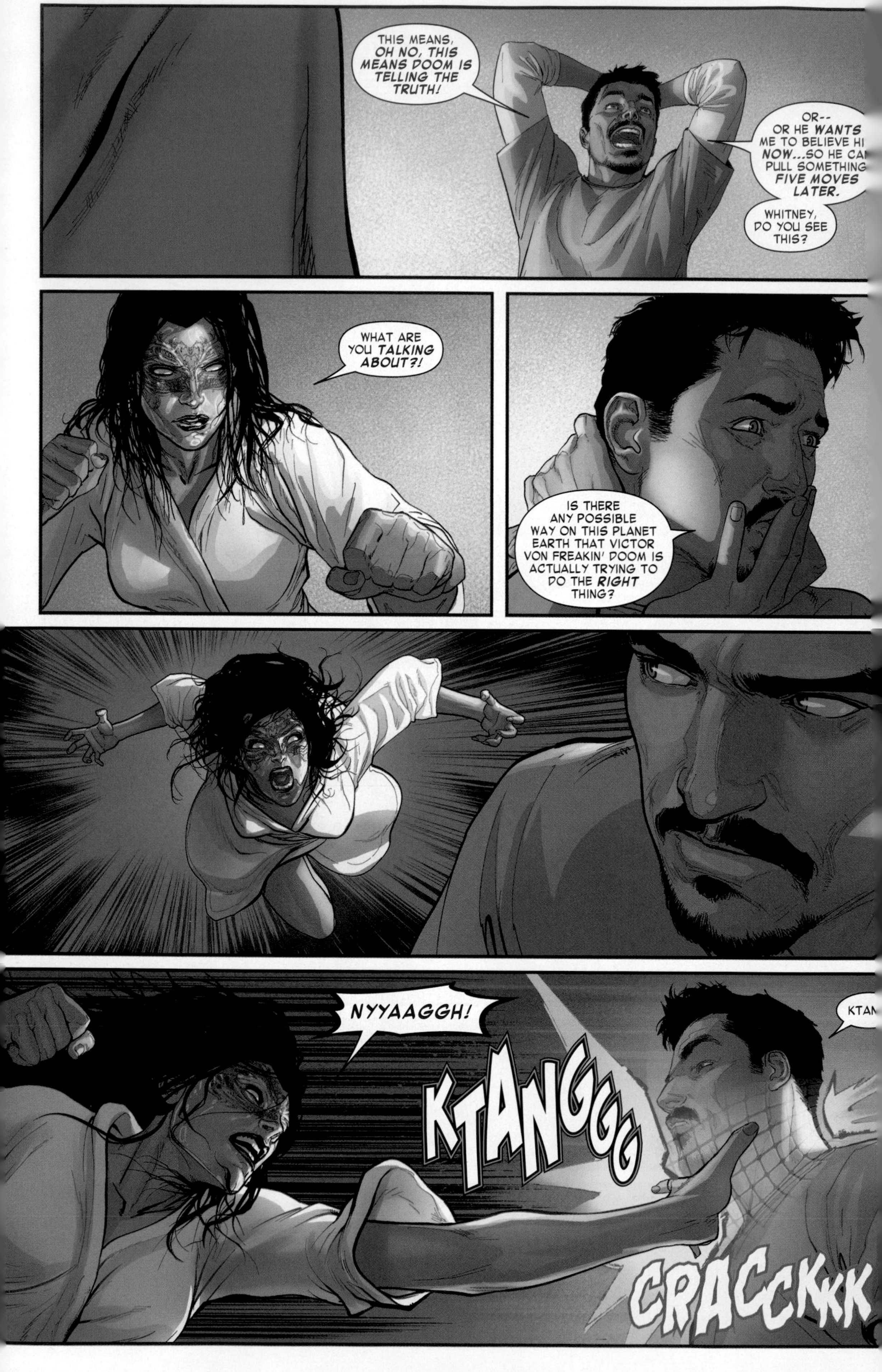
THIS MEANS, OH NO, THIS MEANS DOOM IS TELLING THE TRUTH!
OR-- OR HE WANTS ME TO BELIEVE HI NOW...SO HE CA PULL SOMETHING FIVE MOVES LATER.
WHITNEY, DO YOU SEE THIS?
WHAT ARE YOU TALKING ABOUT?!
IS THERE ANY POSSIBLE WAY ON THIS PLANET EARTH THAT VICTOR VON FREAKIN' DOOM IS ACTUALLY TRYING TO DO THE RIGHT THING?
NYYAAGGH!
KTANGGG
KTAN
CRACCKKK

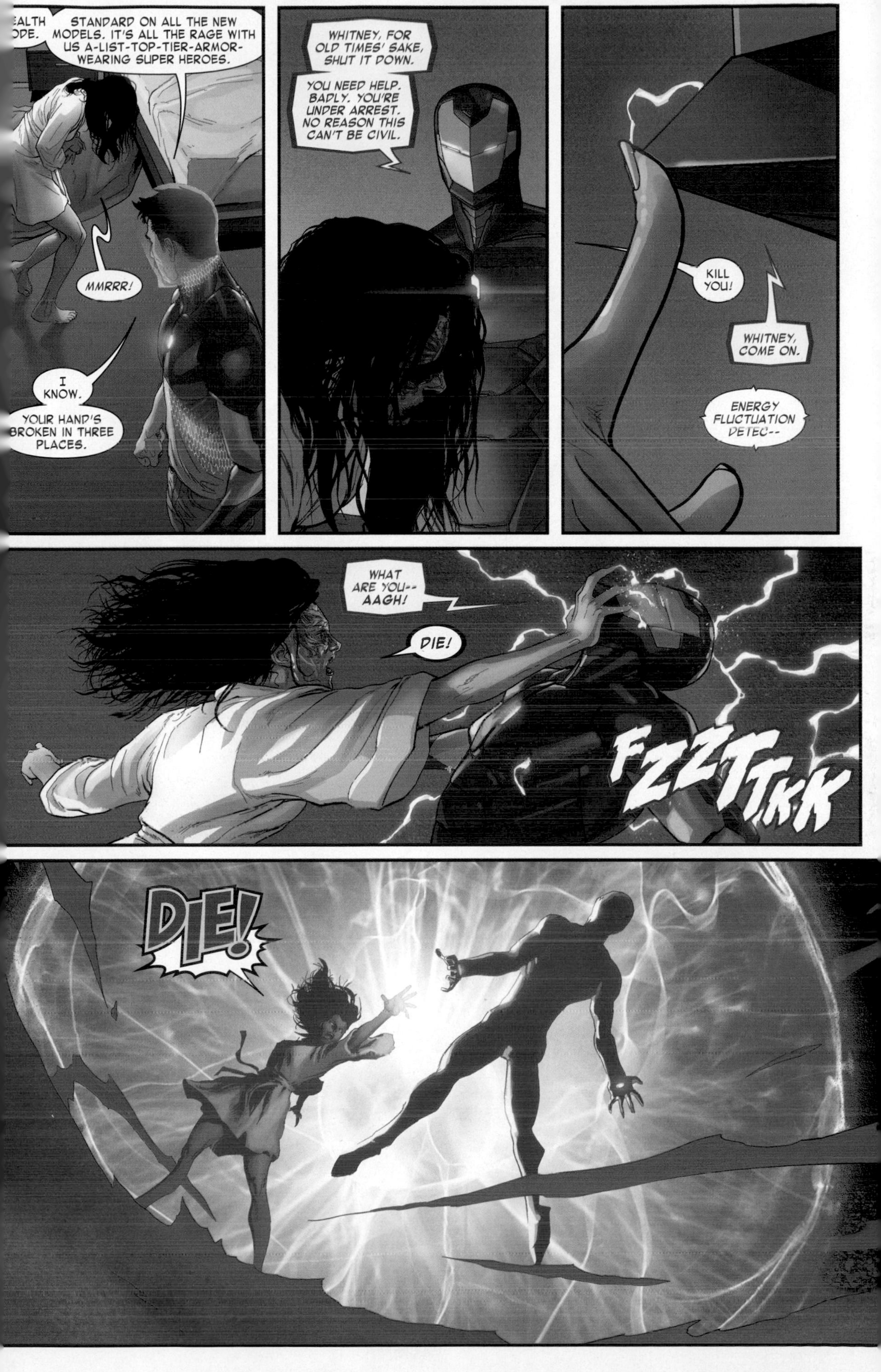
EALTH ODE.
STANDARD ON ALL THE NEW MODELS. IT'S ALL THE RAGE WITH US A-LIST-TOP-TIER-ARMOR-WEARING SUPER HEROES.
MMRRR!
I KNOW.
YOUR HAND'S BROKEN IN THREE PLACES.
WHITNEY, FOR OLD TIMES' SAKE, SHUT IT DOWN.
YOU NEED HELP. BADLY. YOU'RE UNDER ARREST. NO REASON THIS CAN'T BE CIVIL.
KILL YOU!
WHITNEY, COME ON.
ENERGY FLUCTUATION DETEC--
WHAT ARE YOU-- AAGH!
DIE!
FZZZTTKK
DIE!

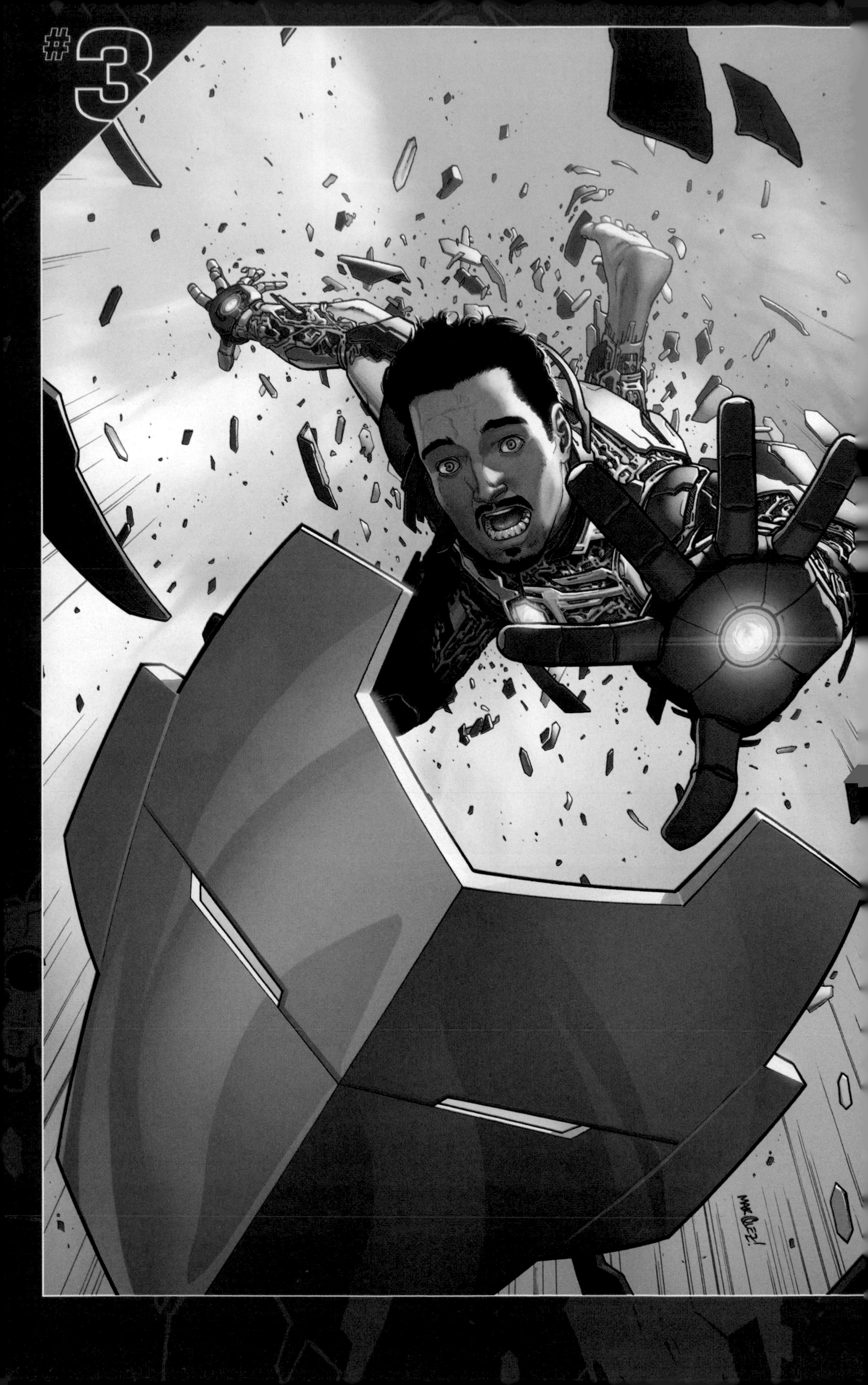
#3

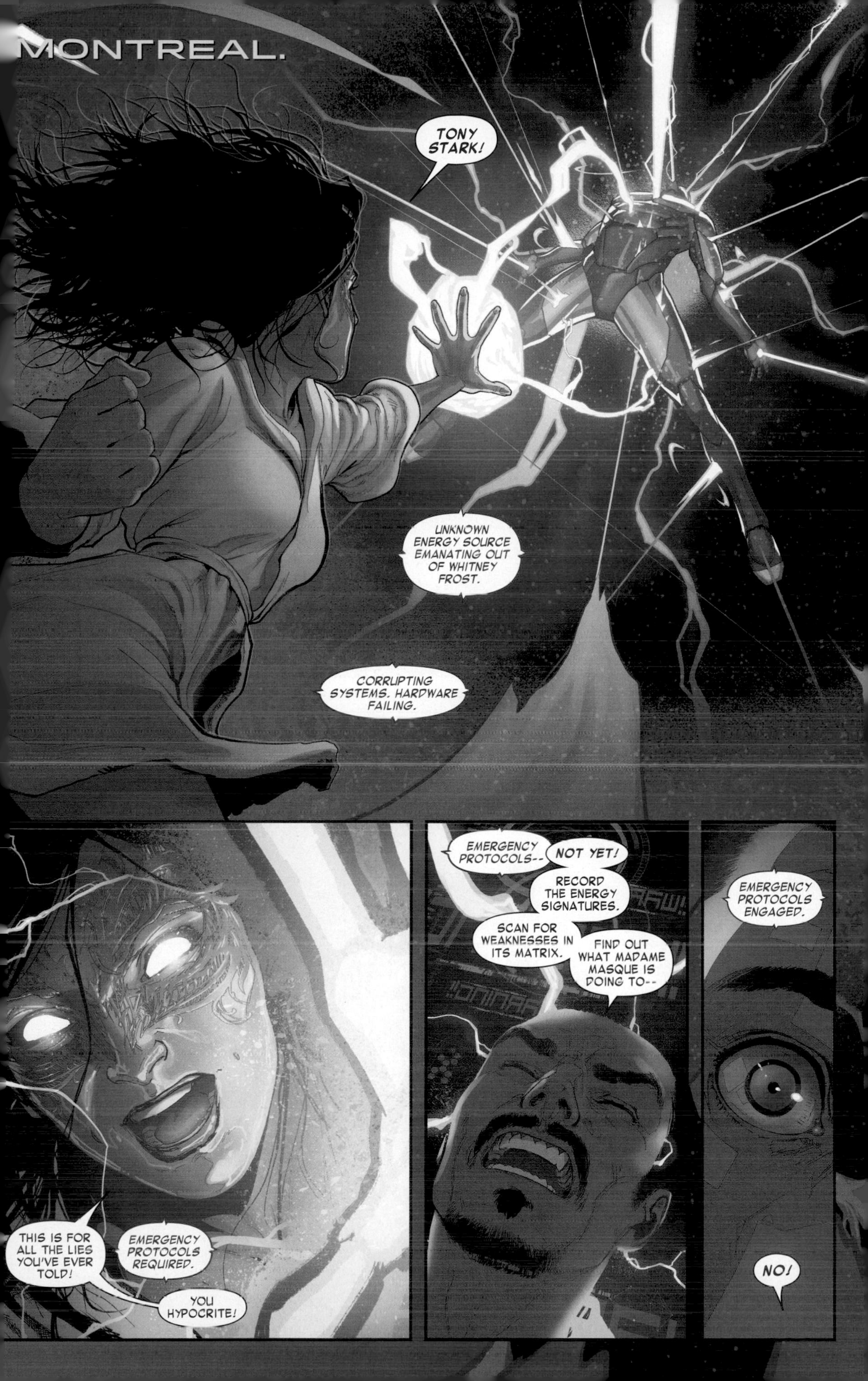
MONTREAL.
TONY STARK!
UNKNOWN ENERGY SOURCE EMANATING OUT OF WHITNEY FROST.
CORRUPTING SYSTEMS. HARDWARE FAILING.
THIS IS FOR ALL THE LIES YOU'VE EVER TOLD!
EMERGENCY PROTOCOLS REQUIRED.
YOU HYPOCRITE!
EMERGENCY PROTOCOLS--
NOT YET!
RECORD THE ENERGY SIGNATURES.
SCAN FOR WEAKNESSES IN ITS MATRIX.
FIND OUT WHAT MADAME MASQUE IS DOING TO--
EMERGENCY PROTOCOLS ENGAGED.
NO!

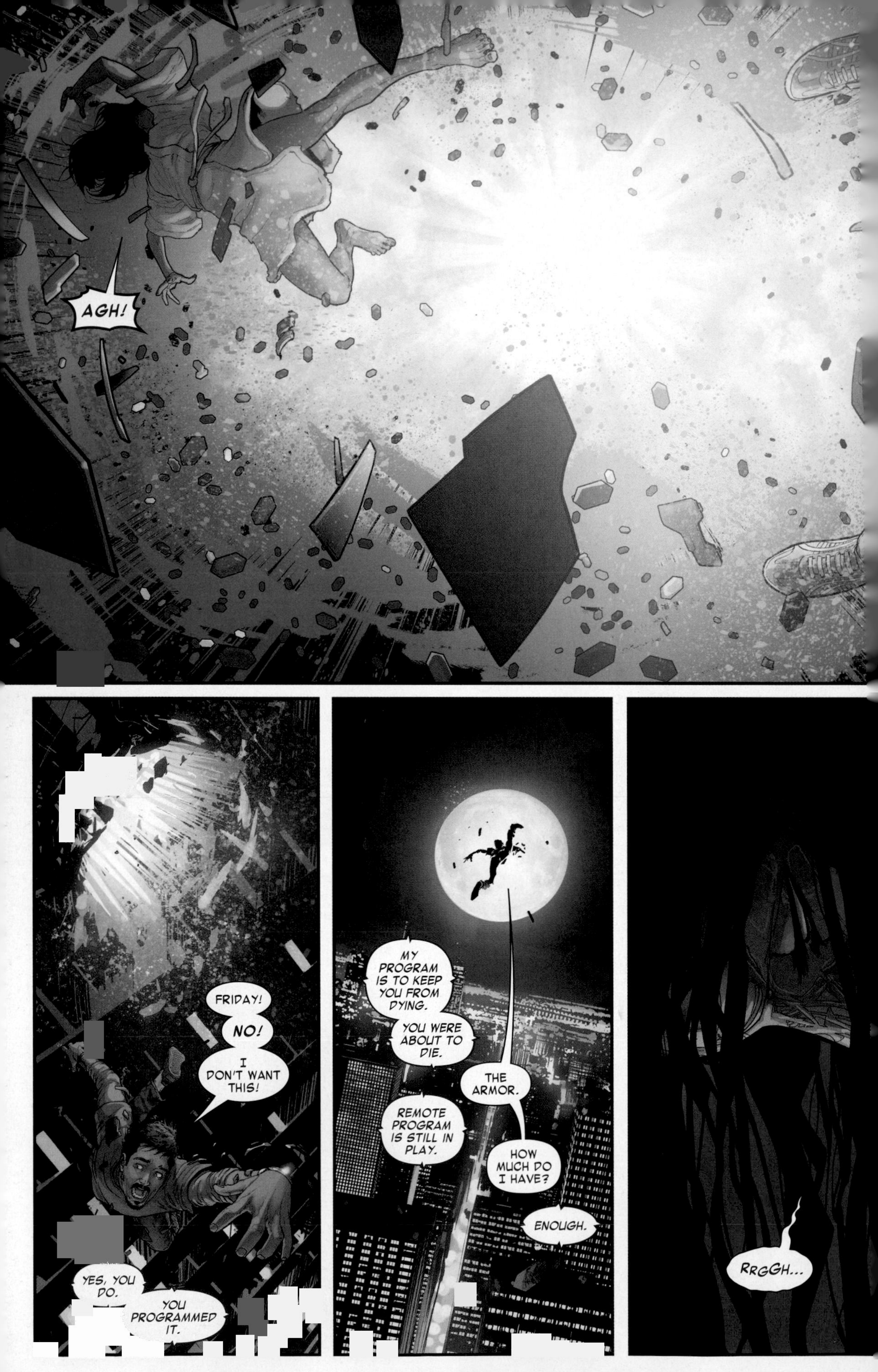
AGH!
FRIDAY!
NO!
I DON'T WANT THIS!
YES, YOU DO.
YOU PROGRAMMED IT.
MY PROGRAM IS TO KEEP YOU FROM DYING.
YOU WERE ABOUT TO DIE.
THE ARMOR.
REMOTE PROGRAM IS STILL IN PLAY.
HOW MUCH DO I HAVE?
ENOUGH.
RRGGH...

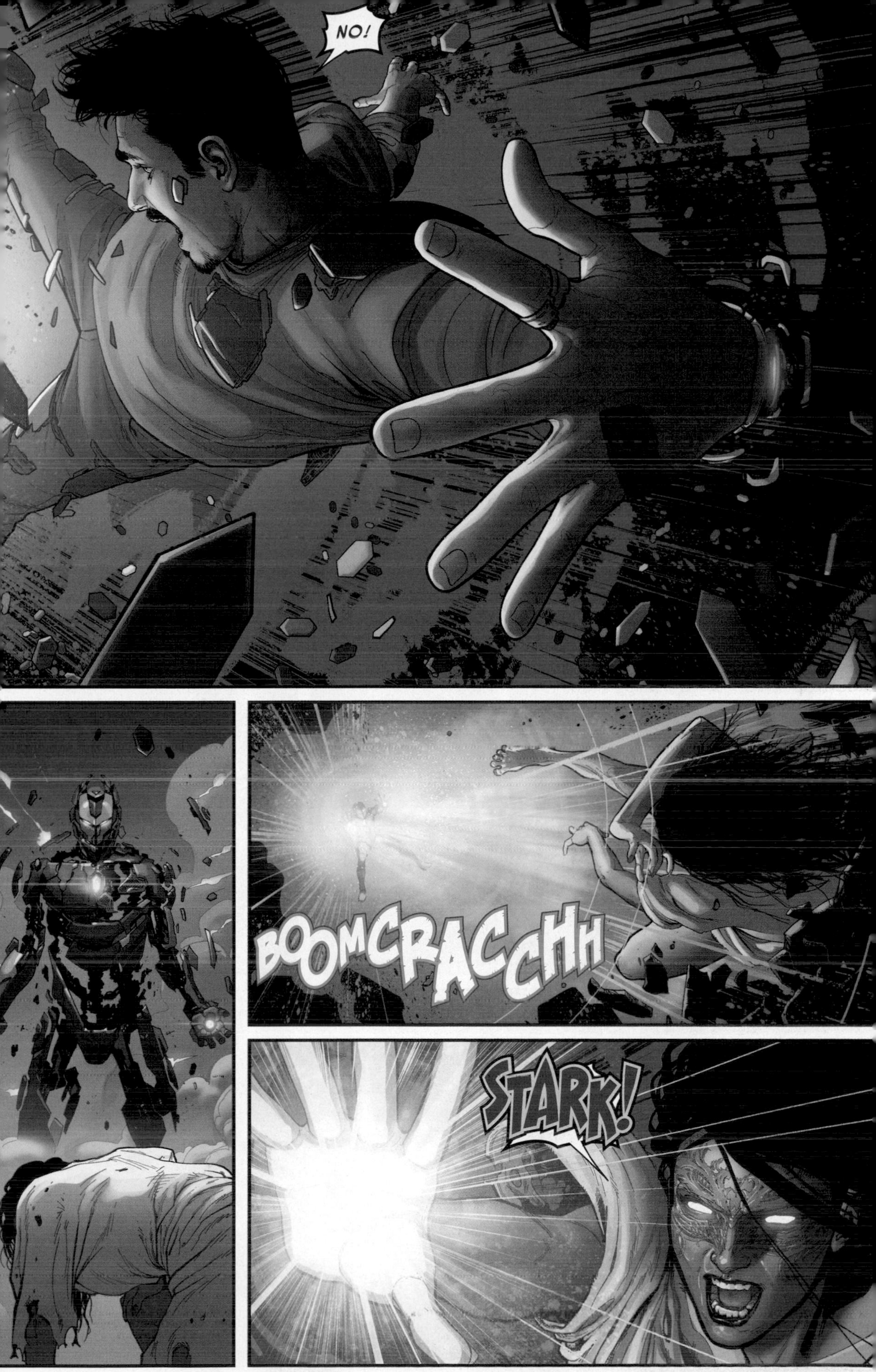
NO!
BOOMCRACCHH
STARK!

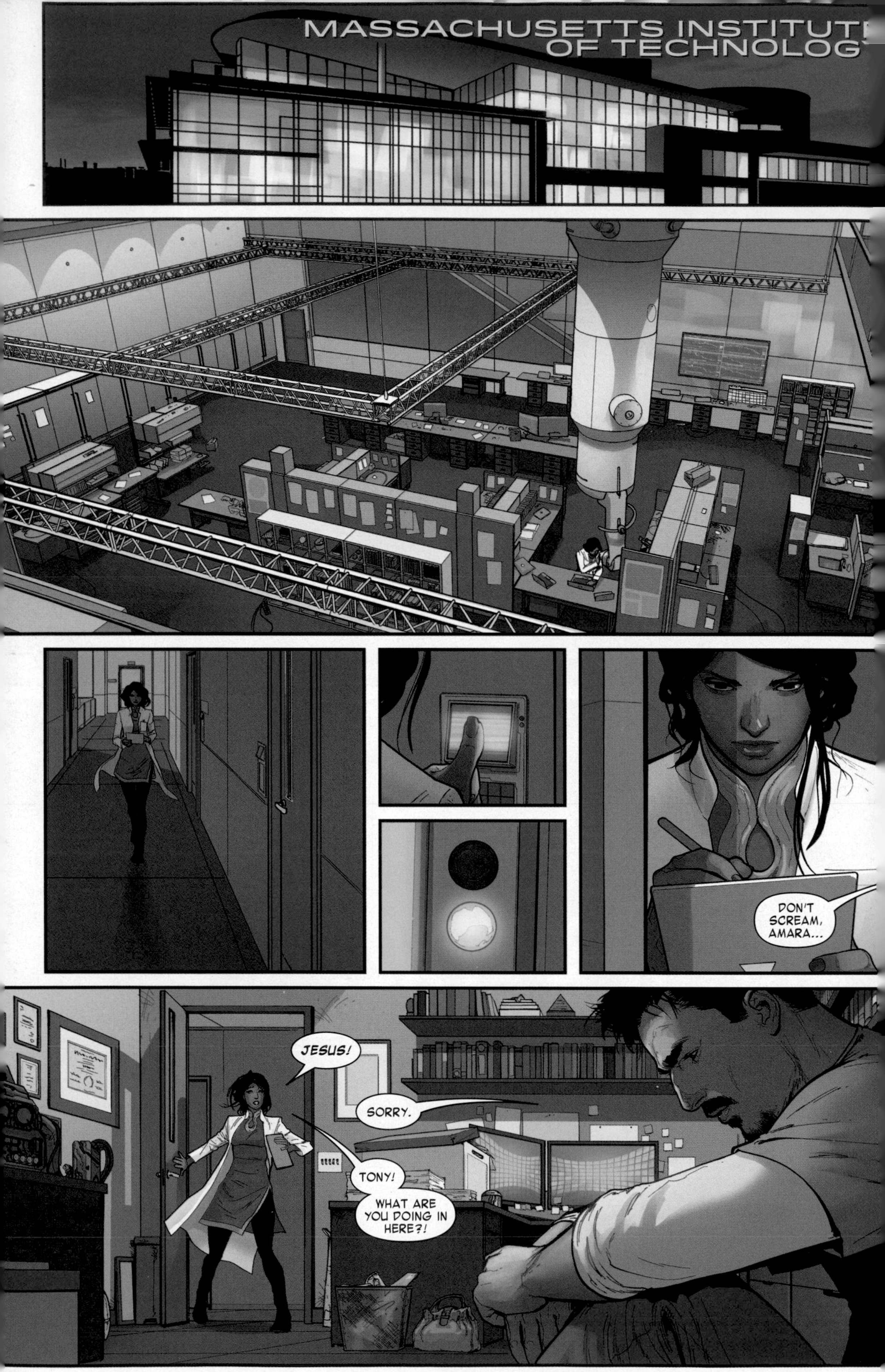
MASSACHUSETTS INSTITUT
OF TECHNOLOG
DON'T SCREAM, AMARA...
JESUS!
SORRY.
TONY!
WHAT ARE YOU DOING IN HERE?!

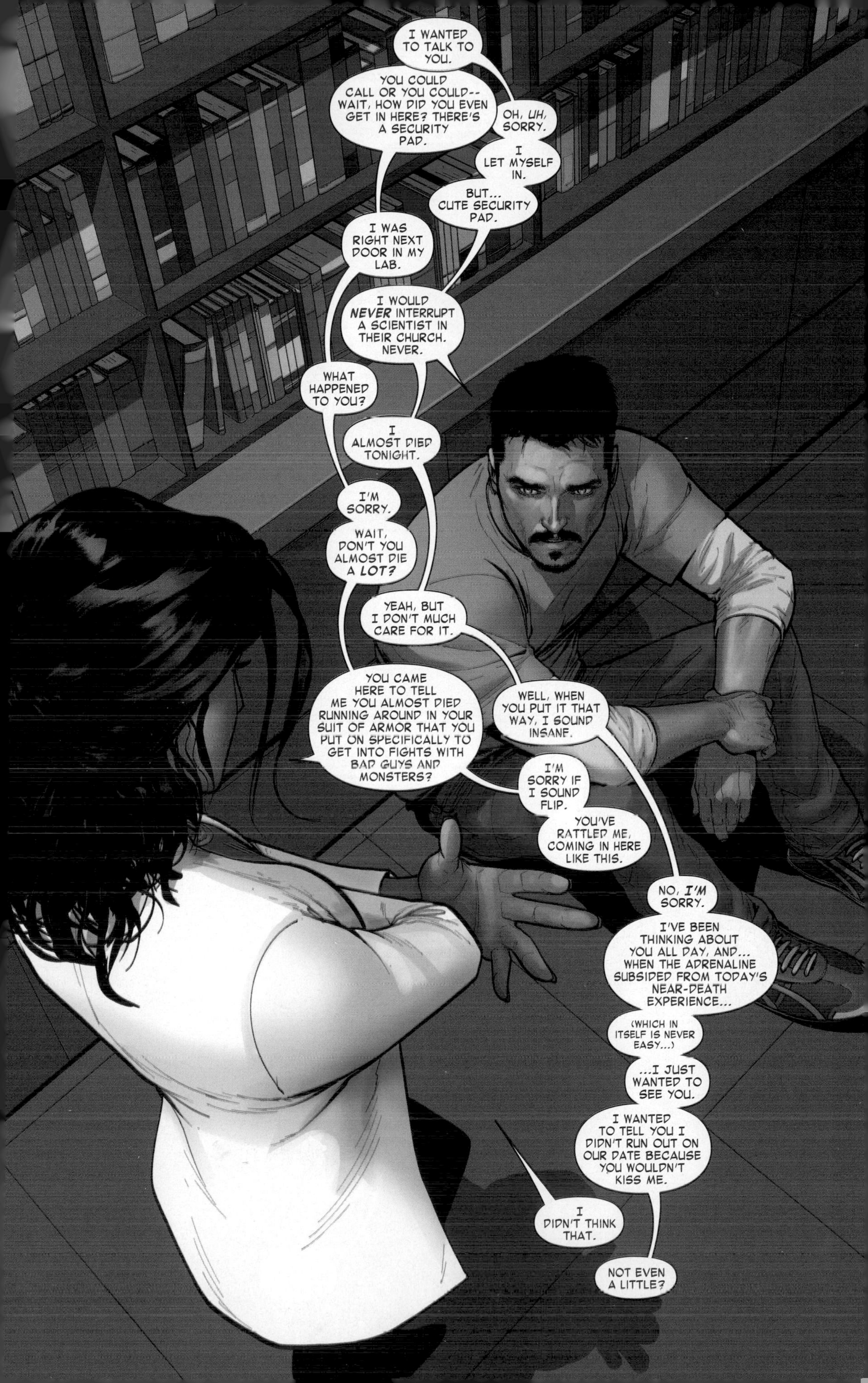
I WANTED TO TALK TO YOU.
YOU COULD CALL OR YOU COULD-- WAIT, HOW DID YOU EVEN GET IN HERE? THERE'S A SECURITY PAD.
OH, UH, SORRY.
I LET MYSELF IN.
BUT... CUTE SECURITY PAD.
I WAS RIGHT NEXT DOOR IN MY LAB.
I WOULD NEVER INTERRUPT A SCIENTIST IN THEIR CHURCH. NEVER.
WHAT HAPPENED TO YOU?
I ALMOST DIED TONIGHT.
I'M SORRY.
WAIT, DON'T YOU ALMOST DIE A LOT?
YEAH, BUT I DON'T MUCH CARE FOR IT.
YOU CAME HERE TO TELL ME YOU ALMOST DIED RUNNING AROUND IN YOUR SUIT OF ARMOR THAT YOU PUT ON SPECIFICALLY TO GET INTO FIGHTS WITH BAD GUYS AND MONSTERS?
WELL, WHEN YOU PUT IT THAT WAY, I SOUND INSANE.
I'M SORRY IF I SOUND FLIP.
YOU'VE RATTLED ME, COMING IN HERE LIKE THIS.
NO, I'M SORRY.
I'VE BEEN THINKING ABOUT YOU ALL DAY, AND... WHEN THE ADRENALINE SUBSIDED FROM TODAY'S NEAR-DEATH EXPERIENCE...
(WHICH IN ITSELF IS NEVER EASY...)
...I JUST WANTED TO SEE YOU.
I WANTED TO TELL YOU I DIDN'T RUN OUT ON OUR DATE BECAUSE YOU WOULDN'T KISS ME.
I DIDN'T THINK THAT.
NOT EVEN A LITTLE?

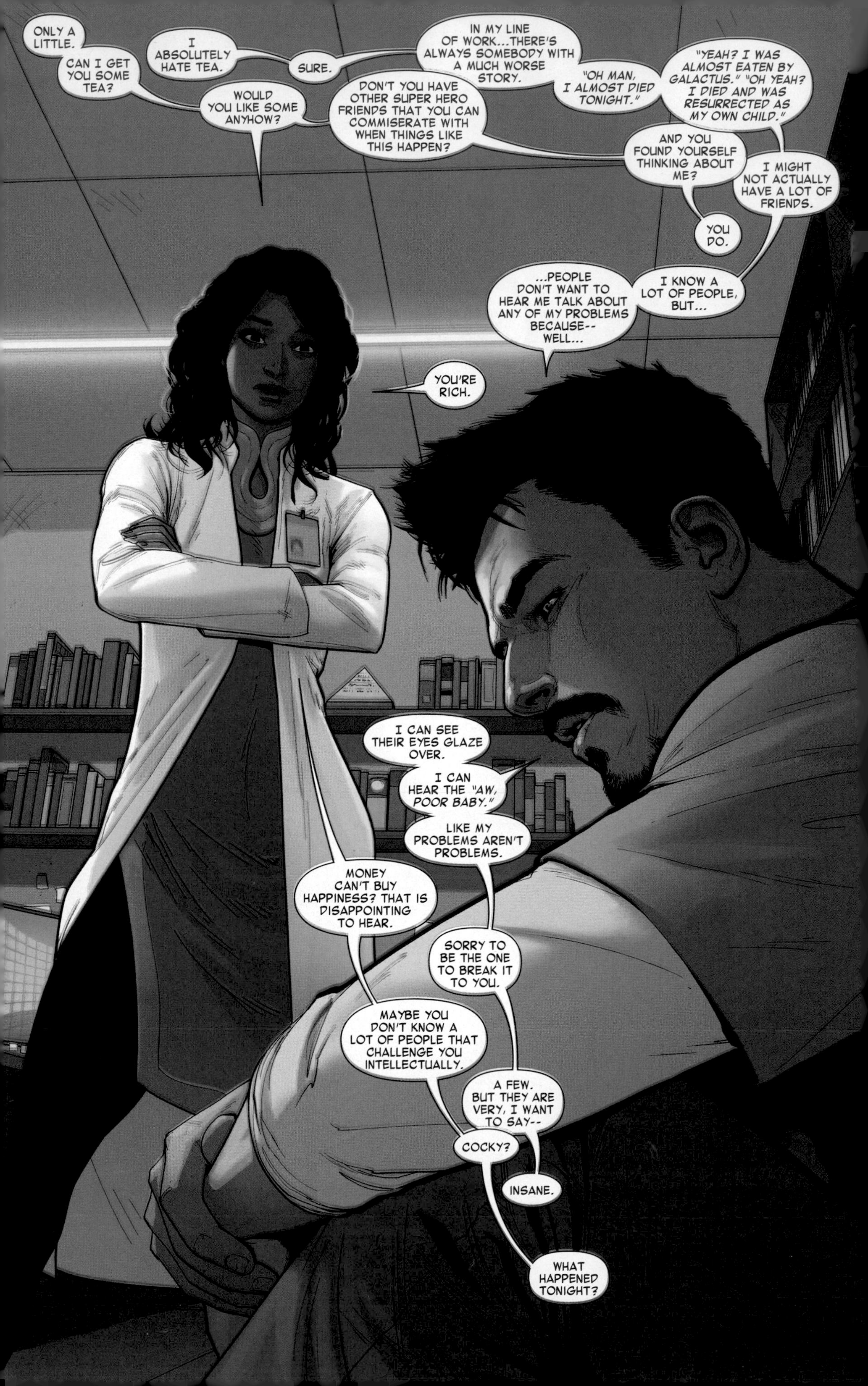

ONLY A LITTLE.
CAN I GET YOU SOME TEA?
I ABSOLUTELY HATE TEA.
WOULD YOU LIKE SOME ANYHOW?
SURE.
IN MY LINE OF WORK...THERE'S ALWAYS SOMEBODY WITH A MUCH WORSE STORY.
DON'T YOU HAVE OTHER SUPER HERO FRIENDS THAT YOU CAN COMMISERATE WITH WHEN THINGS LIKE THIS HAPPEN?
"OH MAN, I ALMOST DIED TONIGHT."
"YEAH? I WAS ALMOST EATEN BY GALACTUS." "OH YEAH? I DIED AND WAS RESURRECTED AS MY OWN CHILD."
AND YOU FOUND YOURSELF THINKING ABOUT ME?
I MIGHT NOT ACTUALLY HAVE A LOT OF FRIENDS.
YOU DO.
I KNOW A LOT OF PEOPLE, BUT...
...PEOPLE DON'T WANT TO HEAR ME TALK ABOUT ANY OF MY PROBLEMS BECAUSE-- WELL...
YOU'RE RICH.
I CAN SEE THEIR EYES GLAZE OVER.
I CAN HEAR THE "AW, POOR BABY."
LIKE MY PROBLEMS AREN'T PROBLEMS.
MONEY CAN'T BUY HAPPINESS? THAT IS DISAPPOINTING TO HEAR.
SORRY TO BE THE ONE TO BREAK IT TO YOU.
MAYBE YOU DON'T KNOW A LOT OF PEOPLE THAT CHALLENGE YOU INTELLECTUALLY.
A FEW. BUT THEY ARE VERY, I WANT TO SAY--
COCKY?
INSANE.
WHAT HAPPENED TONIGHT?

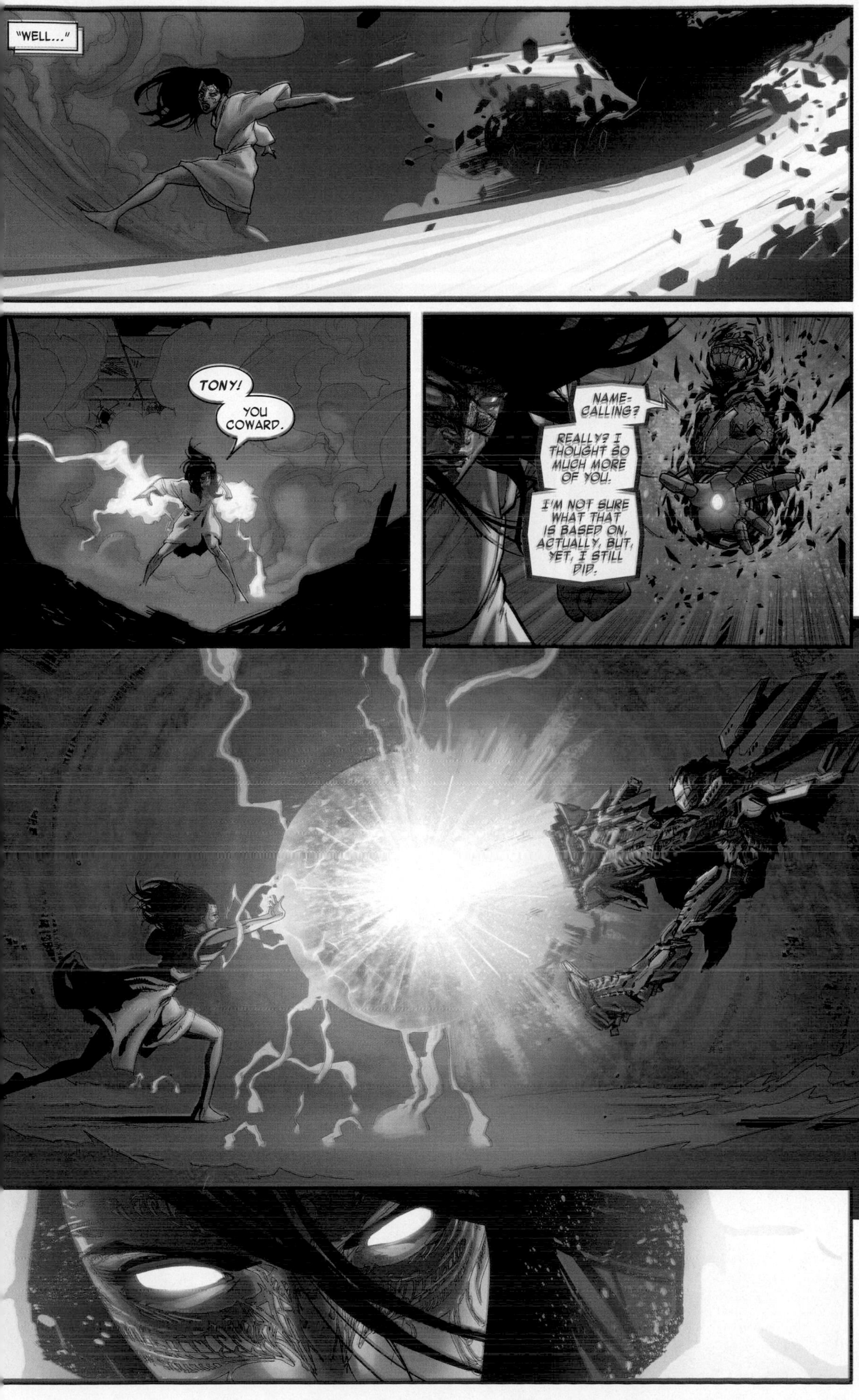
"WELL..."
TONY!
YOU COWARD.
NAME-CALLING?
REALLY? I THOUGHT SO MUCH MORE OF YOU.
I'M NOT SURE WHAT THAT IS BASED ON, ACTUALLY, BUT, YET, I STILL DID.

WHAT IS GOING ON WITH YOU, WHITNEY? YOU'RE RUNNING AROUND MURDERING AND STEALING...

HOW DO YOU THINK IT'S GOING TO END FOR YOU IF YOU KEEP MESSING AROUND LIKE THIS?

RRRAAGGHH!

SMAAASSHH

SIGNAL LOST. REACQUIRING...

RUDE.

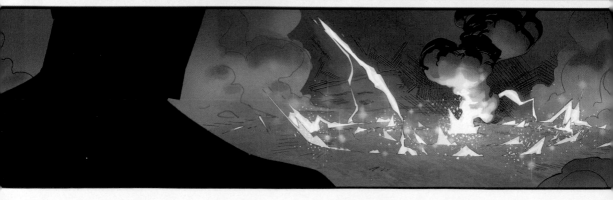

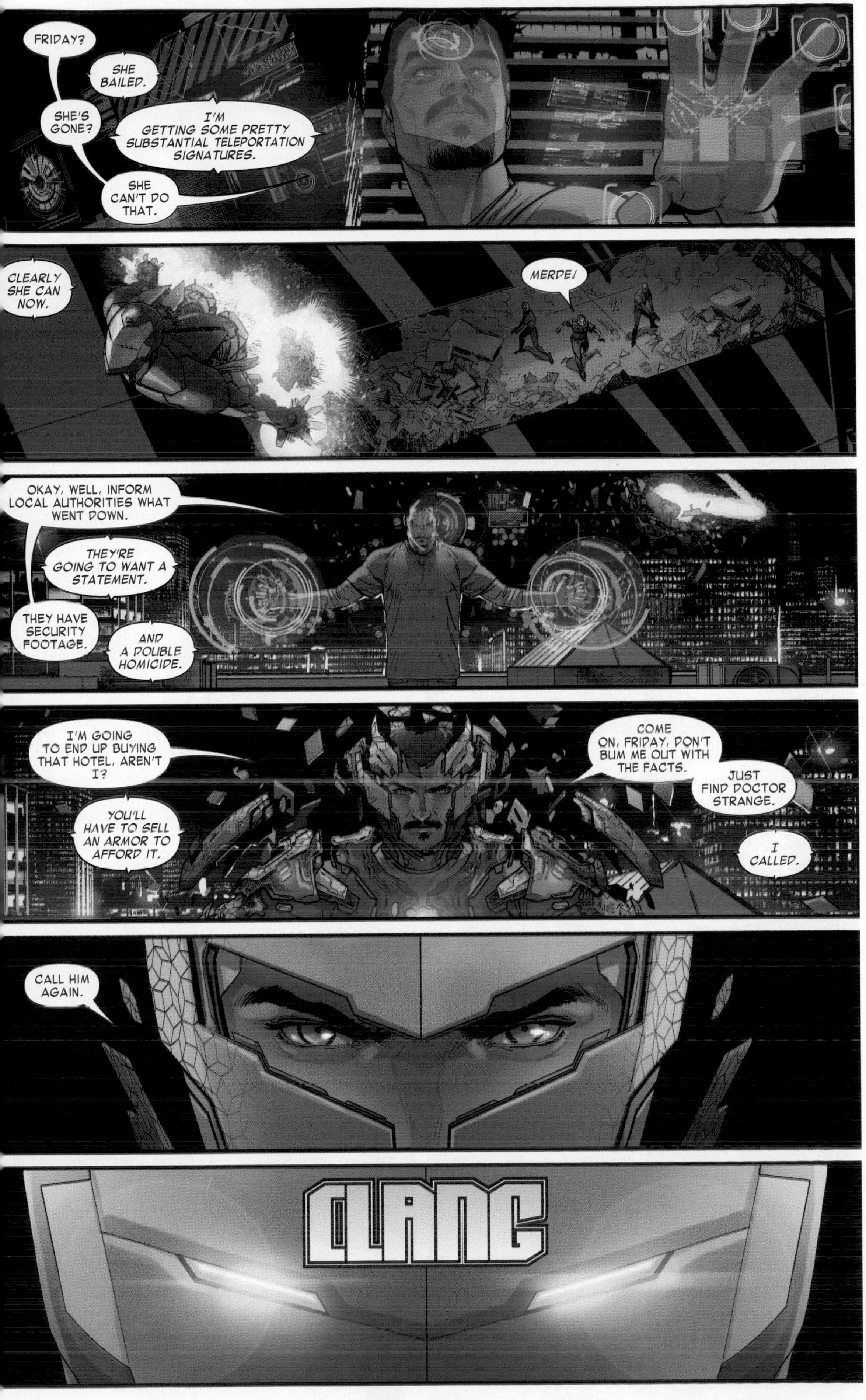
FRIDAY?
SHE BAILED.
SHE'S GONE?
I'M GETTING SOME PRETTY SUBSTANTIAL TELEPORTATION SIGNATURES.
SHE CAN'T DO THAT.
CLEARLY SHE CAN NOW.
MERDE!
OKAY, WELL, INFORM LOCAL AUTHORITIES WHAT WENT DOWN.
THEY'RE GOING TO WANT A STATEMENT.
THEY HAVE SECURITY FOOTAGE.
AND A DOUBLE HOMICIDE.
I'M GOING TO END UP BUYING THAT HOTEL, AREN'T I?
YOU'LL HAVE TO SELL AN ARMOR TO AFFORD IT.
COME ON, FRIDAY, DON'T BUM ME OUT WITH THE FACTS.
JUST FIND DOCTOR STRANGE.
I CALLED.
CALL HIM AGAIN.
CLANG

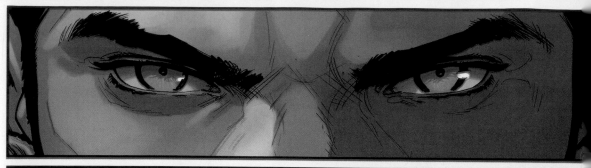

YOU CHASED HER OFF.

NO.

YOU STOPPED HER.

NOT BEFORE SHE MURDERED TWO PEOPLE.

SURE, NOT THE BEST *QUALITY* OF PEOPLE, BUT STILL...

TECHNICALLY, PEOPLE.

DO YOU GET THIS WAY AFTER EVERY IRON MAN KERFUFFLE?

NO. JUST THE ONES I CAN'T FIGURE OUT.

SEE, THIS IS NOT MADAME MASQUE'S NORMAL M.O.

AND IT'S A POWER SET I CAN'T IDENTIFY.

SHE IS GATHERING POWERFUL ITEMS FOR A NIGHTMARE AGENDA I CAN ONLY GUESS AT...

...AND DOCTOR DOOM IS SO DAMN HELPFUL AND SO DAMN HANDSOME NOW...

...I THINK YOU CAN UNDERSTAND THIS WITHOUT IT SOUNDING TOO ARROGANT, BUT I'M TOO SMART FOR THIS NOT TO JUST PISS ME OFF.

WHY DID YOU COME HERE?

I TOLD YOU.

YOU JUST MET ME.

I JUST MET YOU AND REALIZED YOU ARE WHOLEHEARTEDLY AND COMPLETELY OUT OF MY LEAGUE.

INTELLECTUALLY, MORALLY, YOU HAVE BETTER HAIR...

BUT WHY DID YOU COME HERE?

I CAN'T SHAKE THE IDEA THAT BECOMING THE MAN THAT WOULD ACTUALLY DESERVE YOU...WOULD BE A VERY GOOD GOAL IN LIFE AT THIS STAGE OF THE GAME.

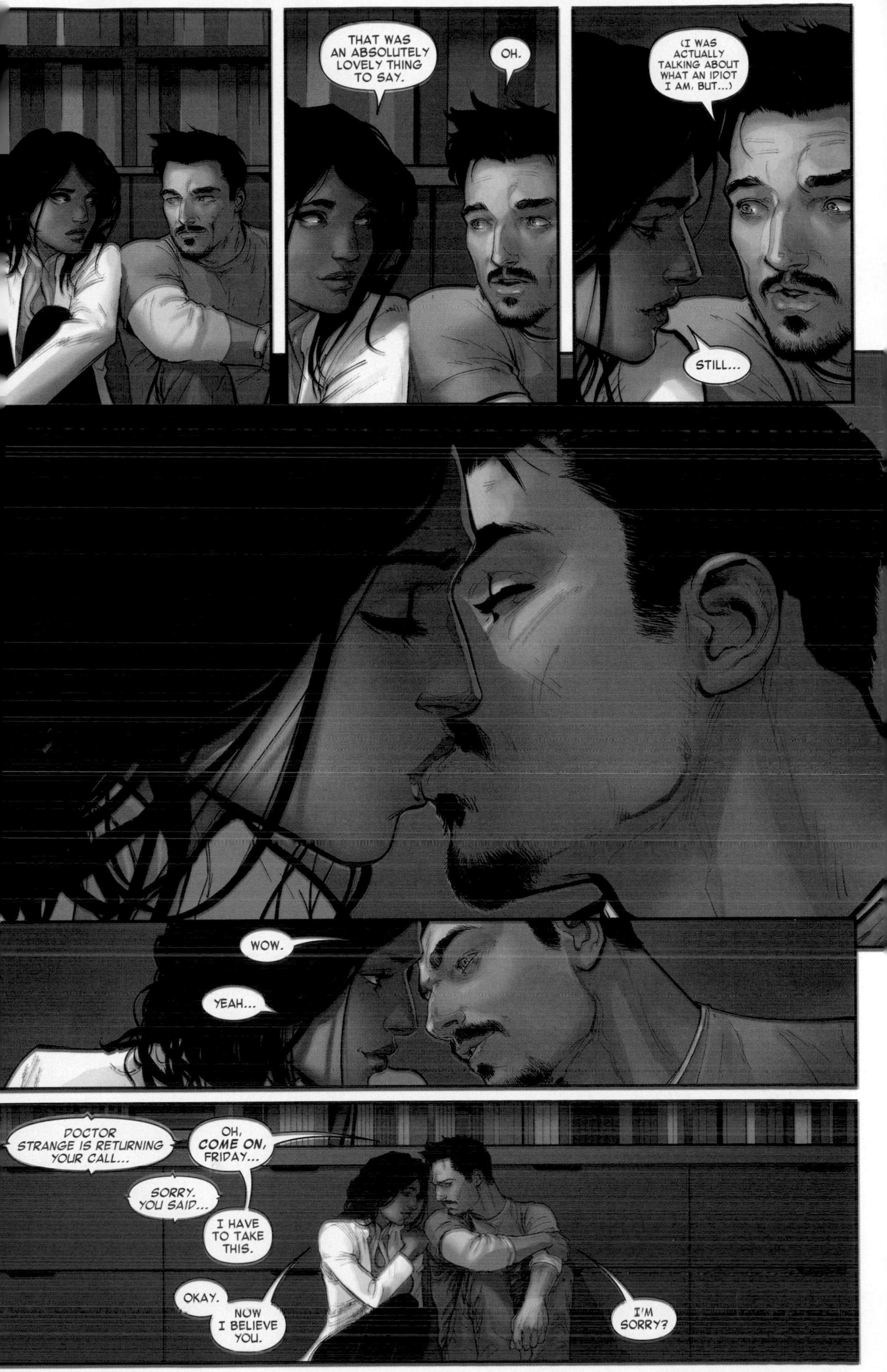
THAT WAS AN ABSOLUTELY LOVELY THING TO SAY.
OH.
(I WAS ACTUALLY TALKING ABOUT WHAT AN IDIOT I AM, BUT...)
STILL...
WOW.
YEAH...
DOCTOR STRANGE IS RETURNING YOUR CALL...
OH, COME ON, FRIDAY...
SORRY. YOU SAID...
I HAVE TO TAKE THIS.
OKAY. NOW I BELIEVE YOU.
I'M SORRY?

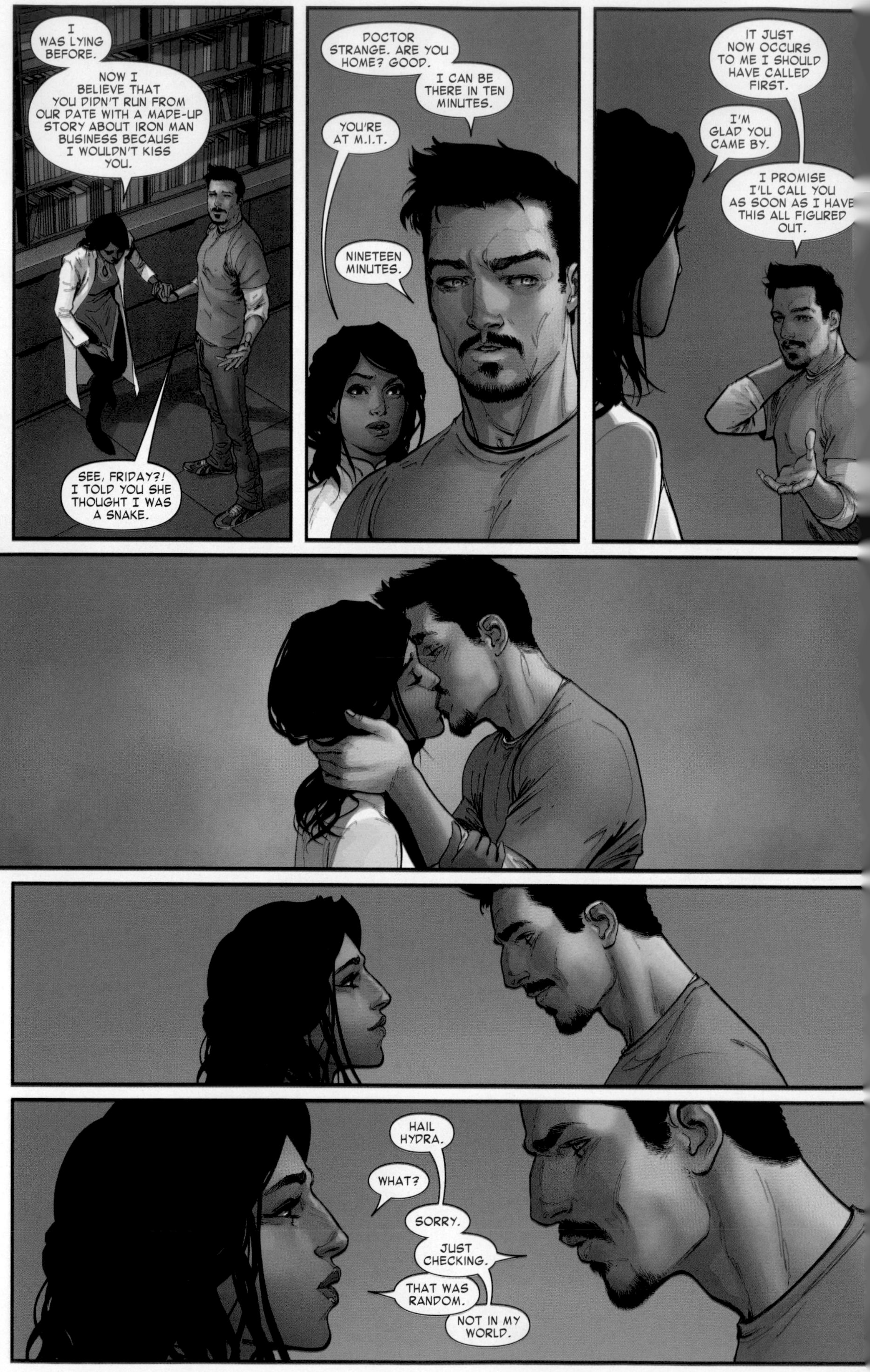
I WAS LYING BEFORE.
NOW I BELIEVE THAT YOU DIDN'T RUN FROM OUR DATE WITH A MADE-UP STORY ABOUT IRON MAN BUSINESS BECAUSE I WOULDN'T KISS YOU.
SEE, FRIDAY?! I TOLD YOU SHE THOUGHT I WAS A SNAKE.
DOCTOR STRANGE. ARE YOU HOME? GOOD.
I CAN BE THERE IN TEN MINUTES.
YOU'RE AT M.I.T.
NINETEEN MINUTES.
IT JUST NOW OCCURS TO ME I SHOULD HAVE CALLED FIRST.
I'M GLAD YOU CAME BY.
I PROMISE I'LL CALL YOU AS SOON AS I HAVE THIS ALL FIGURED OUT.
HAIL HYDRA.
WHAT?
SORRY.
JUST CHECKING.
THAT WAS RANDOM.
NOT IN MY WORLD.

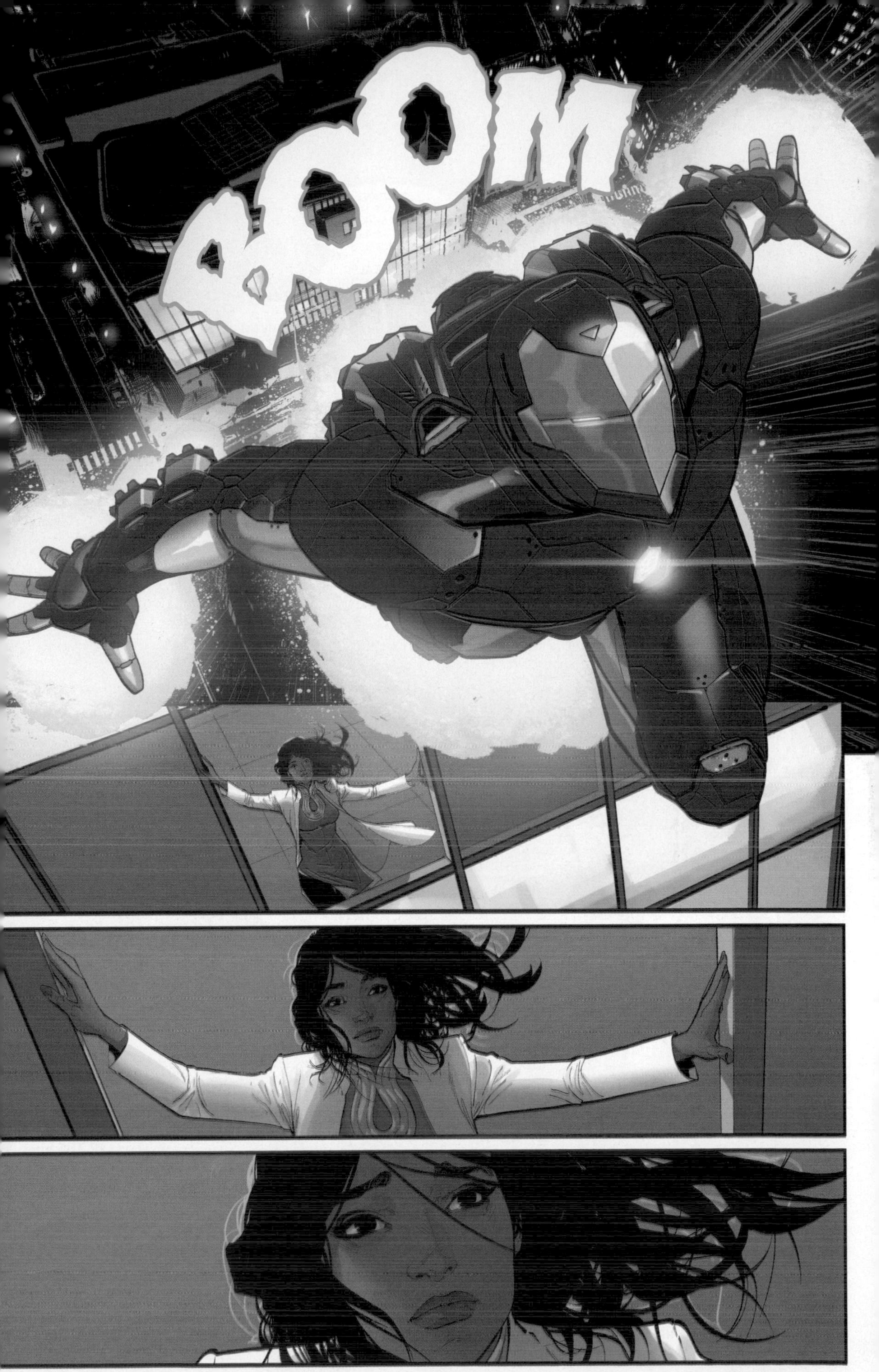
BOOM

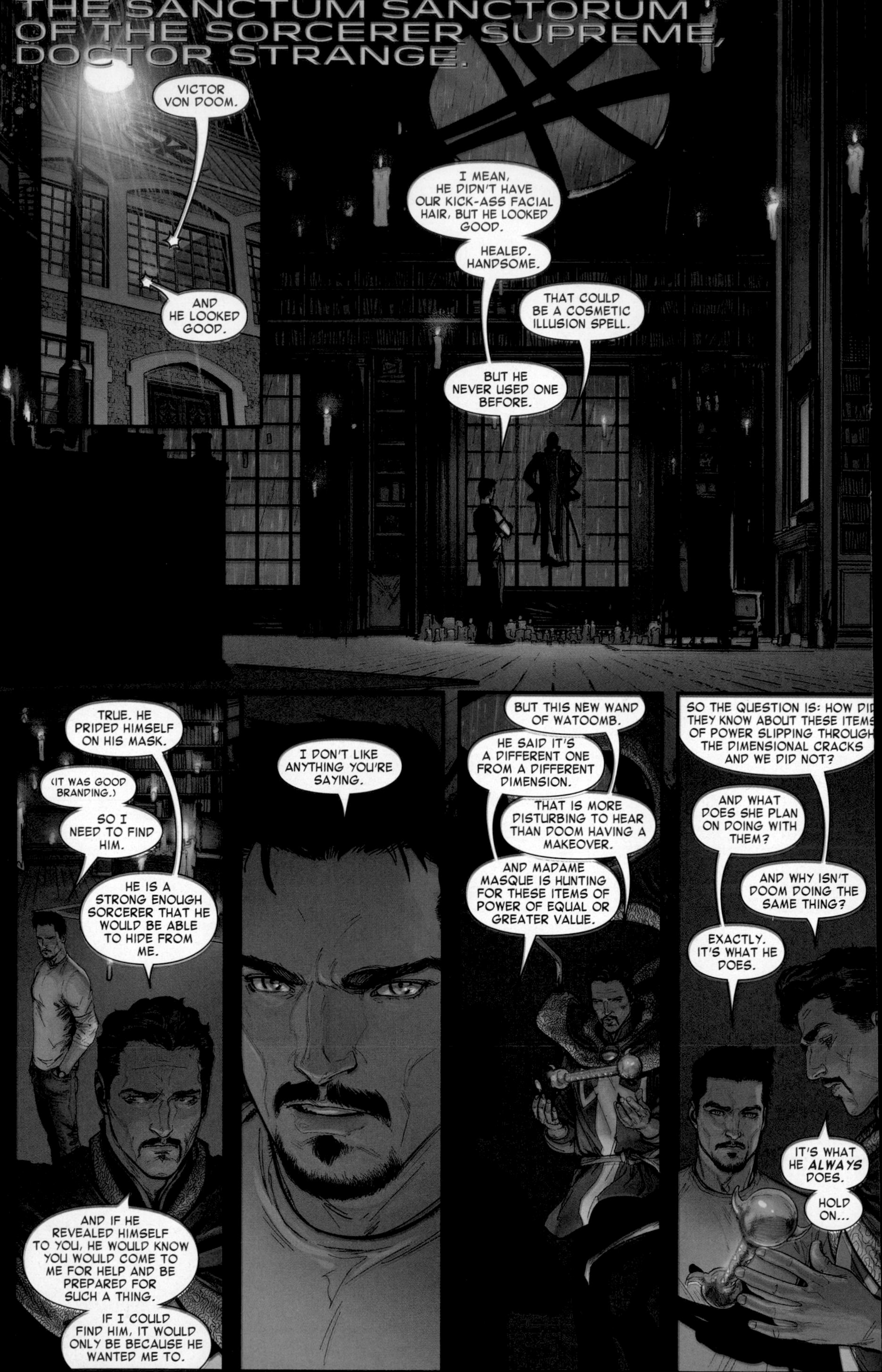
THE SANCTUM SANCTORUM OF THE SORCERER SUPREME, DOCTOR STRANGE.
VICTOR VON DOOM.
AND HE LOOKED GOOD.
I MEAN, HE DIDN'T HAVE OUR KICK-ASS FACIAL HAIR, BUT HE LOOKED GOOD.
HEALED. HANDSOME.
THAT COULD BE A COSMETIC ILLUSION SPELL.
BUT HE NEVER USED ONE BEFORE.
TRUE. HE PRIDED HIMSELF ON HIS MASK.
(IT WAS GOOD BRANDING.)
SO I NEED TO FIND HIM.
HE IS A STRONG ENOUGH SORCERER THAT HE WOULD BE ABLE TO HIDE FROM ME.
AND IF HE REVEALED HIMSELF TO YOU, HE WOULD KNOW YOU WOULD COME TO ME FOR HELP AND BE PREPARED FOR SUCH A THING.
IF I COULD FIND HIM, IT WOULD ONLY BE BECAUSE HE WANTED ME TO.
I DON'T LIKE ANYTHING YOU'RE SAYING.
BUT THIS NEW WAND OF WATOOMB.
HE SAID IT'S A DIFFERENT ONE FROM A DIFFERENT DIMENSION.
THAT IS MORE DISTURBING TO HEAR THAN DOOM HAVING A MAKEOVER.
AND MADAME MASQUE IS HUNTING FOR THESE ITEMS OF POWER OF EQUAL OR GREATER VALUE.
SO THE QUESTION IS: HOW DID THEY KNOW ABOUT THESE ITEMS OF POWER SLIPPING THROUGH THE DIMENSIONAL CRACKS AND WE DID NOT?
AND WHAT DOES SHE PLAN ON DOING WITH THEM?
AND WHY ISN'T DOOM DOING THE SAME THING?
EXACTLY. IT'S WHAT HE DOES.
IT'S WHAT HE *ALWAYS* DOES.
HOLD ON...

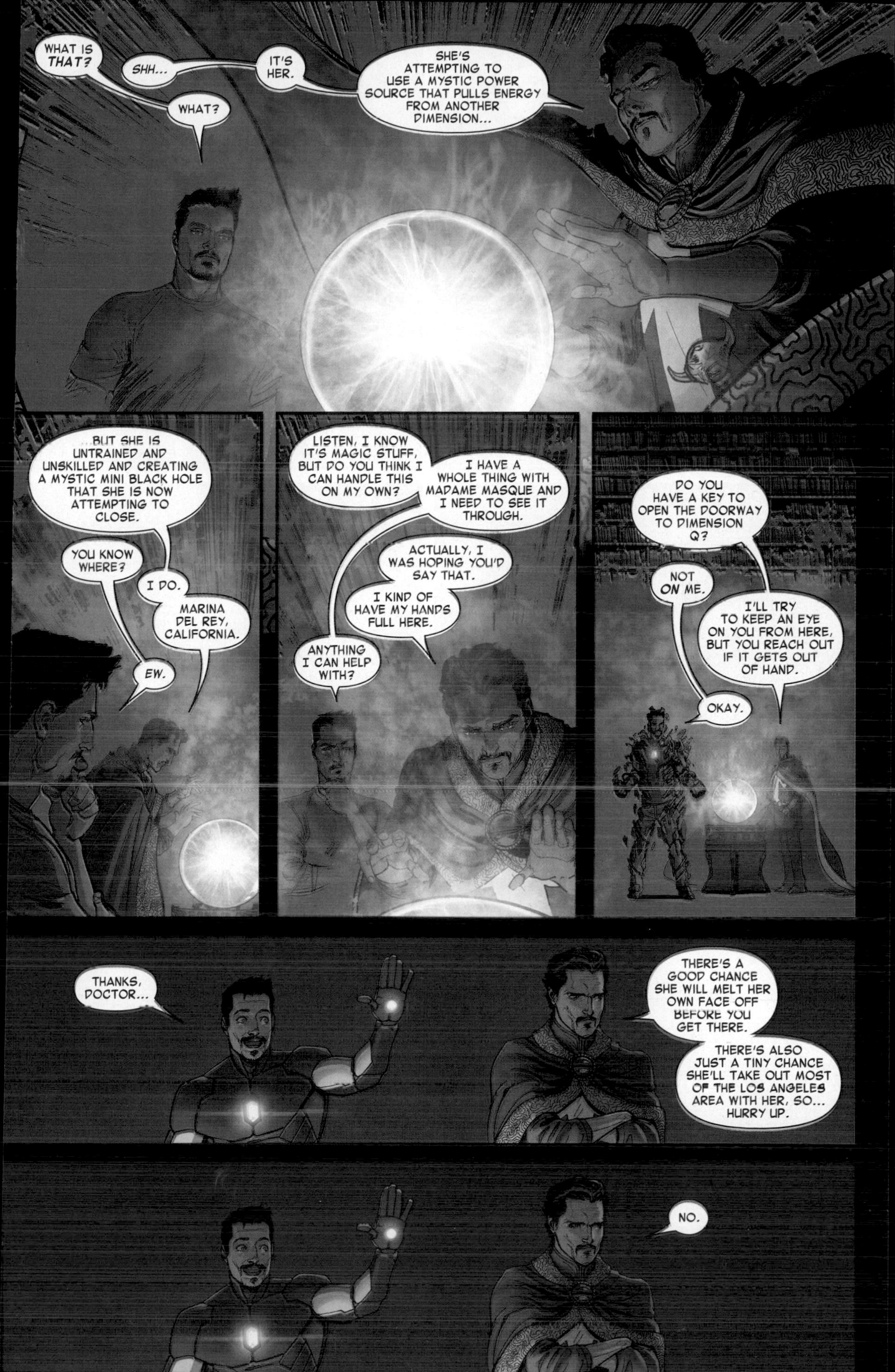
WHAT IS THAT?
SHH...
IT'S HER.
WHAT?
SHE'S ATTEMPTING TO USE A MYSTIC POWER SOURCE THAT PULLS ENERGY FROM ANOTHER DIMENSION...
...BUT SHE IS UNTRAINED AND UNSKILLED AND CREATING A MYSTIC MINI BLACK HOLE THAT SHE IS NOW ATTEMPTING TO CLOSE.
YOU KNOW WHERE?
I DO.
MARINA DEL REY, CALIFORNIA.
EW.
LISTEN, I KNOW IT'S MAGIC STUFF, BUT DO YOU THINK I CAN HANDLE THIS ON MY OWN?
I HAVE A WHOLE THING WITH MADAME MASQUE AND I NEED TO SEE IT THROUGH.
ACTUALLY, I WAS HOPING YOU'D SAY THAT.
I KIND OF HAVE MY HANDS FULL HERE.
ANYTHING I CAN HELP WITH?
DO YOU HAVE A KEY TO OPEN THE DOORWAY TO DIMENSION Q?
NOT ON ME.
I'LL TRY TO KEEP AN EYE ON YOU FROM HERE, BUT YOU REACH OUT IF IT GETS OUT OF HAND.
OKAY.
THANKS, DOCTOR...
THERE'S A GOOD CHANCE SHE WILL MELT HER OWN FACE OFF BEFORE YOU GET THERE.
THERE'S ALSO JUST A TINY CHANCE SHE'LL TAKE OUT MOST OF THE LOS ANGELES AREA WITH HER, SO... HURRY UP.
NO.

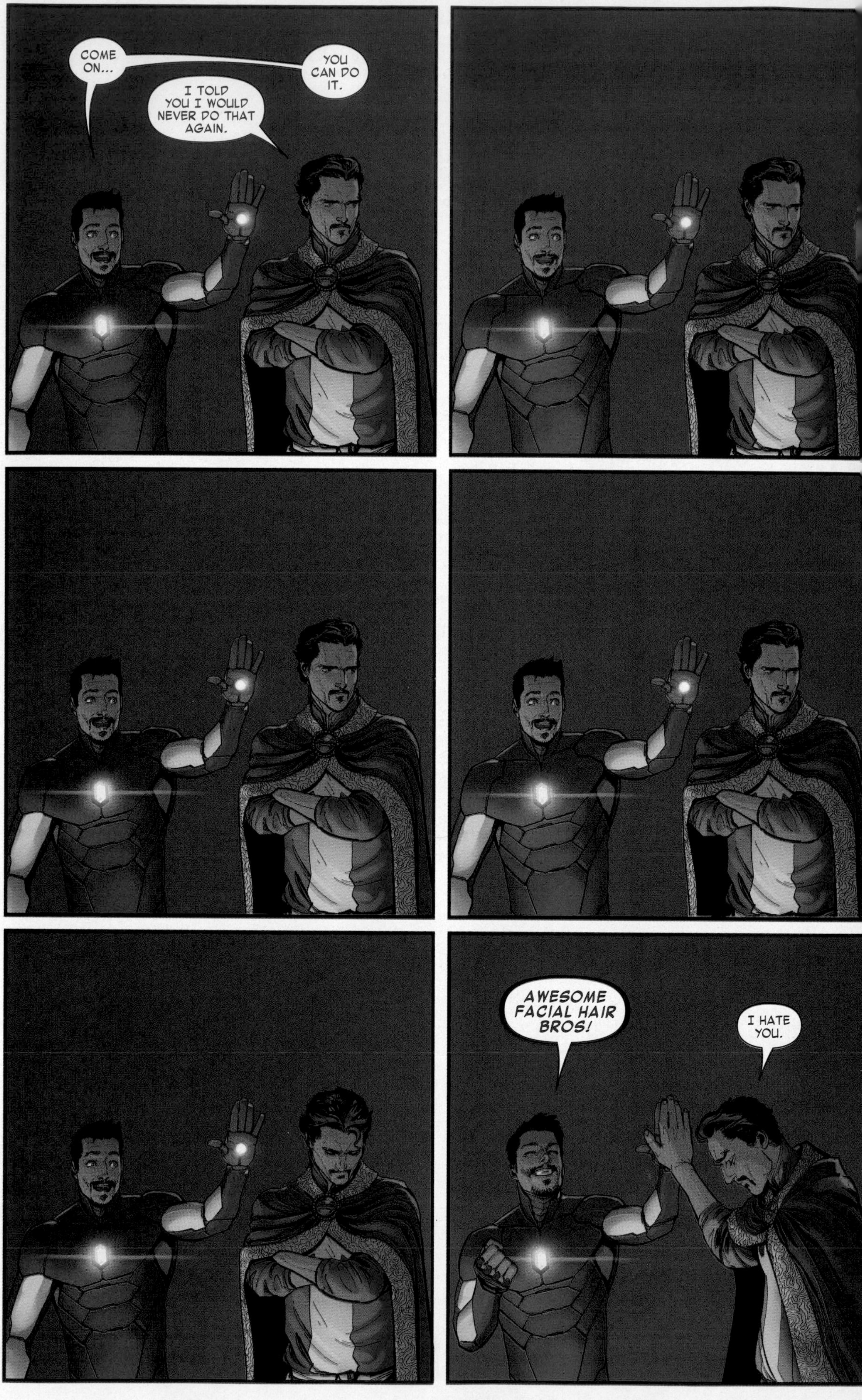
COME ON...
I TOLD YOU I WOULD NEVER DO THAT AGAIN.
YOU CAN DO IT.
AWESOME FACIAL HAIR BROS!
I HATE YOU.

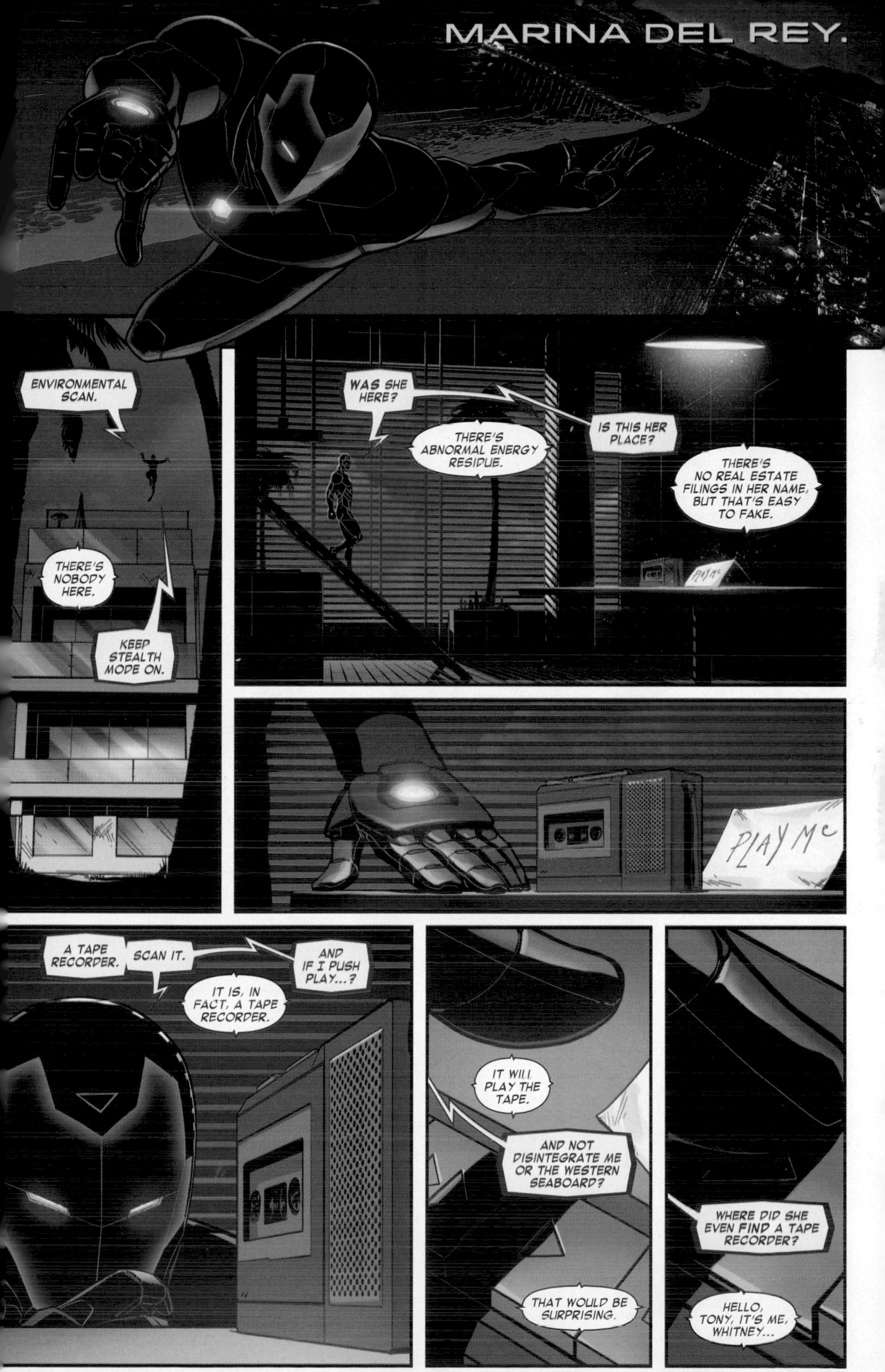
MARINA DEL REY.
ENVIRONMENTAL SCAN.
THERE'S NOBODY HERE.
KEEP STEALTH MODE ON.
WAS SHE HERE?
THERE'S ABNORMAL ENERGY RESIDUE.
IS THIS HER PLACE?
THERE'S NO REAL ESTATE FILINGS IN HER NAME, BUT THAT'S EASY TO FAKE.
PLAY ME
A TAPE RECORDER.
SCAN IT.
IT IS, IN FACT, A TAPE RECORDER.
AND IF I PUSH PLAY...?
IT WILL PLAY THE TAPE.
AND NOT DISINTEGRATE ME OR THE WESTERN SEABOARD?
THAT WOULD BE SURPRISING.
WHERE DID SHE EVEN FIND A TAPE RECORDER?
HELLO, TONY, IT'S ME, WHITNEY...

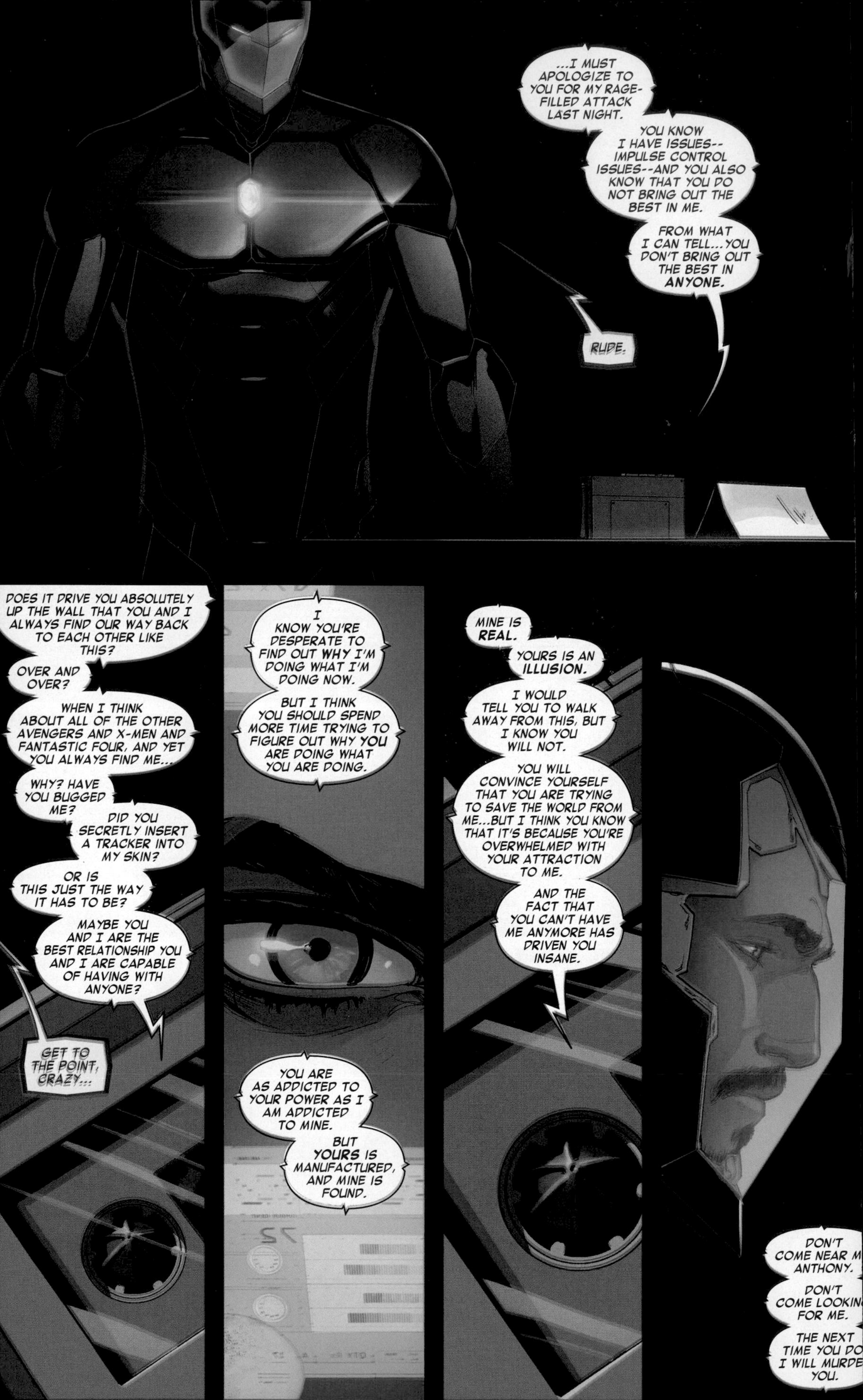
...I MUST APOLOGIZE TO YOU FOR MY RAGE-FILLED ATTACK LAST NIGHT.
YOU KNOW I HAVE ISSUES-- IMPULSE CONTROL ISSUES--AND YOU ALSO KNOW THAT YOU DO NOT BRING OUT THE BEST IN ME.
FROM WHAT I CAN TELL...YOU DON'T BRING OUT THE BEST IN ANYONE.
RUDE.
DOES IT DRIVE YOU ABSOLUTELY UP THE WALL THAT YOU AND I ALWAYS FIND OUR WAY BACK TO EACH OTHER LIKE THIS?
OVER AND OVER?
WHEN I THINK ABOUT ALL OF THE OTHER AVENGERS AND X-MEN AND FANTASTIC FOUR, AND YET YOU ALWAYS FIND ME...
WHY? HAVE YOU BUGGED ME?
DID YOU SECRETLY INSERT A TRACKER INTO MY SKIN?
OR IS THIS JUST THE WAY IT HAS TO BE?
MAYBE YOU AND I ARE THE BEST RELATIONSHIP YOU AND I ARE CAPABLE OF HAVING WITH ANYONE?
GET TO THE POINT, CRAZY...
I KNOW YOU'RE DESPERATE TO FIND OUT WHY I'M DOING WHAT I'M DOING NOW.
BUT I THINK YOU SHOULD SPEND MORE TIME TRYING TO FIGURE OUT WHY YOU ARE DOING WHAT YOU ARE DOING.
YOU ARE AS ADDICTED TO YOUR POWER AS I AM ADDICTED TO MINE.
BUT YOURS IS MANUFACTURED, AND MINE IS FOUND.
MINE IS REAL.
YOURS IS AN ILLUSION.
I WOULD TELL YOU TO WALK AWAY FROM THIS, BUT I KNOW YOU WILL NOT.
YOU WILL CONVINCE YOURSELF THAT YOU ARE TRYING TO SAVE THE WORLD FROM ME...BUT I THINK YOU KNOW THAT IT'S BECAUSE YOU'RE OVERWHELMED WITH YOUR ATTRACTION TO ME.
AND THE FACT THAT YOU CAN'T HAVE ME ANYMORE HAS DRIVEN YOU INSANE.
DON'T COME NEAR M ANTHONY.
DON'T COME LOOKIN FOR ME.
THE NEXT TIME YOU DO I WILL MURDE YOU.

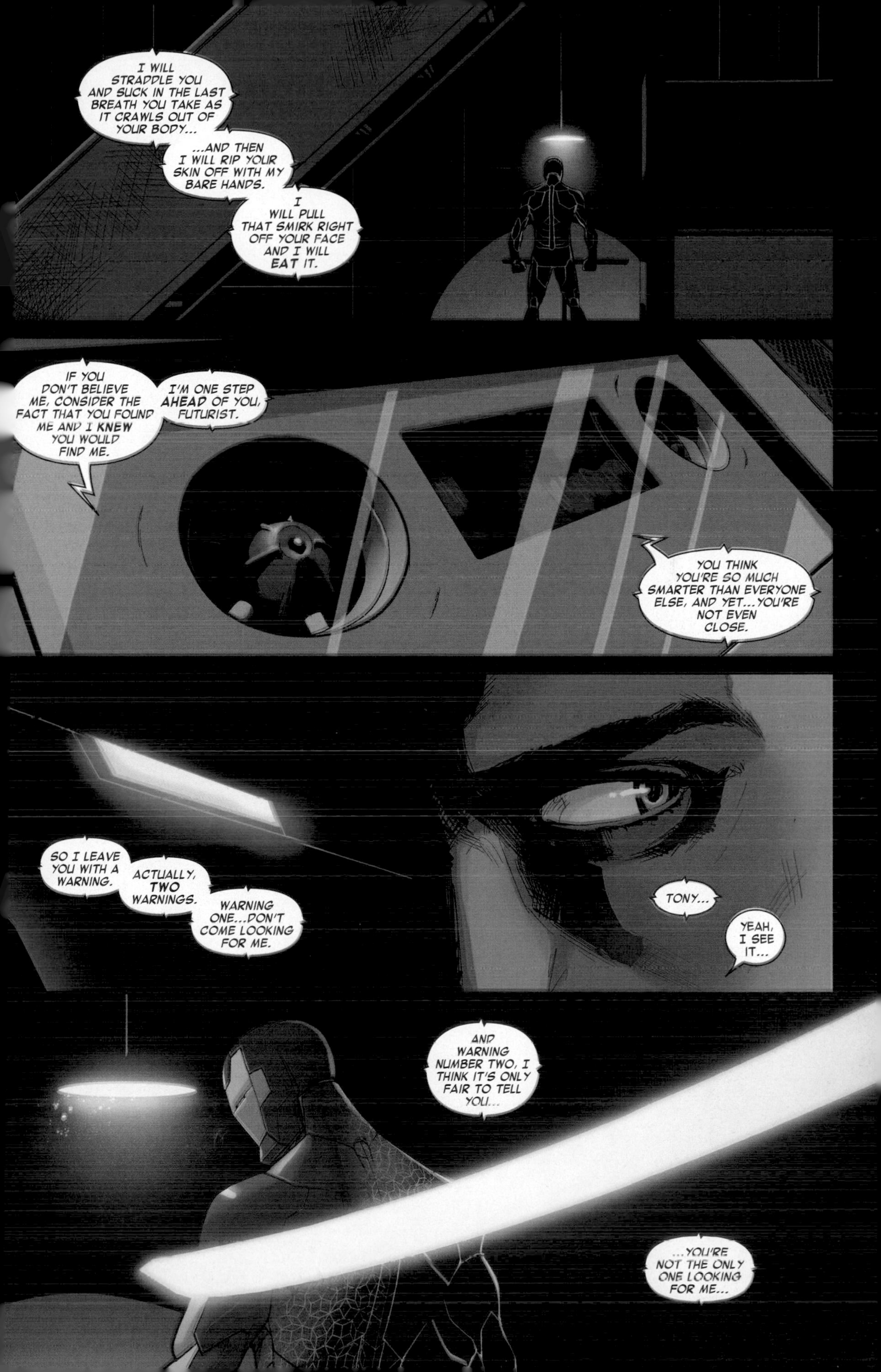
I WILL STRADDLE YOU AND SUCK IN THE LAST BREATH YOU TAKE AS IT CRAWLS OUT OF YOUR BODY...
...AND THEN I WILL RIP YOUR SKIN OFF WITH MY BARE HANDS.
I WILL PULL THAT SMIRK RIGHT OFF YOUR FACE AND I WILL EAT IT.
IF YOU DON'T BELIEVE ME, CONSIDER THE FACT THAT YOU FOUND ME AND I KNEW YOU WOULD FIND ME.
I'M ONE STEP AHEAD OF YOU, FUTURIST.
YOU THINK YOU'RE SO MUCH SMARTER THAN EVERYONE ELSE, AND YET... YOU'RE NOT EVEN CLOSE.
SO I LEAVE YOU WITH A WARNING.
ACTUALLY, TWO WARNINGS.
WARNING ONE... DON'T COME LOOKING FOR ME.
TONY...
YEAH, I SEE IT...
AND WARNING NUMBER TWO, I THINK IT'S ONLY FAIR TO TELL YOU...
...YOU'RE NOT THE ONLY ONE LOOKING FOR ME...

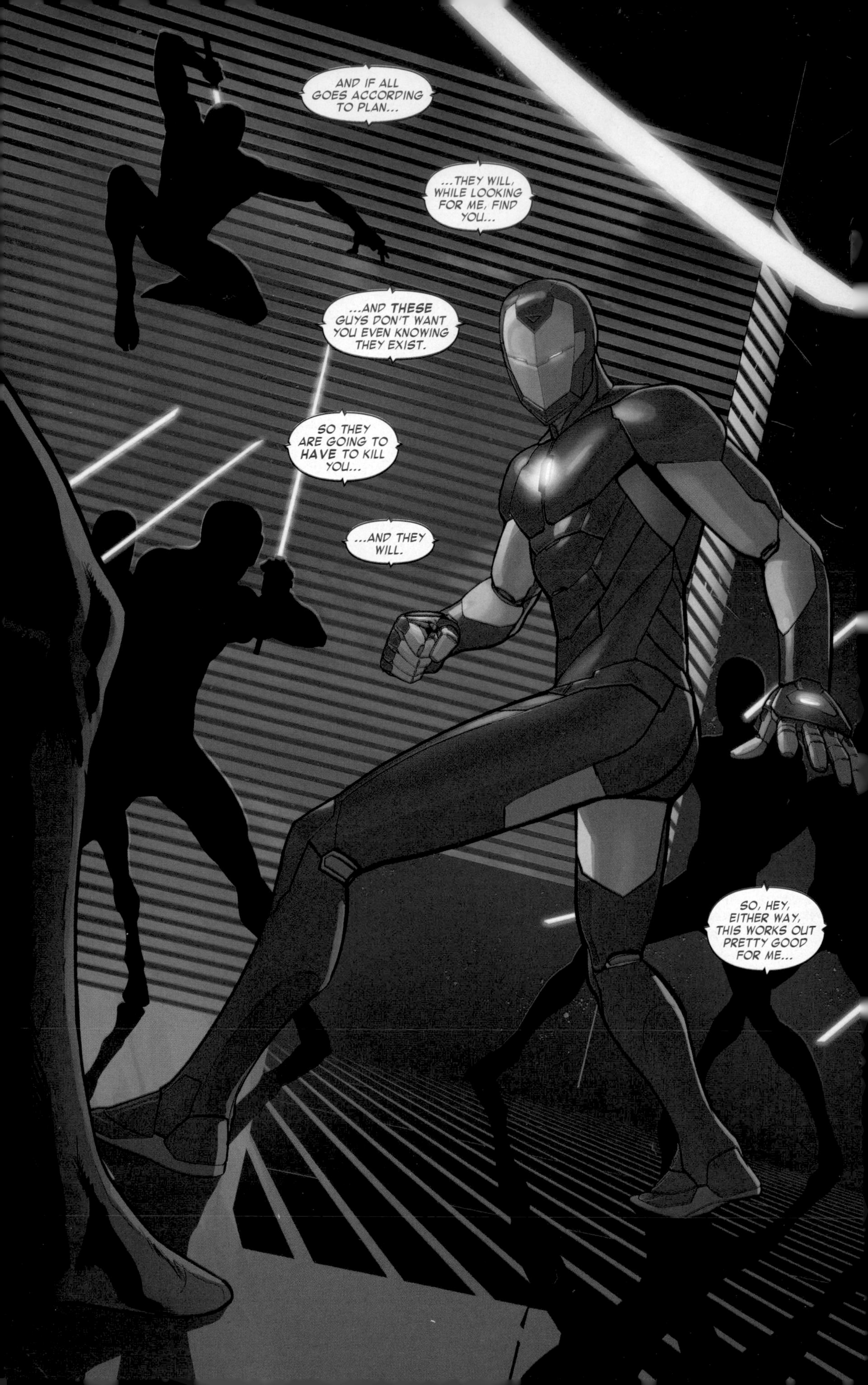
AND IF ALL GOES ACCORDING TO PLAN...
...THEY WILL, WHILE LOOKING FOR ME, FIND YOU...
...AND THESE GUYS DON'T WANT YOU EVEN KNOWING THEY EXIST.
SO THEY ARE GOING TO HAVE TO KILL YOU...
...AND THEY WILL.
SO, HEY, EITHER WAY, THIS WORKS OUT PRETTY GOOD FOR ME...

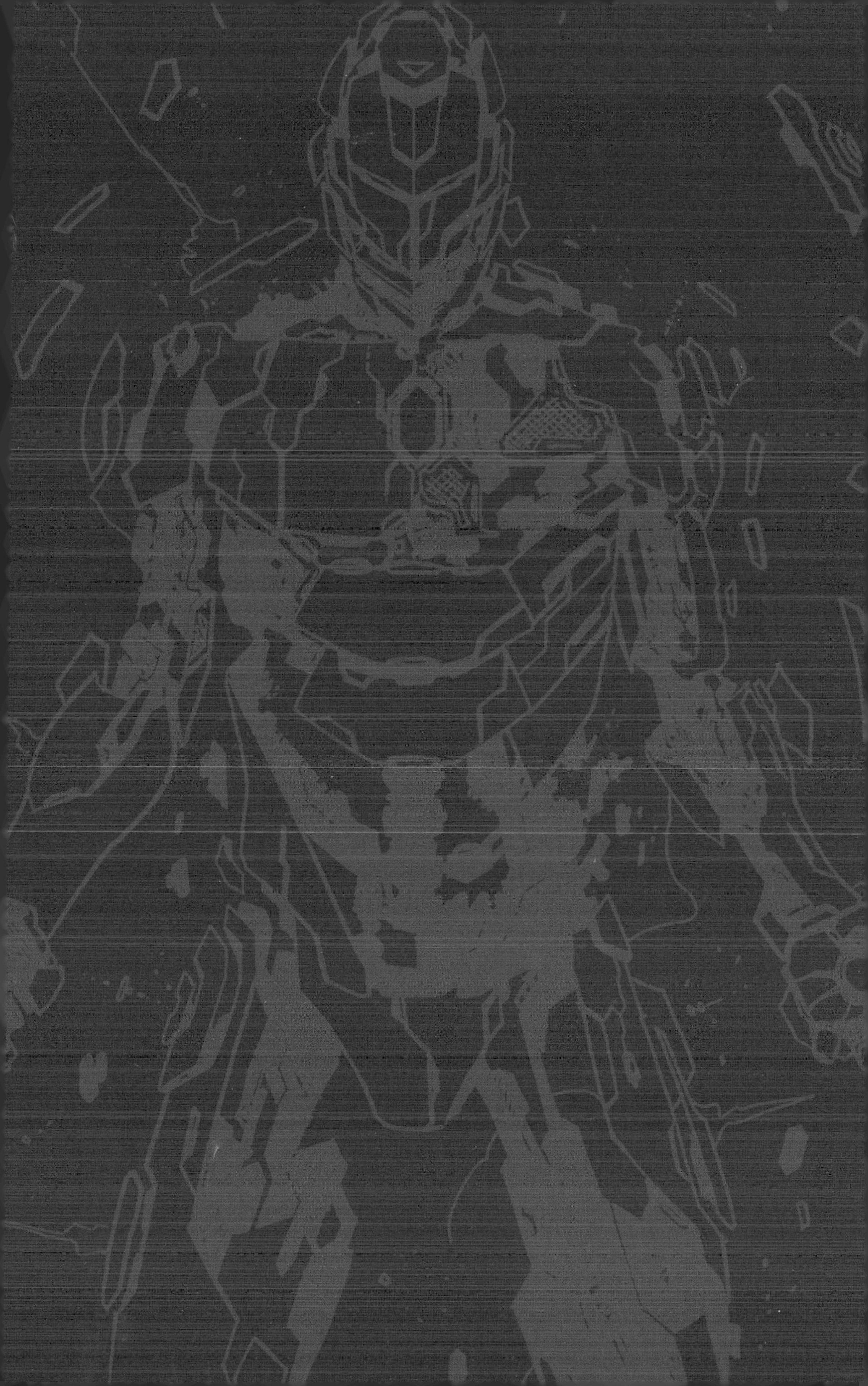

#4

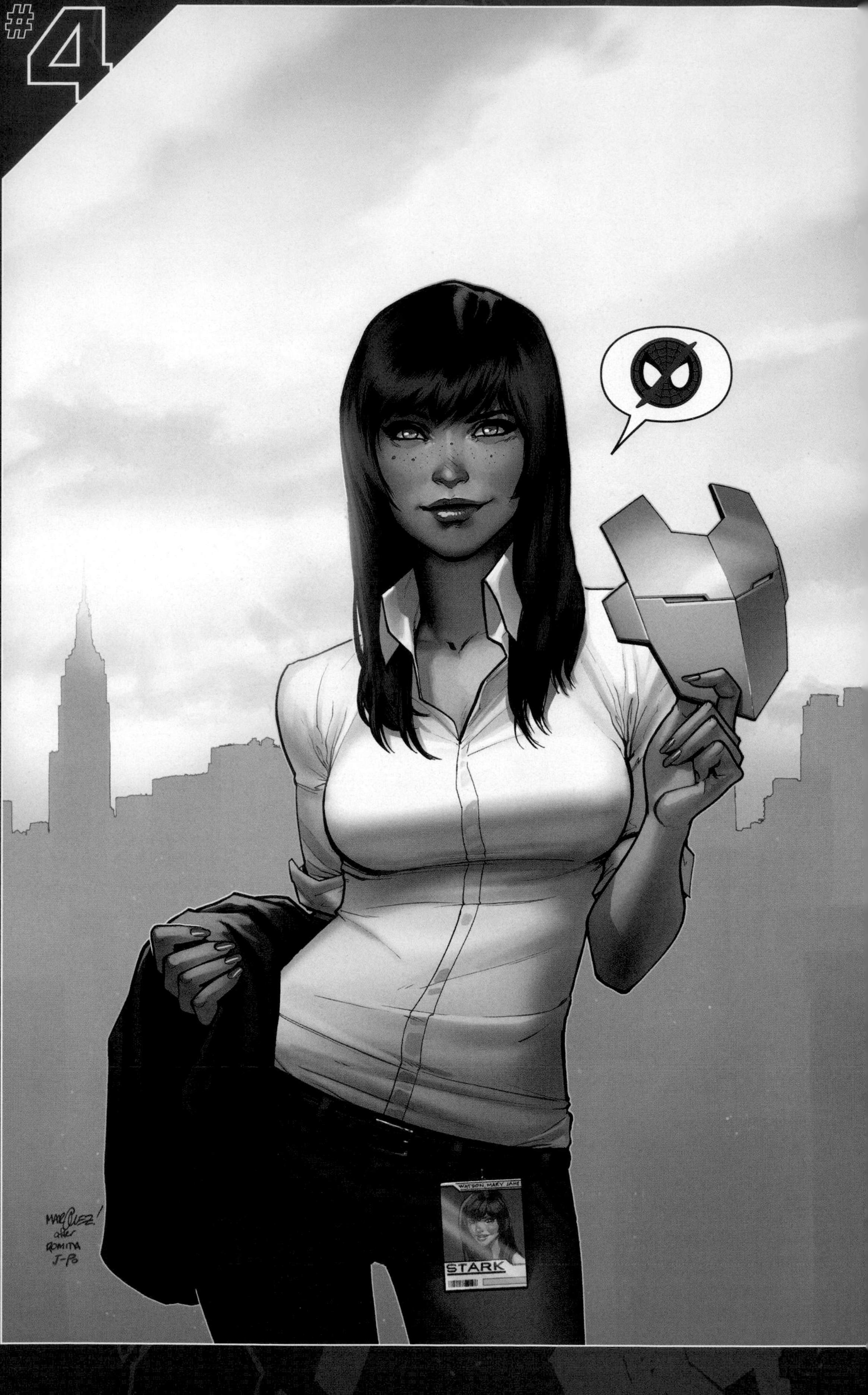
WATSON MARY JANE
STARK

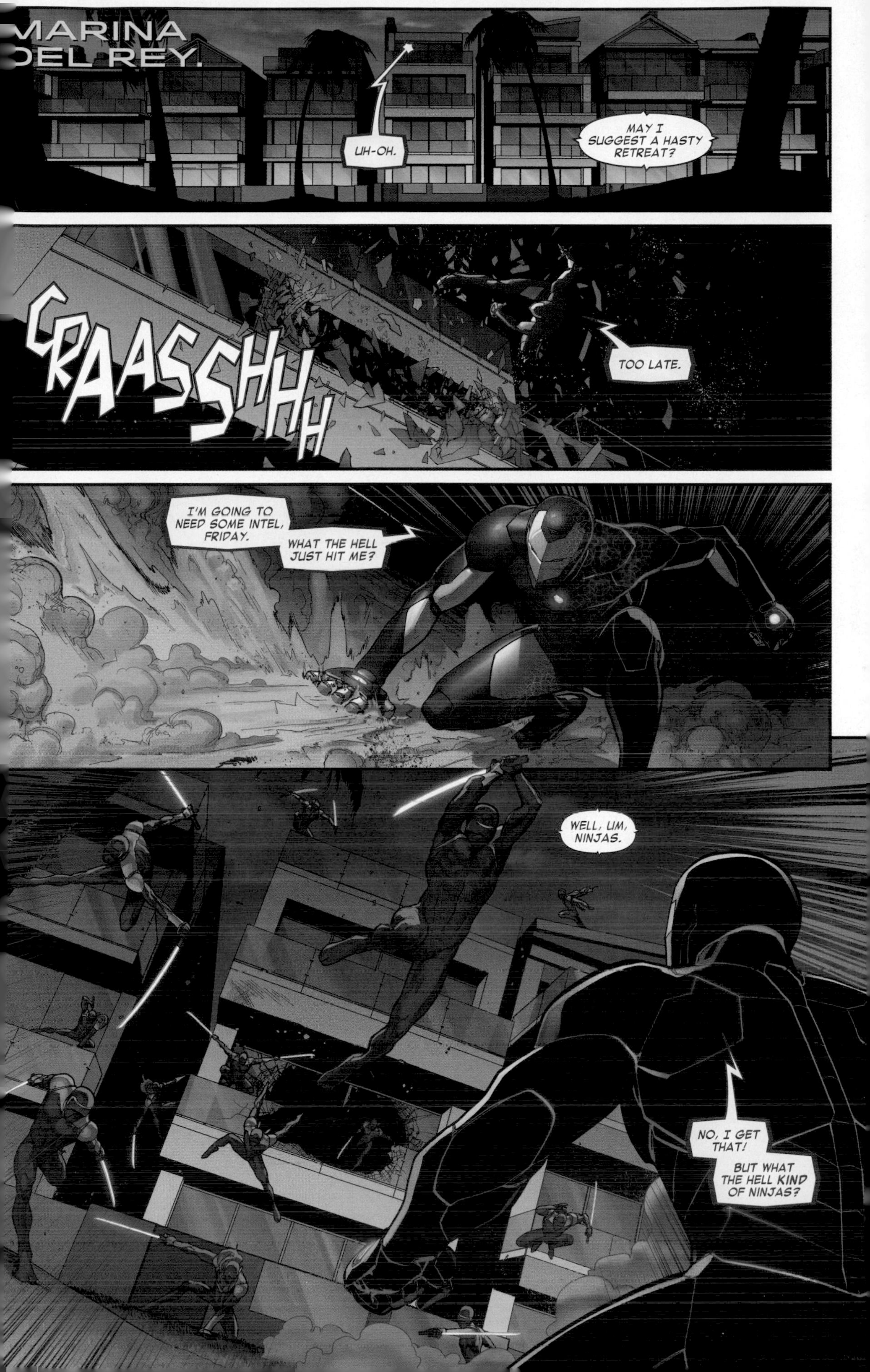
MARINA DEL REY.
UH-OH.
MAY I SUGGEST A HASTY RETREAT?
CRAASSHHH
TOO LATE.
I'M GOING TO NEED SOME INTEL, FRIDAY.
WHAT THE HELL JUST HIT ME?
WELL, UM, NINJAS.
NO, I GET THAT!
BUT WHAT THE HELL KIND OF NINJAS?

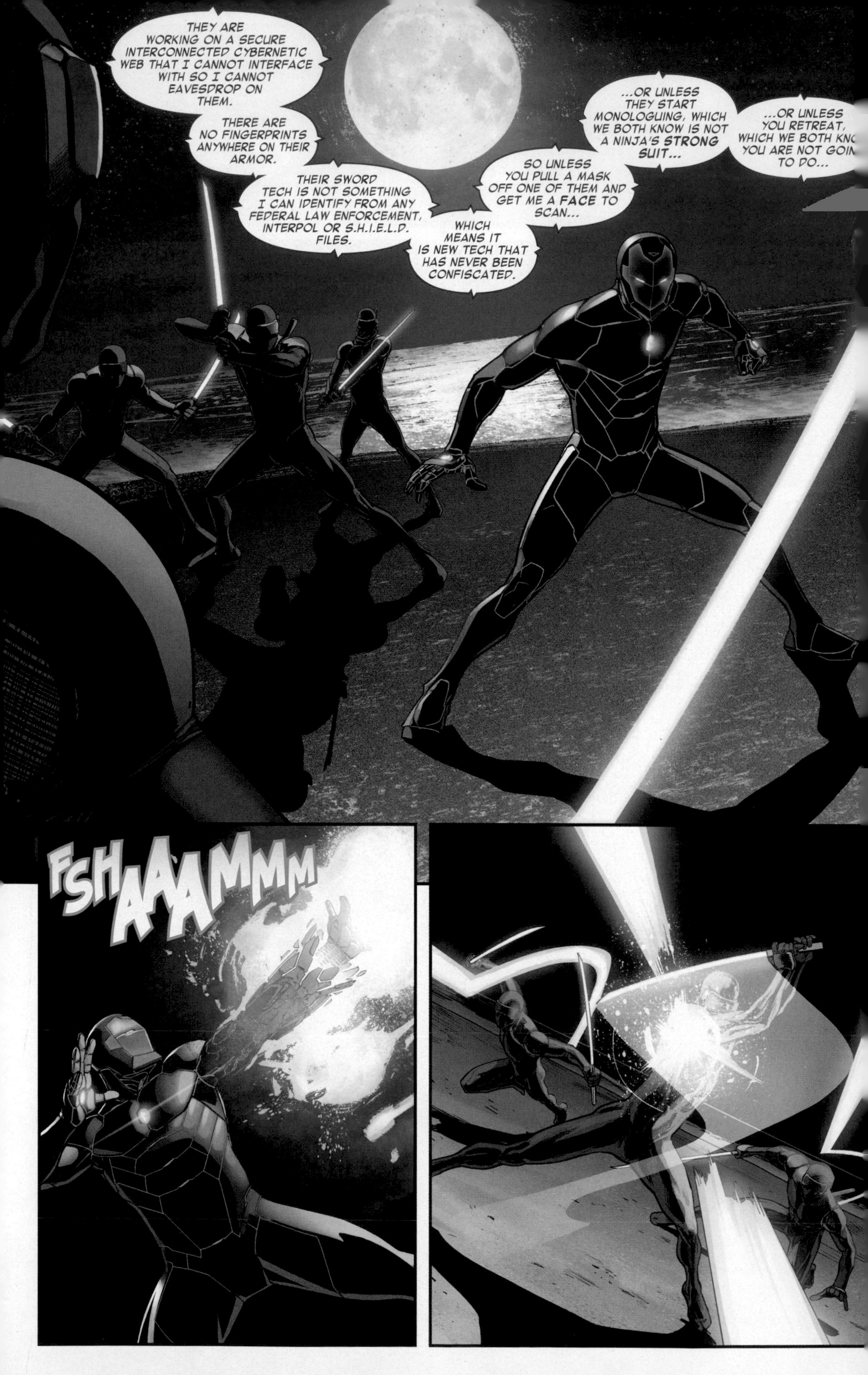
THEY ARE WORKING ON A SECURE INTERCONNECTED CYBERNETIC WEB THAT I CANNOT INTERFACE WITH SO I CANNOT EAVESDROP ON THEM.
THERE ARE NO FINGERPRINTS ANYWHERE ON THEIR ARMOR.
THEIR SWORD TECH IS NOT SOMETHING I CAN IDENTIFY FROM ANY FEDERAL LAW ENFORCEMENT, INTERPOL OR S.H.I.E.L.D. FILES.
WHICH MEANS IT IS NEW TECH THAT HAS NEVER BEEN CONFISCATED.
SO UNLESS YOU PULL A MASK OFF ONE OF THEM AND GET ME A **FACE** TO SCAN...
...OR UNLESS THEY START MONOLOGUING, WHICH WE BOTH KNOW IS NOT A NINJA'S **STRONG SUIT...**
...OR UNLESS YOU RETREAT, WHICH WE BOTH KNO YOU ARE NOT GOIN TO DO...
FSHAAAMMMM

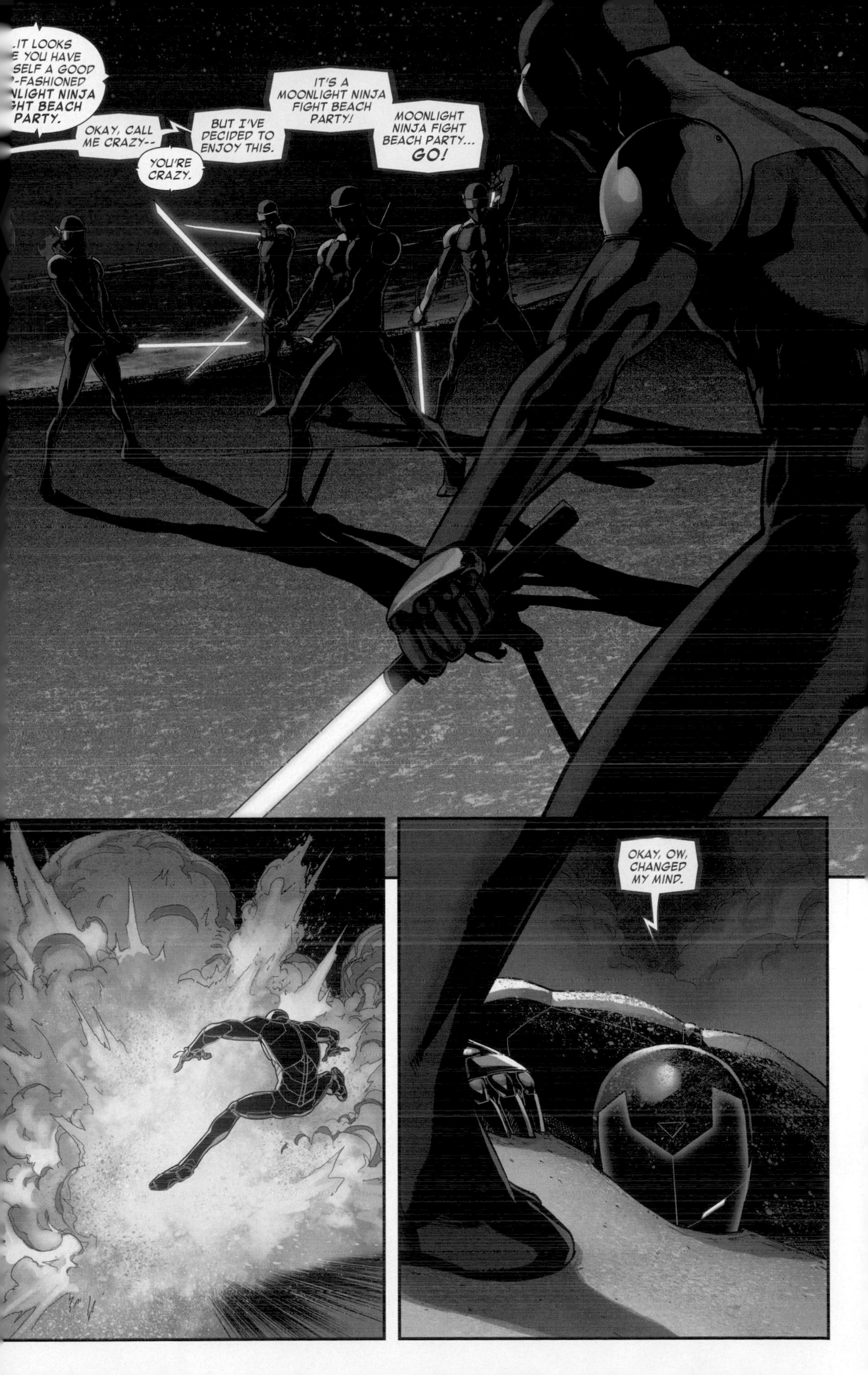

.IT LOOKS E YOU HAVE SELF A GOOD -FASHIONED NLIGHT NINJA GHT BEACH PARTY.
OKAY, CALL ME CRAZY--
YOU'RE CRAZY.
BUT I'VE DECIDED TO ENJOY THIS.
IT'S A MOONLIGHT NINJA FIGHT BEACH PARTY!
MOONLIGHT NINJA FIGHT BEACH PARTY... GO!
OKAY, OW, CHANGED MY MIND.

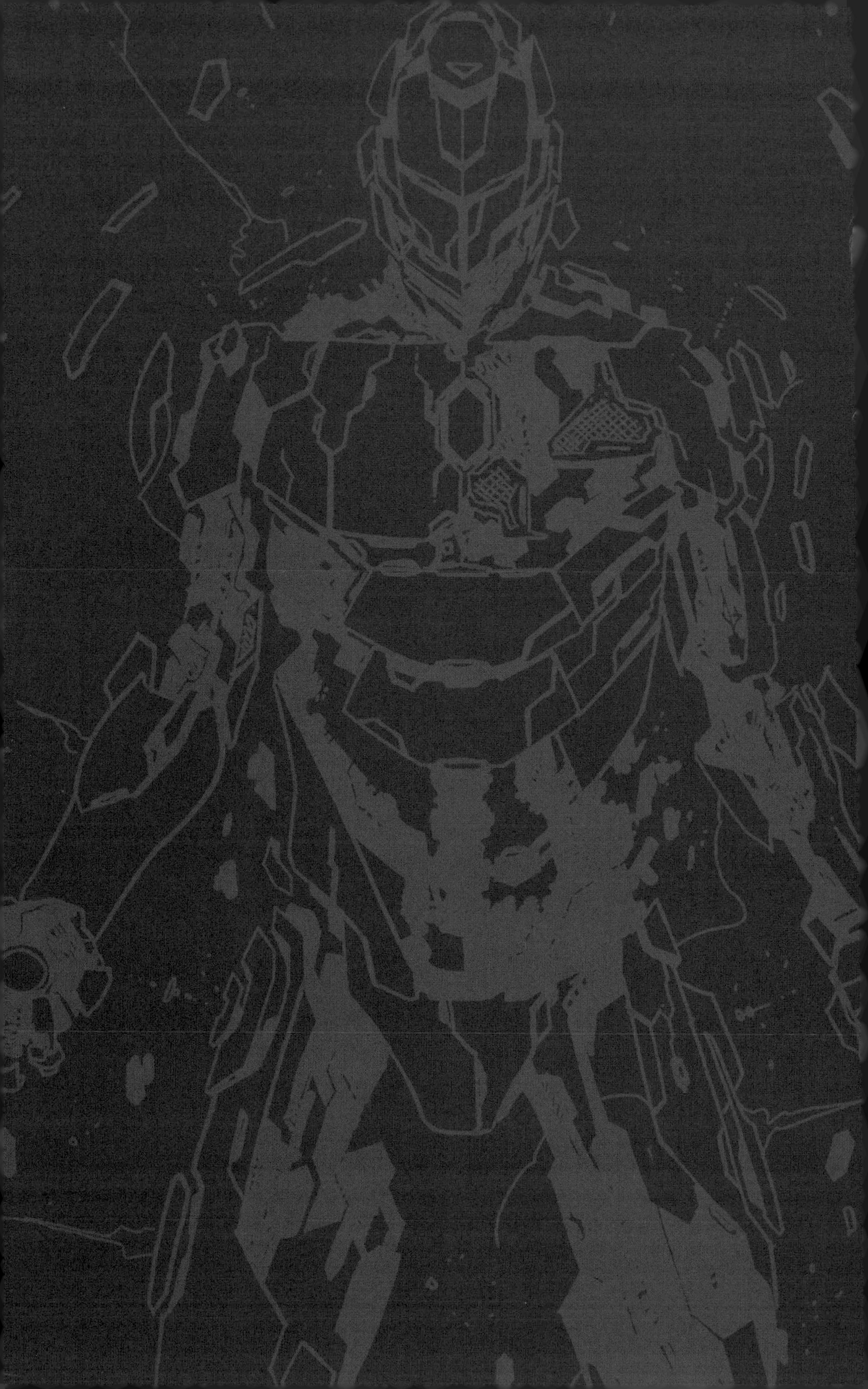

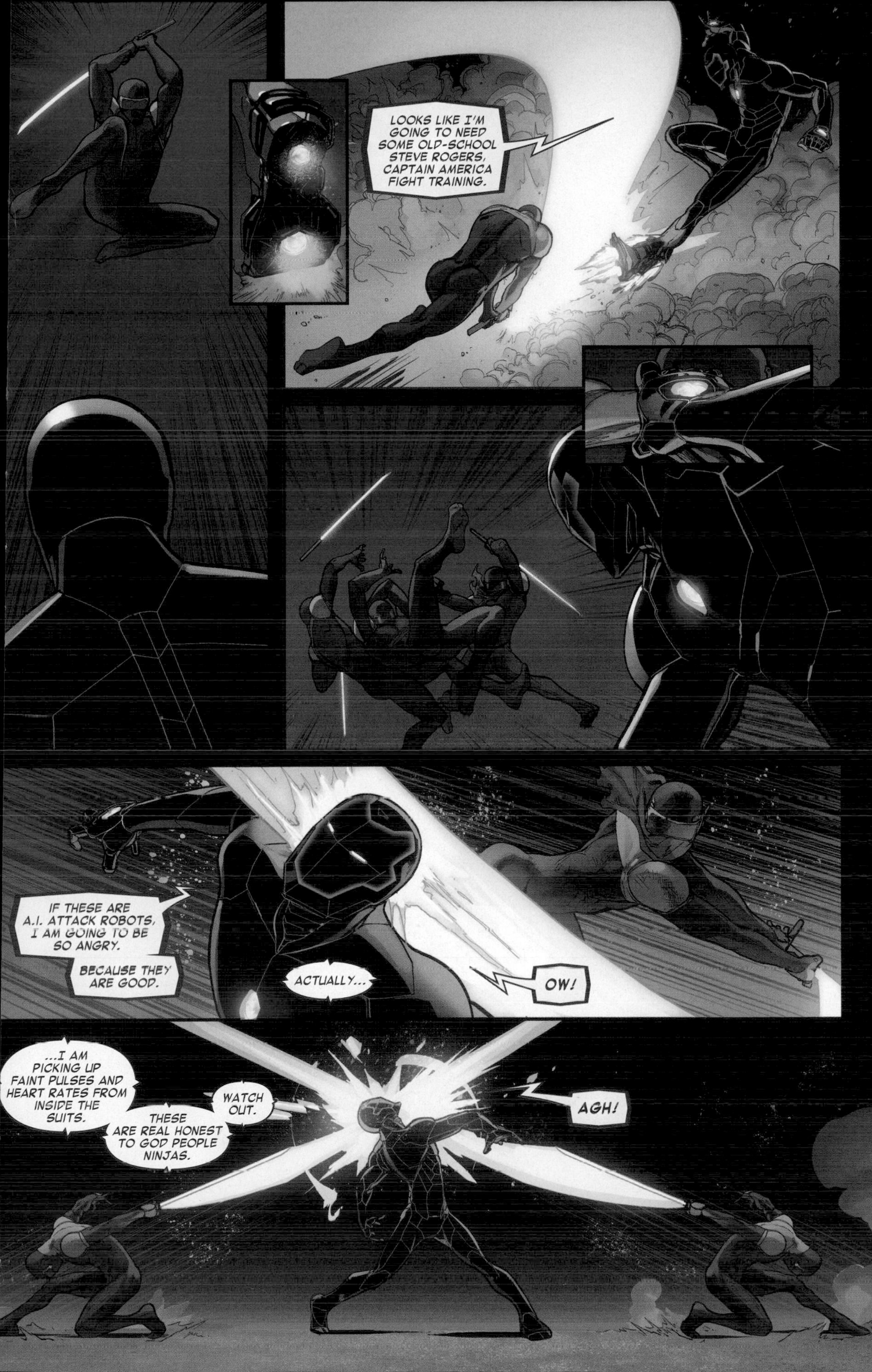

LOOKS LIKE I'M GOING TO NEED SOME OLD-SCHOOL STEVE ROGERS, CAPTAIN AMERICA FIGHT TRAINING.
IF THESE ARE A.I. ATTACK ROBOTS, I AM GOING TO BE SO ANGRY.
BECAUSE THEY ARE GOOD.
ACTUALLY...
OW!
...I AM PICKING UP FAINT PULSES AND HEART RATES FROM INSIDE THE SUITS.
THESE ARE REAL HONEST TO GOD PEOPLE NINJAS.
WATCH OUT.
AGH!

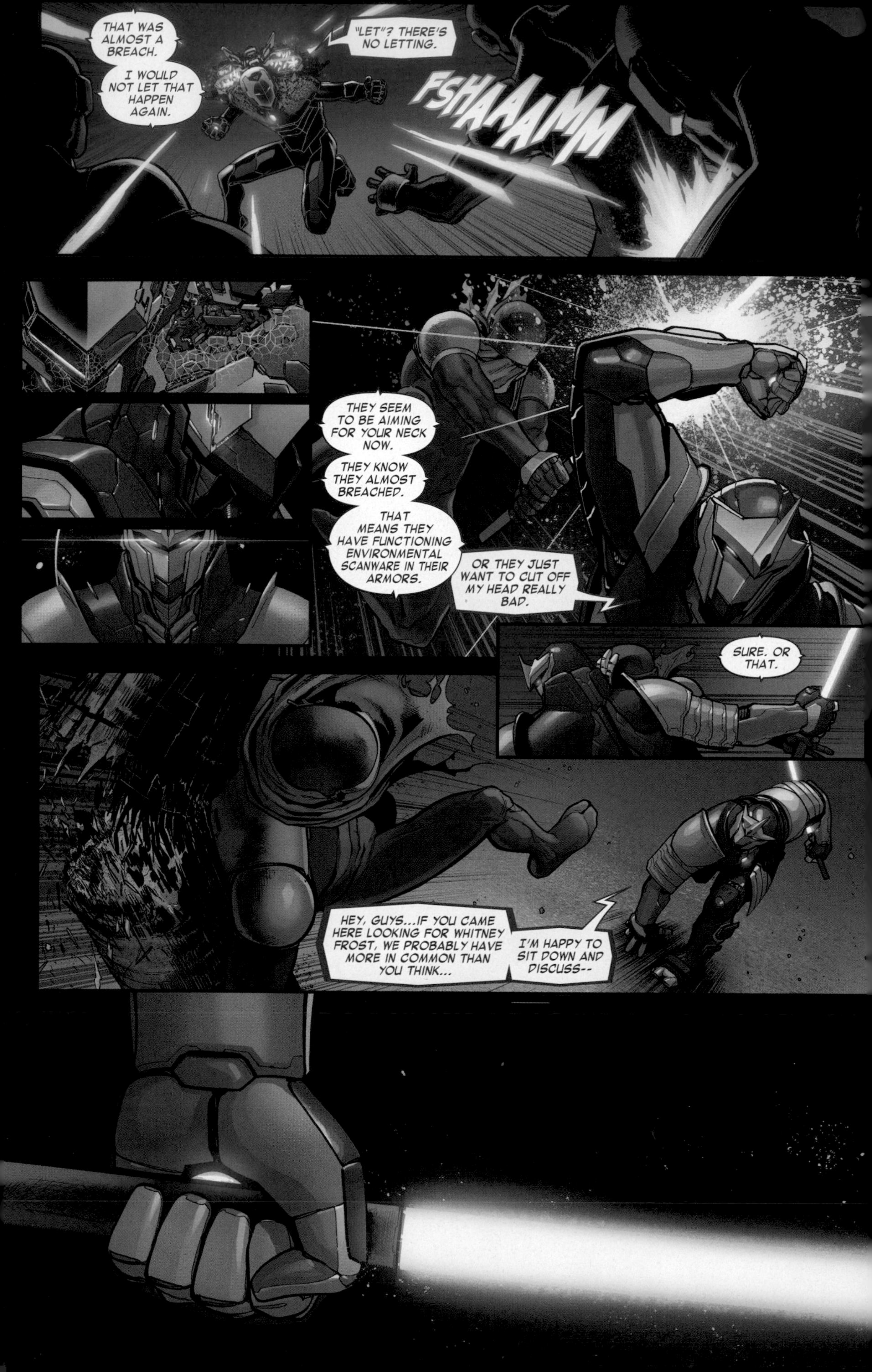
THAT WAS ALMOST A BREACH.
I WOULD NOT LET THAT HAPPEN AGAIN.
"LET"? THERE'S NO LETTING.
FSHAAAMM
THEY SEEM TO BE AIMING FOR YOUR NECK NOW.
THEY KNOW THEY ALMOST BREACHED.
THAT MEANS THEY HAVE FUNCTIONING ENVIRONMENTAL SCANWARE IN THEIR ARMORS.
OR THEY JUST WANT TO CUT OFF MY HEAD REALLY BAD.
SURE. OR THAT.
HEY, GUYS...IF YOU CAME HERE LOOKING FOR WHITNEY FROST, WE PROBABLY HAVE MORE IN COMMON THAN YOU THINK...
I'M HAPPY TO SIT DOWN AND DISCUSS--

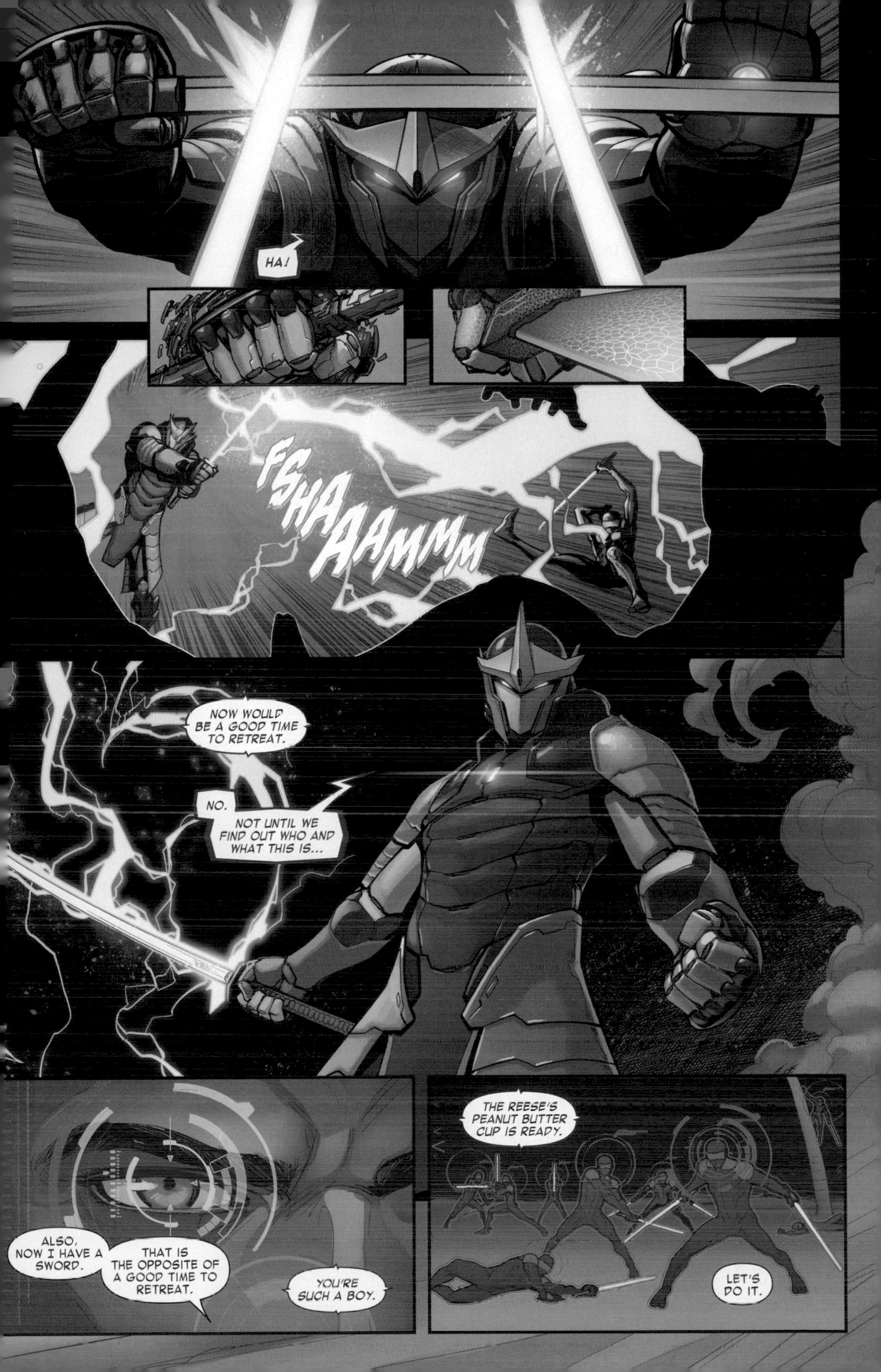
HA!
FSHAAAMMM
NOW WOULD BE A GOOD TIME TO RETREAT.
NO.
NOT UNTIL WE FIND OUT WHO AND WHAT THIS IS...
ALSO, NOW I HAVE A SWORD.
THAT IS THE OPPOSITE OF A GOOD TIME TO RETREAT.
YOU'RE SUCH A BOY.
THE REESE'S PEANUT BUTTER CUP IS READY.
LET'S DO IT.

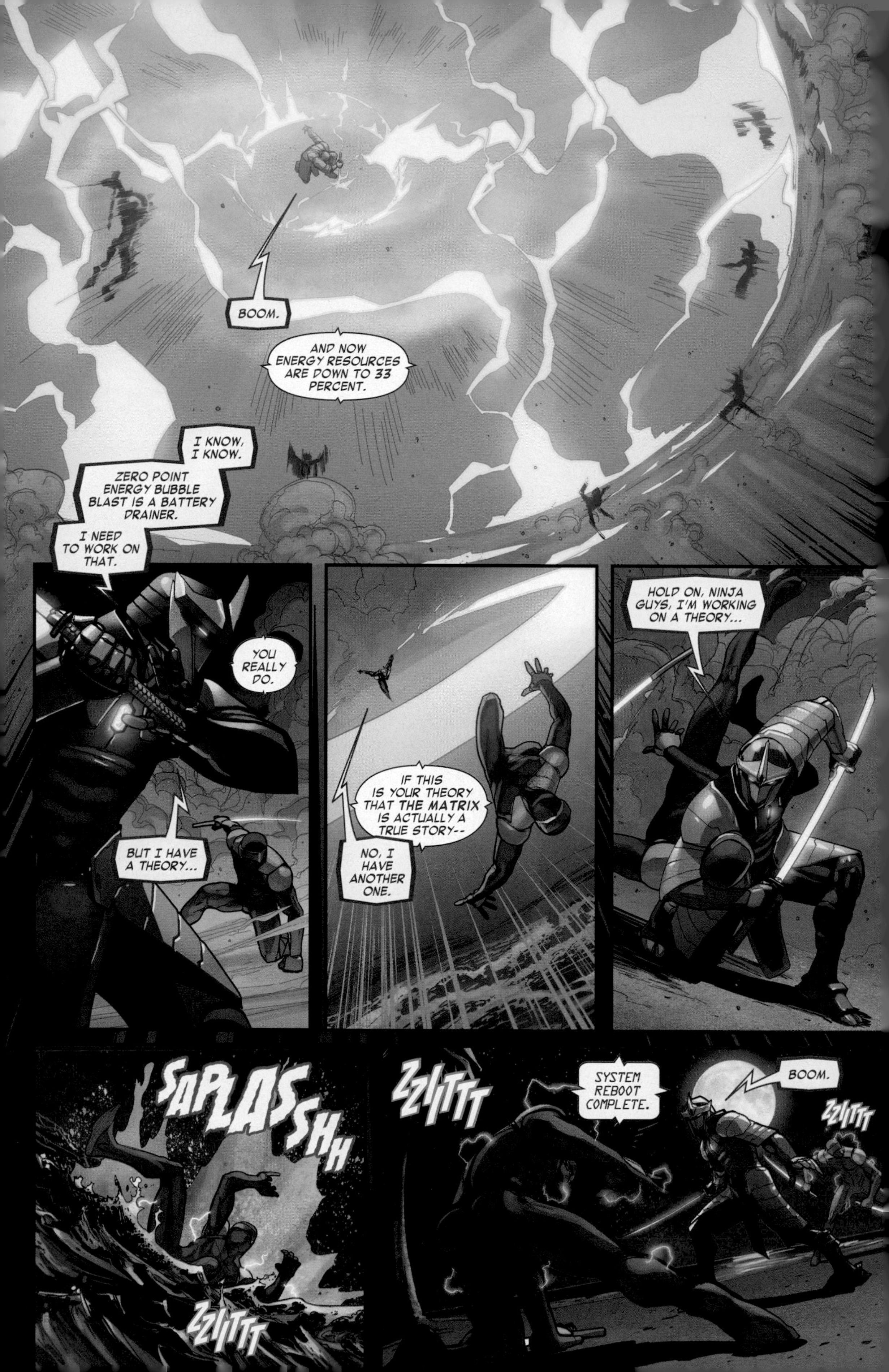

BOOM.
AND NOW ENERGY RESOURCES ARE DOWN TO 33 PERCENT.
I KNOW, I KNOW.
ZERO POINT ENERGY BUBBLE BLAST IS A BATTERY DRAINER.
I NEED TO WORK ON THAT.
YOU REALLY DO.
BUT I HAVE A THEORY...
IF THIS IS YOUR THEORY THAT THE MATRIX IS ACTUALLY A TRUE STORY--
NO, I HAVE ANOTHER ONE.
HOLD ON, NINJA GUYS, I'M WORKING ON A THEORY...
SPLASSHH
ZZIITTT
ZZIITTT
SYSTEM REBOOT COMPLETE.
BOOM.
ZZIITTT

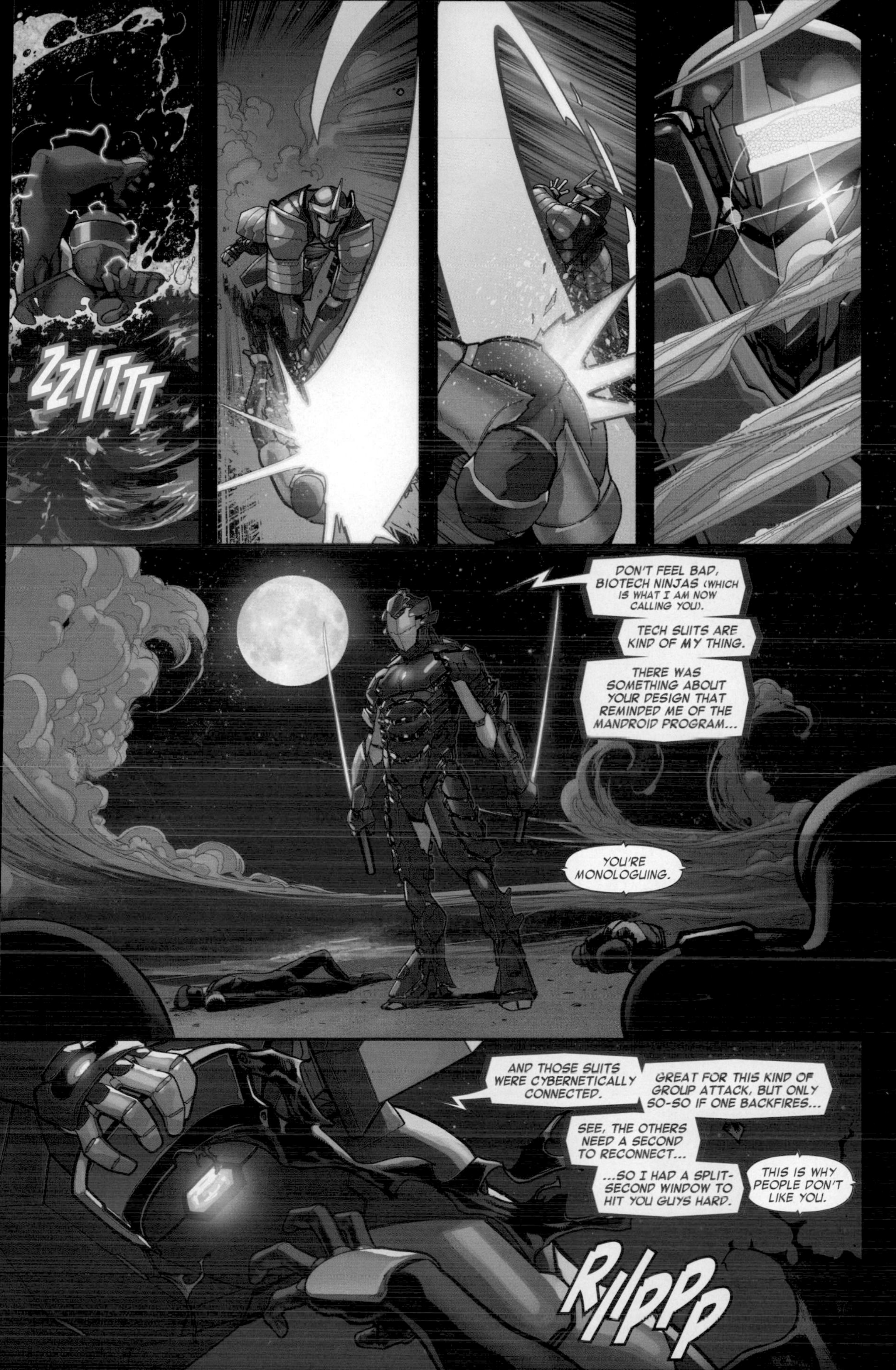
ZZIITTTT
DON'T FEEL BAD, BIOTECH NINJAS (WHICH IS WHAT I AM NOW CALLING YOU).
TECH SUITS ARE KIND OF MY THING.
THERE WAS SOMETHING ABOUT YOUR DESIGN THAT REMINDED ME OF THE MANDROID PROGRAM...
YOU'RE MONOLOGUING.
AND THOSE SUITS WERE CYBERNETICALLY CONNECTED.
GREAT FOR THIS KIND OF GROUP ATTACK, BUT ONLY SO-SO IF ONE BACKFIRES...
SEE, THE OTHERS NEED A SECOND TO RECONNECT...
...SO I HAD A SPLIT-SECOND WINDOW TO HIT YOU GUYS HARD.
THIS IS WHY PEOPLE DON'T LIKE YOU.
RIIPPP

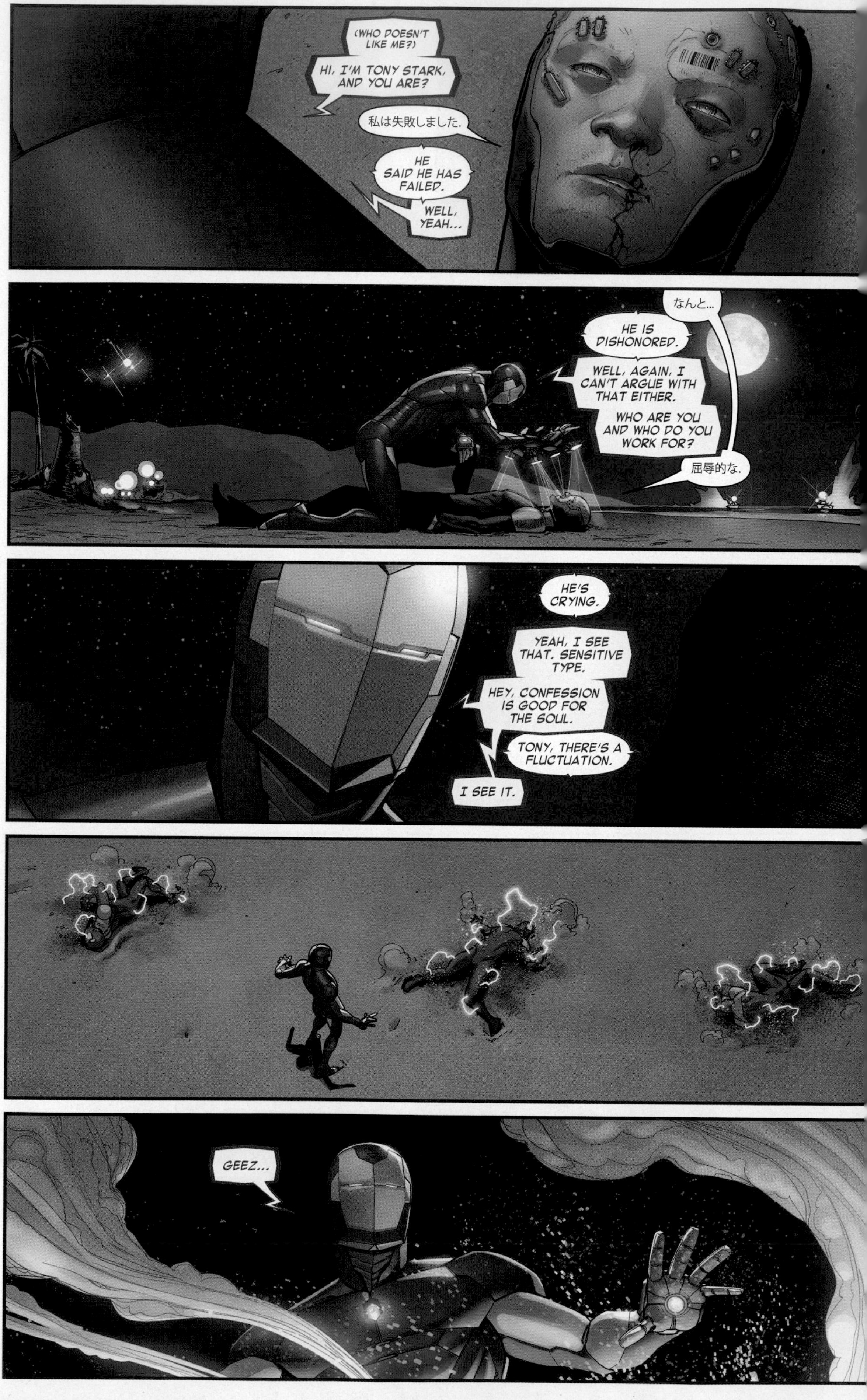
(WHO DOESN'T LIKE ME?)
HI, I'M TONY STARK, AND YOU ARE?
私は失敗しました.
HE SAID HE HAS FAILED.
WELL, YEAH...
なんと...
HE IS DISHONORED.
WELL, AGAIN, I CAN'T ARGUE WITH THAT EITHER.
WHO ARE YOU AND WHO DO YOU WORK FOR?
屈辱的な.
HE'S CRYING.
YEAH, I SEE THAT. SENSITIVE TYPE.
HEY, CONFESSION IS GOOD FOR THE SOUL.
TONY, THERE'S A FLUCTUATION.
I SEE IT.
GEEZ...

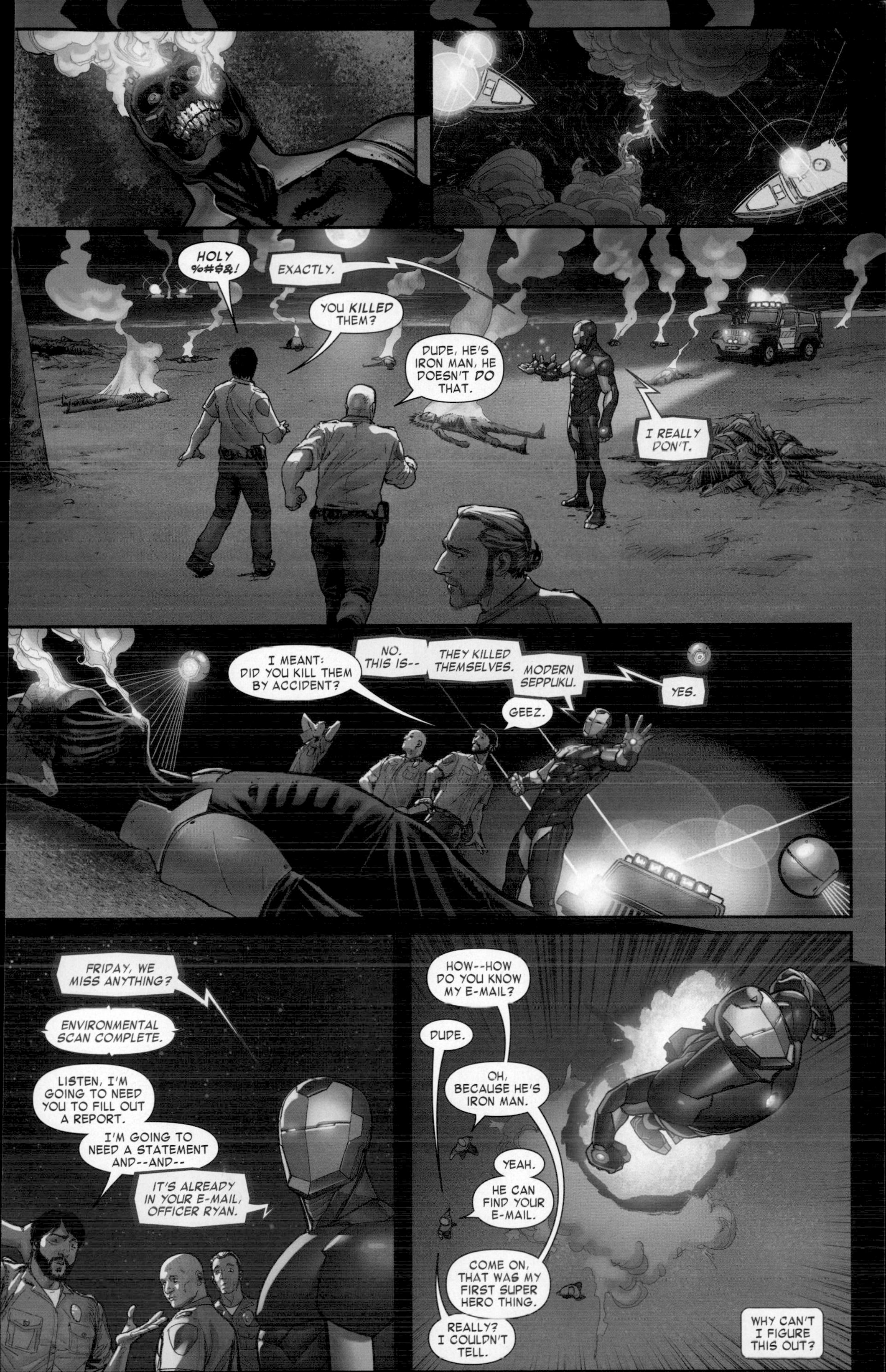
HOLY %#$&!
EXACTLY.
YOU KILLED THEM?
DUDE, HE'S IRON MAN, HE DOESN'T DO THAT.
I REALLY DON'T.
I MEANT: DID YOU KILL THEM BY ACCIDENT?
NO. THIS IS--
THEY KILLED THEMSELVES.
MODERN SEPPUKU.
YES.
GEEZ.
FRIDAY, WE MISS ANYTHING?
ENVIRONMENTAL SCAN COMPLETE.
LISTEN, I'M GOING TO NEED YOU TO FILL OUT A REPORT.
I'M GOING TO NEED A STATEMENT AND--AND--
IT'S ALREADY IN YOUR E-MAIL, OFFICER RYAN.
HOW--HOW DO YOU KNOW MY E-MAIL?
DUDE.
OH, BECAUSE HE'S IRON MAN.
YEAH.
HE CAN FIND YOUR E-MAIL.
COME ON, THAT WAS MY FIRST SUPER HERO THING.
REALLY? I COULDN'T TELL.
WHY CAN'T I FIGURE THIS OUT?

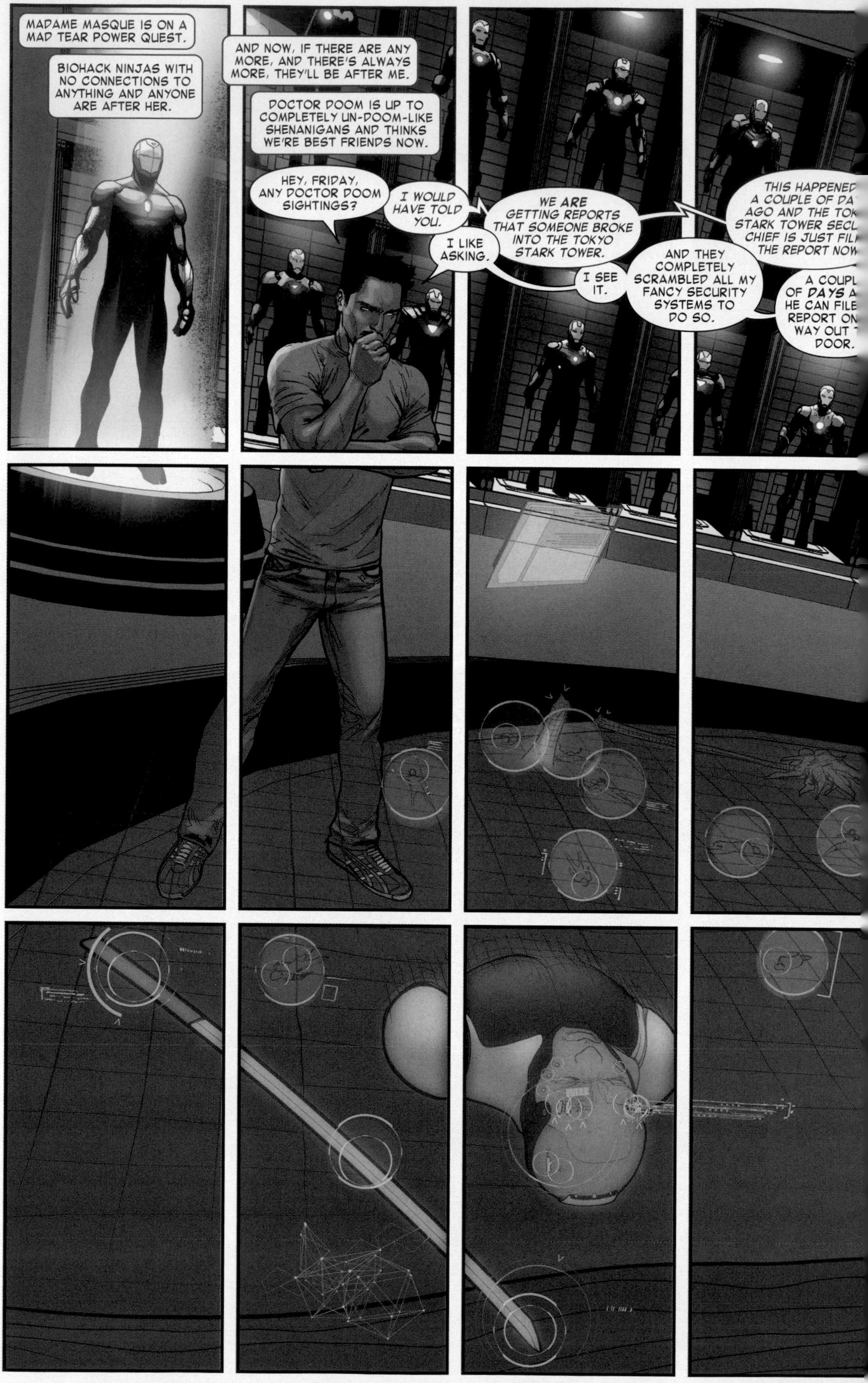
MADAME MASQUE IS ON A MAD TEAR POWER QUEST.
BIOHACK NINJAS WITH NO CONNECTIONS TO ANYTHING AND ANYONE ARE AFTER HER.
AND NOW, IF THERE ARE ANY MORE, AND THERE'S ALWAYS MORE, THEY'LL BE AFTER ME.
DOCTOR DOOM IS UP TO COMPLETELY UN-DOOM-LIKE SHENANIGANS AND THINKS WE'RE BEST FRIENDS NOW.
HEY, FRIDAY, ANY DOCTOR DOOM SIGHTINGS?
I WOULD HAVE TOLD YOU.
I LIKE ASKING.
WE ARE GETTING REPORTS THAT SOMEONE BROKE INTO THE TOKYO STARK TOWER.
I SEE IT.
AND THEY COMPLETELY SCRAMBLED ALL MY FANCY SECURITY SYSTEMS TO DO SO.

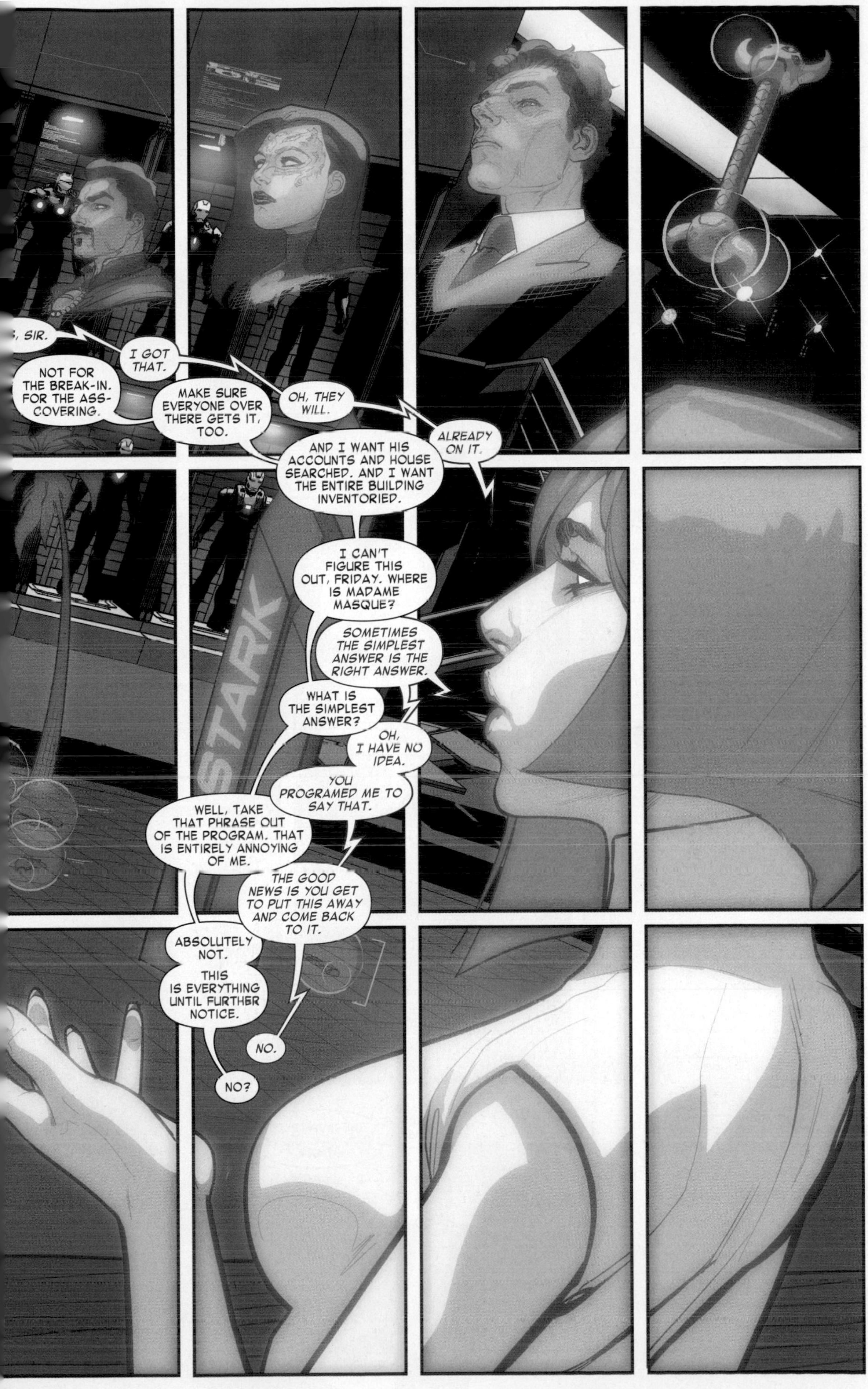

, SIR.
I GOT THAT.
NOT FOR THE BREAK-IN. FOR THE ASS-COVERING.
MAKE SURE EVERYONE OVER THERE GETS IT, TOO.
OH, THEY WILL.
ALREADY ON IT.
AND I WANT HIS ACCOUNTS AND HOUSE SEARCHED. AND I WANT THE ENTIRE BUILDING INVENTORIED.
STARK
I CAN'T FIGURE THIS OUT, FRIDAY. WHERE IS MADAME MASQUE?
SOMETIMES THE SIMPLEST ANSWER IS THE RIGHT ANSWER.
WHAT IS THE SIMPLEST ANSWER?
OH, I HAVE NO IDEA.
YOU PROGRAMED ME TO SAY THAT.
WELL, TAKE THAT PHRASE OUT OF THE PROGRAM. THAT IS ENTIRELY ANNOYING OF ME.
THE GOOD NEWS IS YOU GET TO PUT THIS AWAY AND COME BACK TO IT.
ABSOLUTELY NOT.
THIS IS EVERYTHING UNTIL FURTHER NOTICE.
NO.
NO?

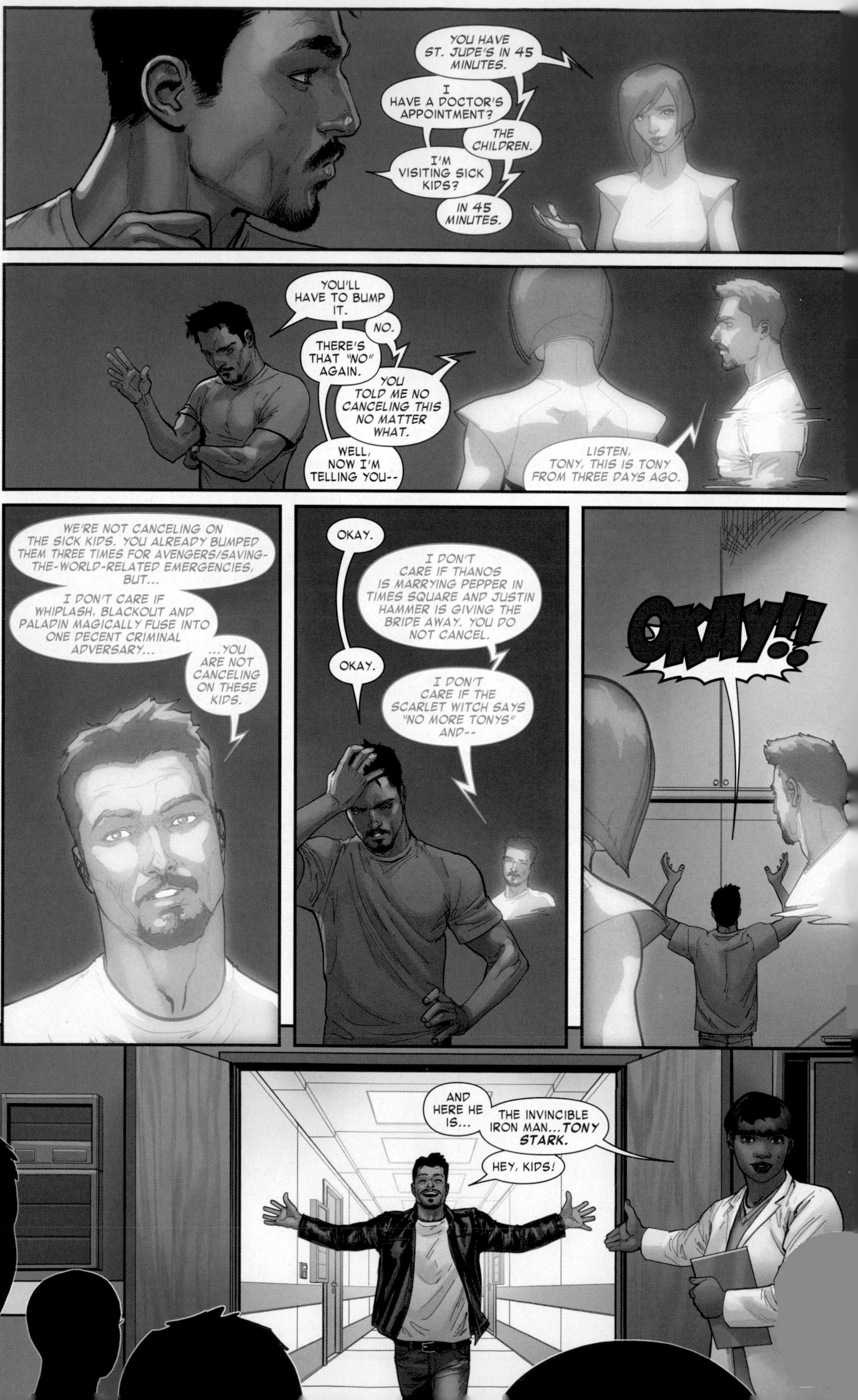
YOU HAVE ST. JUDE'S IN 45 MINUTES.
I HAVE A DOCTOR'S APPOINTMENT?
THE CHILDREN.
I'M VISITING SICK KIDS?
IN 45 MINUTES.
YOU'LL HAVE TO BUMP IT.
NO.
THERE'S THAT "NO" AGAIN.
YOU TOLD ME NO CANCELING THIS NO MATTER WHAT.
WELL, NOW I'M TELLING YOU--
LISTEN, TONY, THIS IS TONY FROM THREE DAYS AGO.
WE'RE NOT CANCELING ON THE SICK KIDS. YOU ALREADY BUMPED THEM THREE TIMES FOR AVENGERS/SAVING-THE-WORLD-RELATED EMERGENCIES, BUT...
I DON'T CARE IF WHIPLASH, BLACKOUT AND PALADIN MAGICALLY FUSE INTO ONE DECENT CRIMINAL ADVERSARY...
...YOU ARE NOT CANCELING ON THESE KIDS.
OKAY.
I DON'T CARE IF THANOS IS MARRYING PEPPER IN TIMES SQUARE AND JUSTIN HAMMER IS GIVING THE BRIDE AWAY. YOU DO NOT CANCEL.
OKAY.
I DON'T CARE IF THE SCARLET WITCH SAYS "NO MORE TONYS" AND--
OKAY!!
AND HERE HE IS...
THE INVINCIBLE IRON MAN...TONY STARK.
HEY, KIDS!

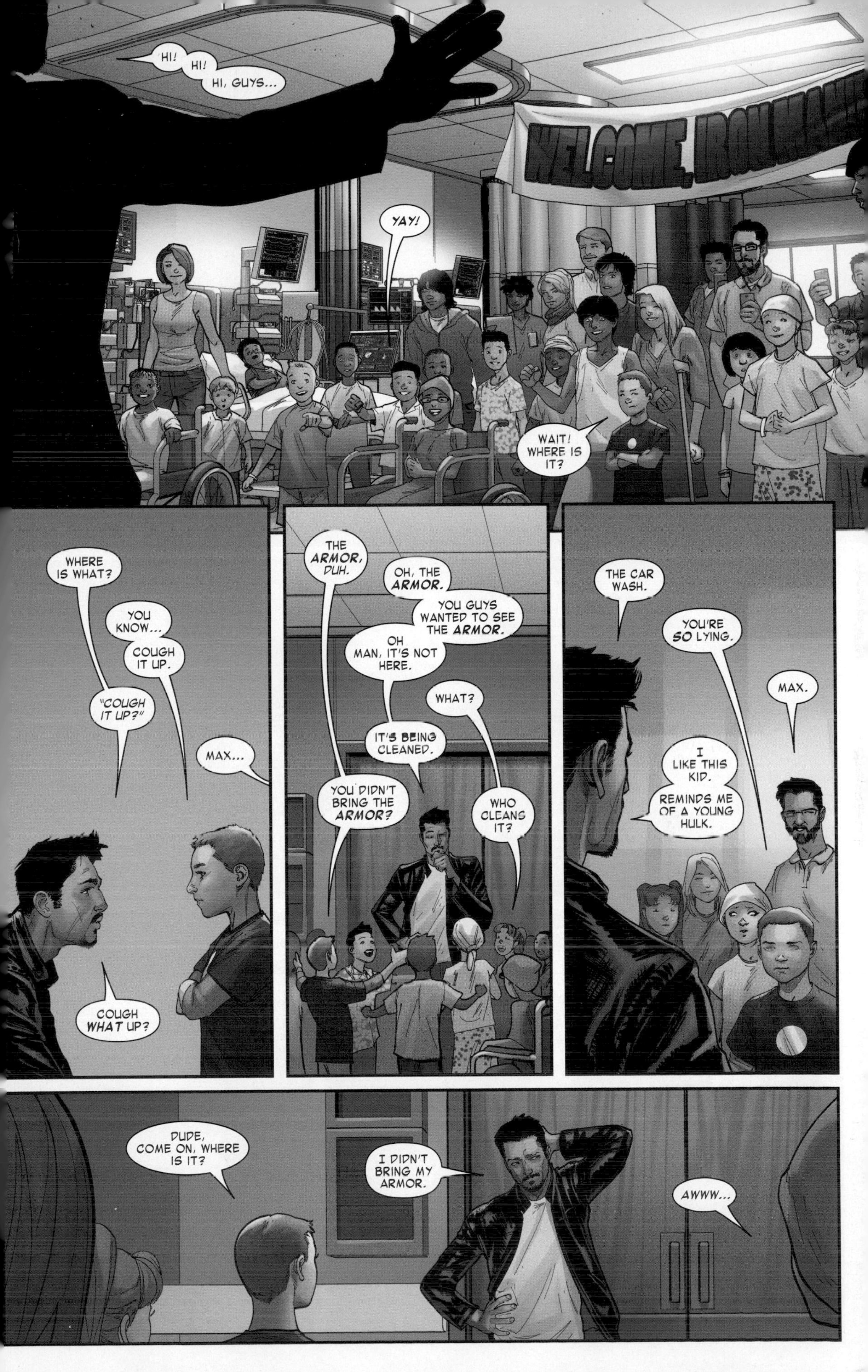
HI! HI! HI, GUYS...
WELCOME, IRON MAN
YAY!
WAIT! WHERE IS IT?
WHERE IS WHAT?
YOU KNOW...
COUGH IT UP.
"COUGH IT UP?"
MAX...
COUGH WHAT UP?
THE ARMOR, DUH.
OH, THE ARMOR.
YOU GUYS WANTED TO SEE THE ARMOR.
OH MAN, IT'S NOT HERE.
WHAT?
IT'S BEING CLEANED.
YOU DIDN'T BRING THE ARMOR?
WHO CLEANS IT?
THE CAR WASH.
YOU'RE SO LYING.
MAX.
I LIKE THIS KID.
REMINDS ME OF A YOUNG HULK.
DUDE, COME ON, WHERE IS IT?
I DIDN'T BRING MY ARMOR.
AWWW...

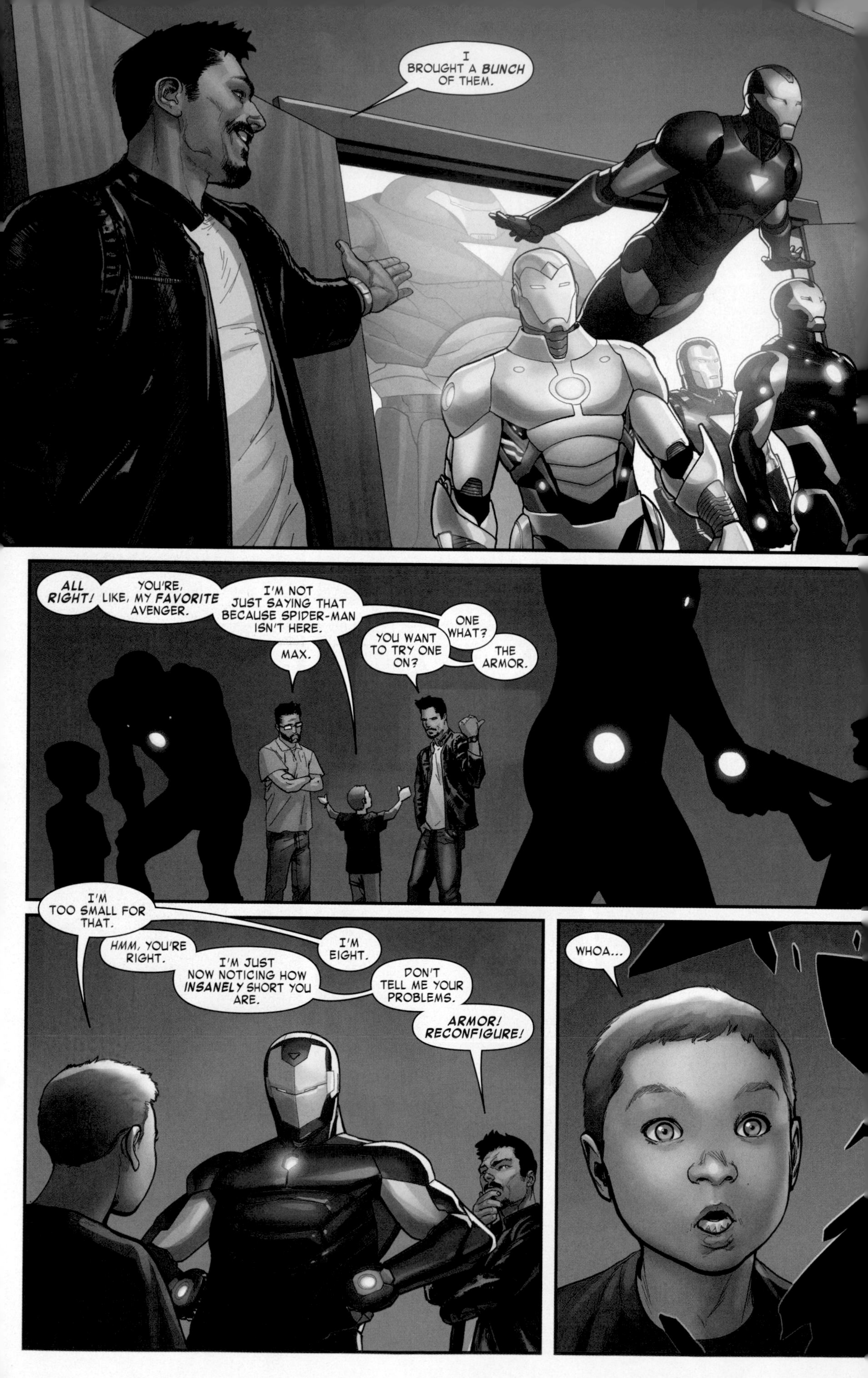
I BROUGHT A BUNCH OF THEM.
ALL RIGHT!
YOU'RE, LIKE, MY FAVORITE AVENGER.
I'M NOT JUST SAYING THAT BECAUSE SPIDER-MAN ISN'T HERE.
MAX.
YOU WANT TO TRY ONE ON?
ONE WHAT?
THE ARMOR.
I'M TOO SMALL FOR THAT.
I'M EIGHT.
HMM, YOU'RE RIGHT.
I'M JUST NOW NOTICING HOW INSANELY SHORT YOU ARE.
DON'T TELL ME YOUR PROBLEMS.
ARMOR! RECONFIGURE!
WHOA...

YEAH!

YES!

DUDE!

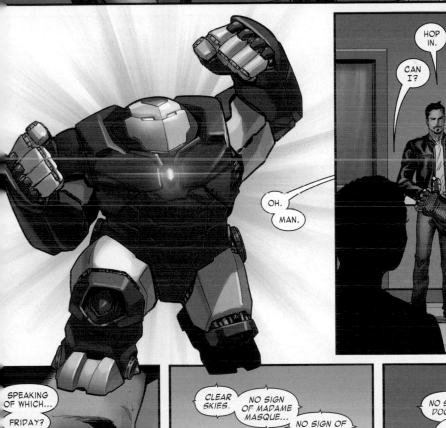

OH. MAN.

HOP IN.

CAN I?

IS IT SAFE?

SURE.

IT'S SAFER *IN THERE* THAN IT IS OUT HERE.

SPEAKING OF WHICH...

FRIDAY?

CLEAR SKIES.

NO SIGN OF MADAME MASQUE...

NO SIGN OF NINJAS...

NO SIGN OF DOCTOR--

OH, COME ON...

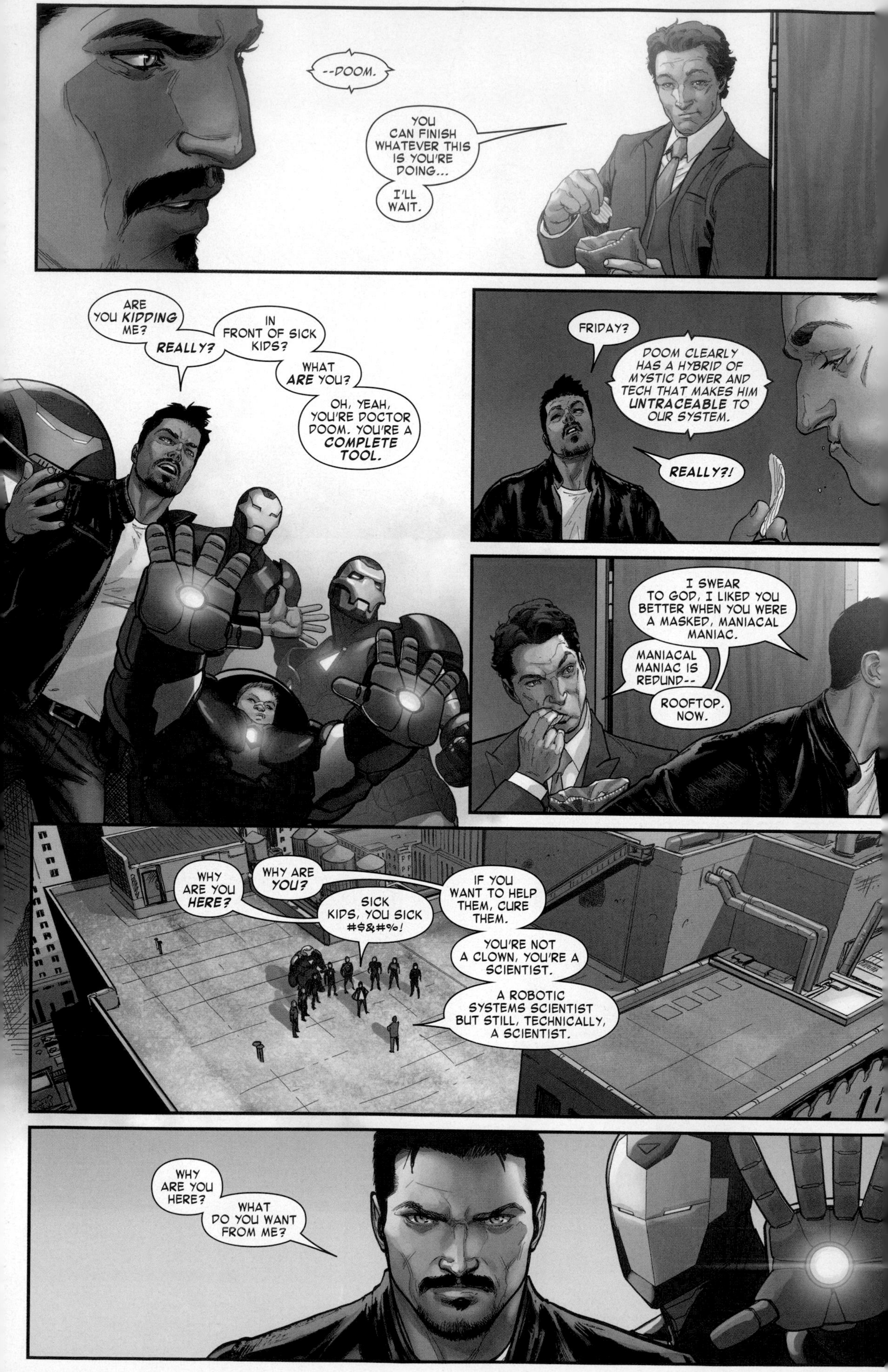
--DOOM.
YOU CAN FINISH WHATEVER THIS IS YOU'RE DOING...
I'LL WAIT.
ARE YOU KIDDING ME?
REALLY?
IN FRONT OF SICK KIDS?
WHAT ARE YOU?
OH, YEAH, YOU'RE DOCTOR DOOM. YOU'RE A COMPLETE TOOL.
FRIDAY?
DOOM CLEARLY HAS A HYBRID OF MYSTIC POWER AND TECH THAT MAKES HIM UNTRACEABLE TO OUR SYSTEM.
REALLY?!
I SWEAR TO GOD, I LIKED YOU BETTER WHEN YOU WERE A MASKED, MANIACAL MANIAC.
MANIACAL MANIAC IS REDUND--
ROOFTOP. NOW.
WHY ARE YOU HERE?
WHY ARE YOU?
SICK KIDS, YOU SICK #$&#%!
IF YOU WANT TO HELP THEM, CURE THEM.
YOU'RE NOT A CLOWN, YOU'RE A SCIENTIST.
A ROBOTIC SYSTEMS SCIENTIST BUT STILL, TECHNICALLY, A SCIENTIST.
WHY ARE YOU HERE?
WHAT DO YOU WANT FROM ME?

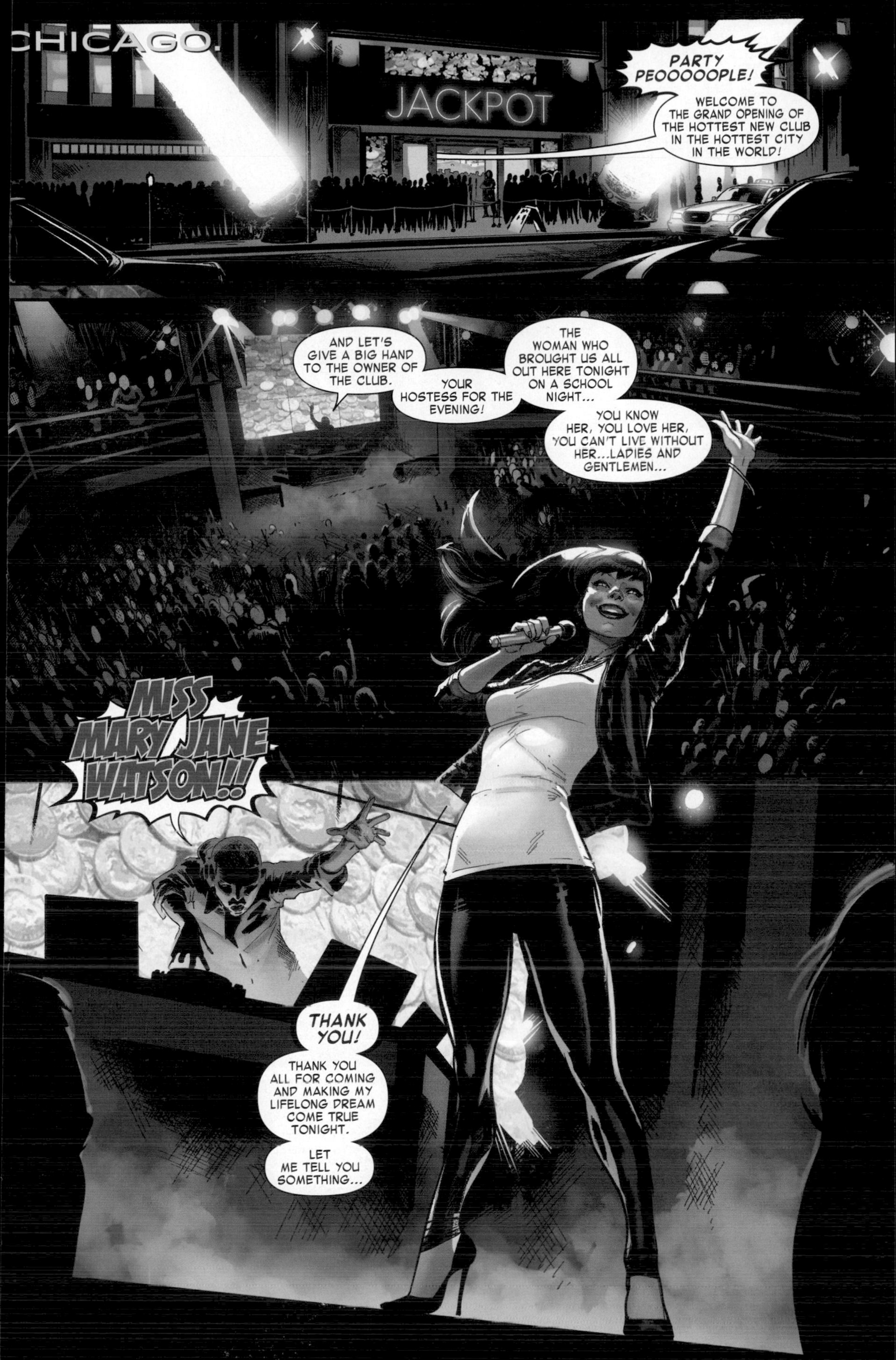

CHICAGO.
JACKPOT
PARTY PEOOOOOPLE!
WELCOME TO THE GRAND OPENING OF THE HOTTEST NEW CLUB IN THE HOTTEST CITY IN THE WORLD!
AND LET'S GIVE A BIG HAND TO THE OWNER OF THE CLUB.
YOUR HOSTESS FOR THE EVENING!
THE WOMAN WHO BROUGHT US ALL OUT HERE TONIGHT ON A SCHOOL NIGHT...
YOU KNOW HER, YOU LOVE HER, YOU CAN'T LIVE WITHOUT HER...LADIES AND GENTLEMEN...
MISS MARY JANE WATSON!!
THANK YOU!
THANK YOU ALL FOR COMING AND MAKING MY LIFELONG DREAM COME TRUE TONIGHT.
LET ME TELL YOU SOMETHING...

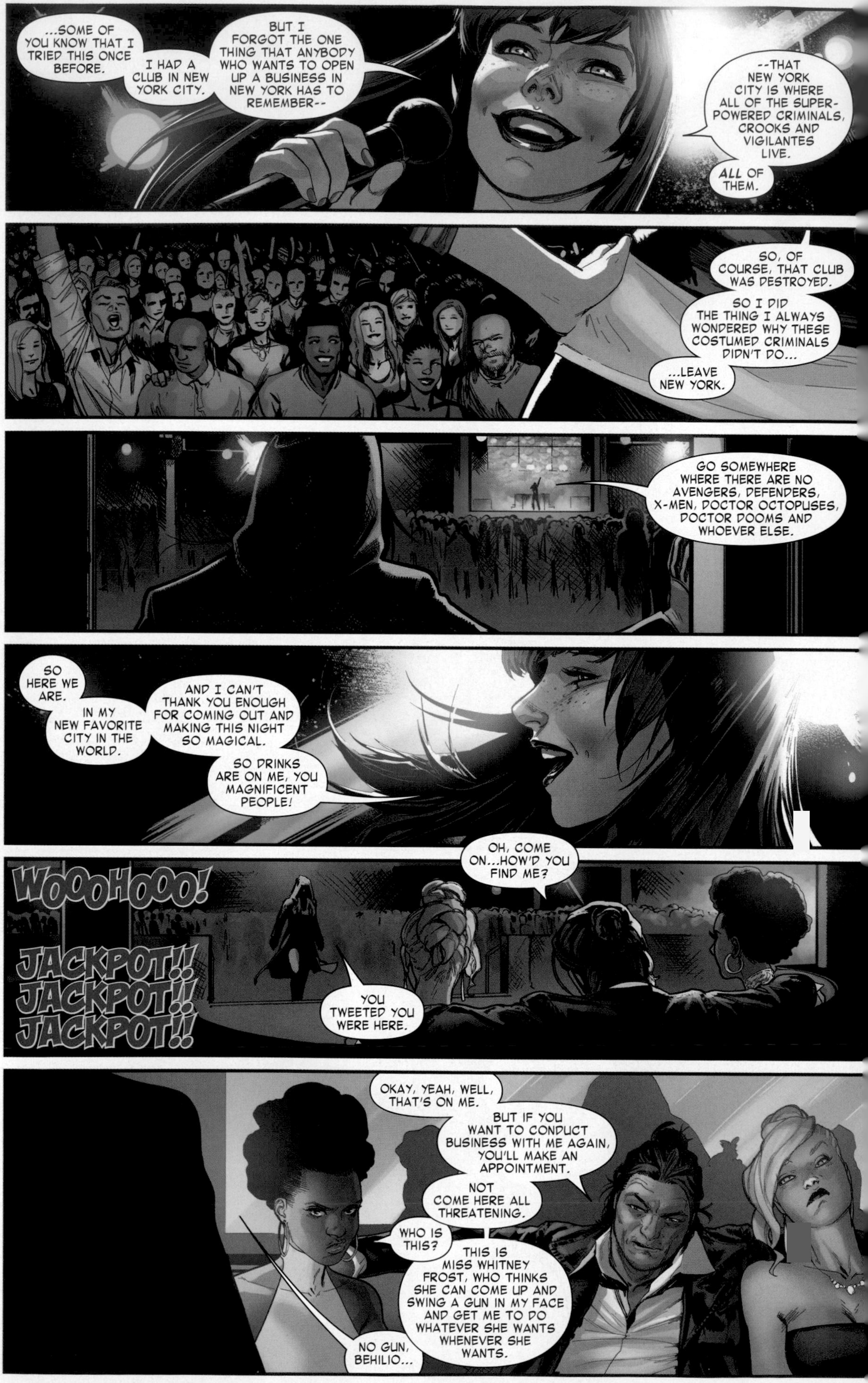
...SOME OF YOU KNOW THAT I TRIED THIS ONCE BEFORE.
I HAD A CLUB IN NEW YORK CITY.
BUT I FORGOT THE ONE THING THAT ANYBODY WHO WANTS TO OPEN UP A BUSINESS IN NEW YORK HAS TO REMEMBER--
--THAT NEW YORK CITY IS WHERE ALL OF THE SUPER-POWERED CRIMINALS, CROOKS AND VIGILANTES LIVE.
ALL OF THEM.
SO, OF COURSE, THAT CLUB WAS DESTROYED.
SO I DID THE THING I ALWAYS WONDERED WHY THESE COSTUMED CRIMINALS DIDN'T DO...
...LEAVE NEW YORK.
GO SOMEWHERE WHERE THERE ARE NO AVENGERS, DEFENDERS, X-MEN, DOCTOR OCTOPUSES, DOCTOR DOOMS AND WHOEVER ELSE.
SO HERE WE ARE.
IN MY NEW FAVORITE CITY IN THE WORLD.
AND I CAN'T THANK YOU ENOUGH FOR COMING OUT AND MAKING THIS NIGHT SO MAGICAL.
SO DRINKS ARE ON ME, YOU MAGNIFICENT PEOPLE!
WOOOHOOO!
JACKPOT!! JACKPOT!! JACKPOT!!
OH, COME ON...HOW'D YOU FIND ME?
YOU TWEETED YOU WERE HERE.
OKAY, YEAH, WELL, THAT'S ON ME.
BUT IF YOU WANT TO CONDUCT BUSINESS WITH ME AGAIN, YOU'LL MAKE AN APPOINTMENT.
NOT COME HERE ALL THREATENING.
WHO IS THIS?
THIS IS MISS WHITNEY FROST, WHO THINKS SHE CAN COME UP AND SWING A GUN IN MY FACE AND GET ME TO DO WHATEVER SHE WANTS WHENEVER SHE WANTS.
NO GUN, BEHILIO...

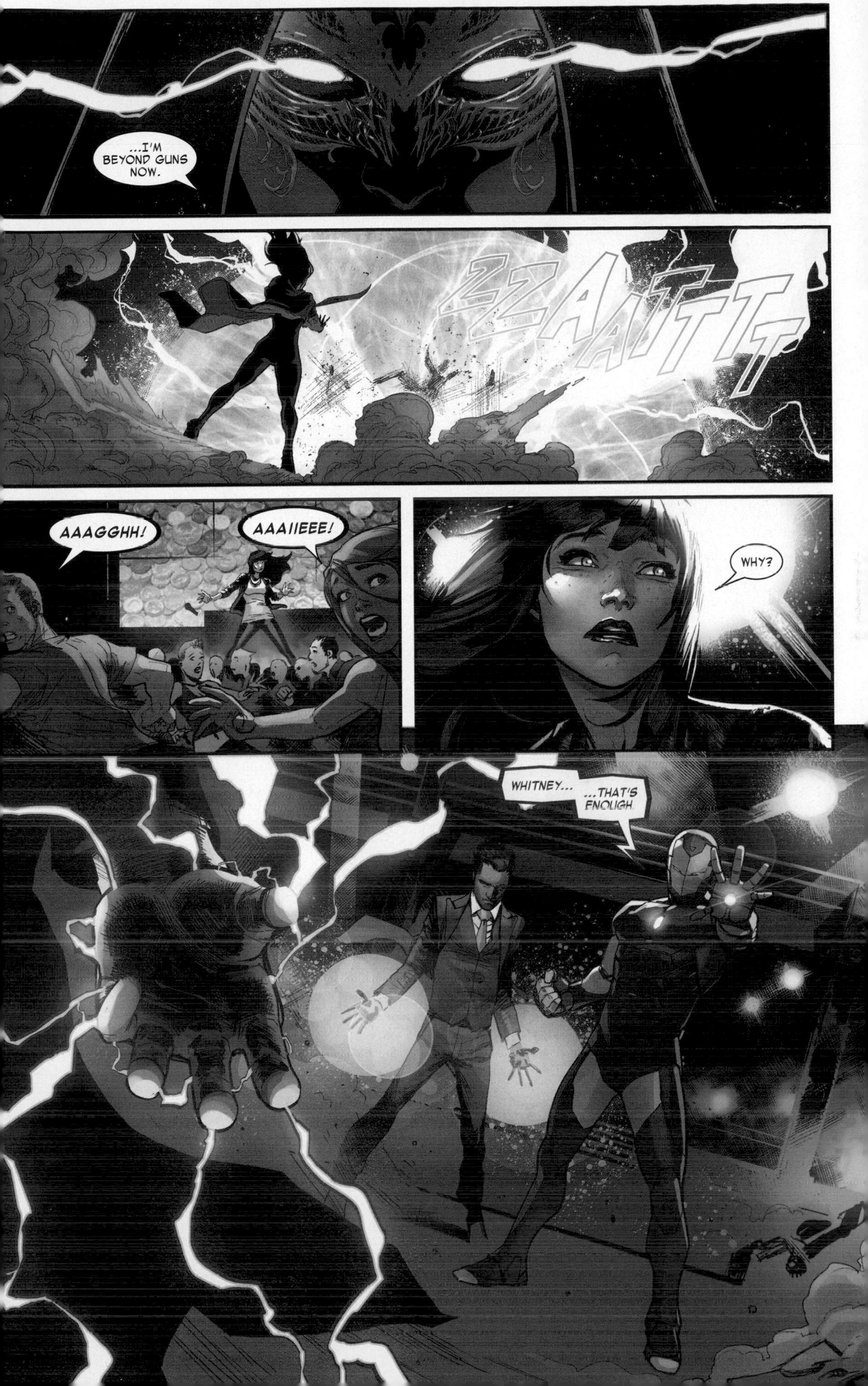
...I'M BEYOND GUNS NOW.
ZZAATTTT
AAAGGHH!
AAAIIEEE!
WHY?
WHITNEY...
...THAT'S ENOUGH.

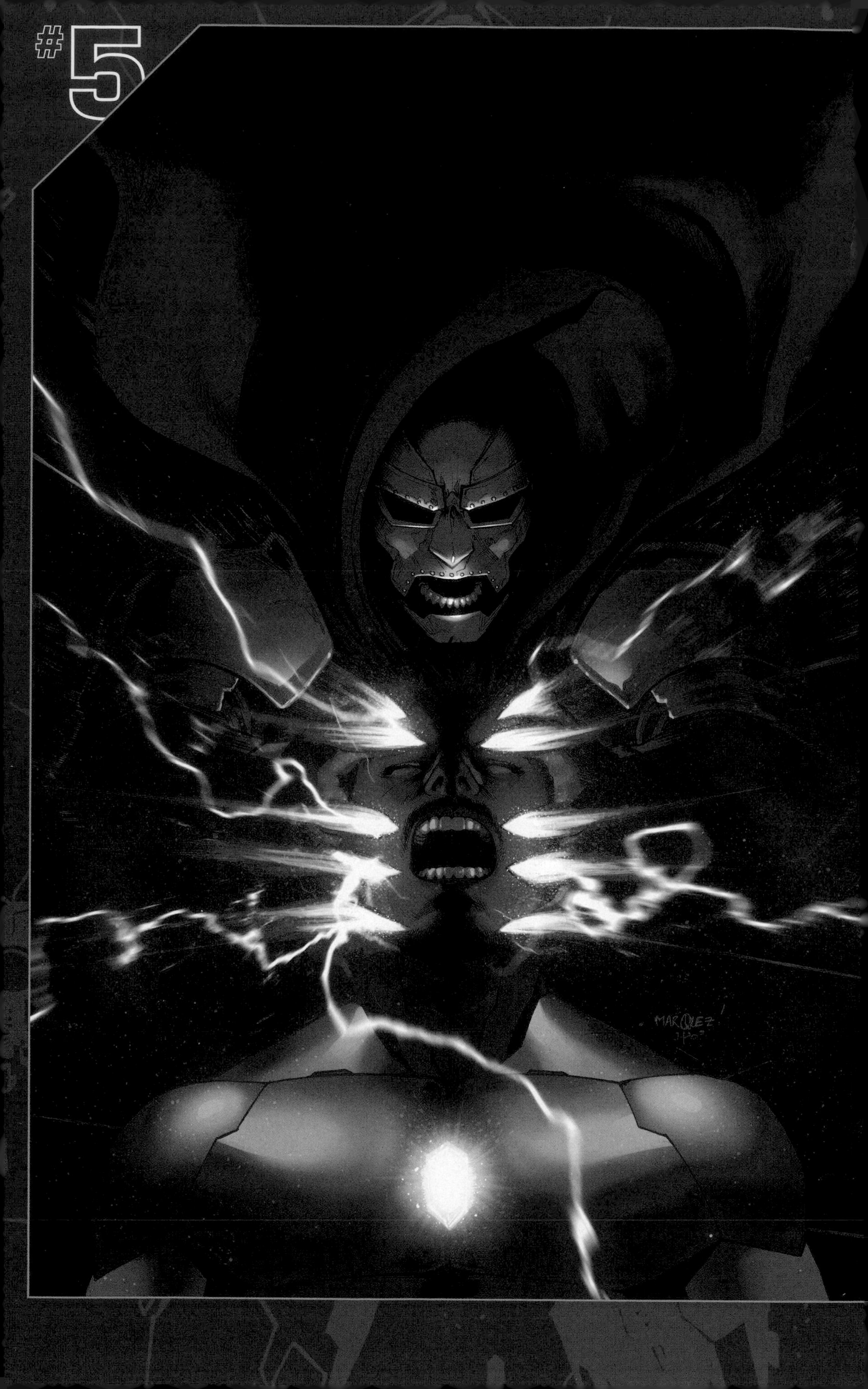
#5
MARQUEZ

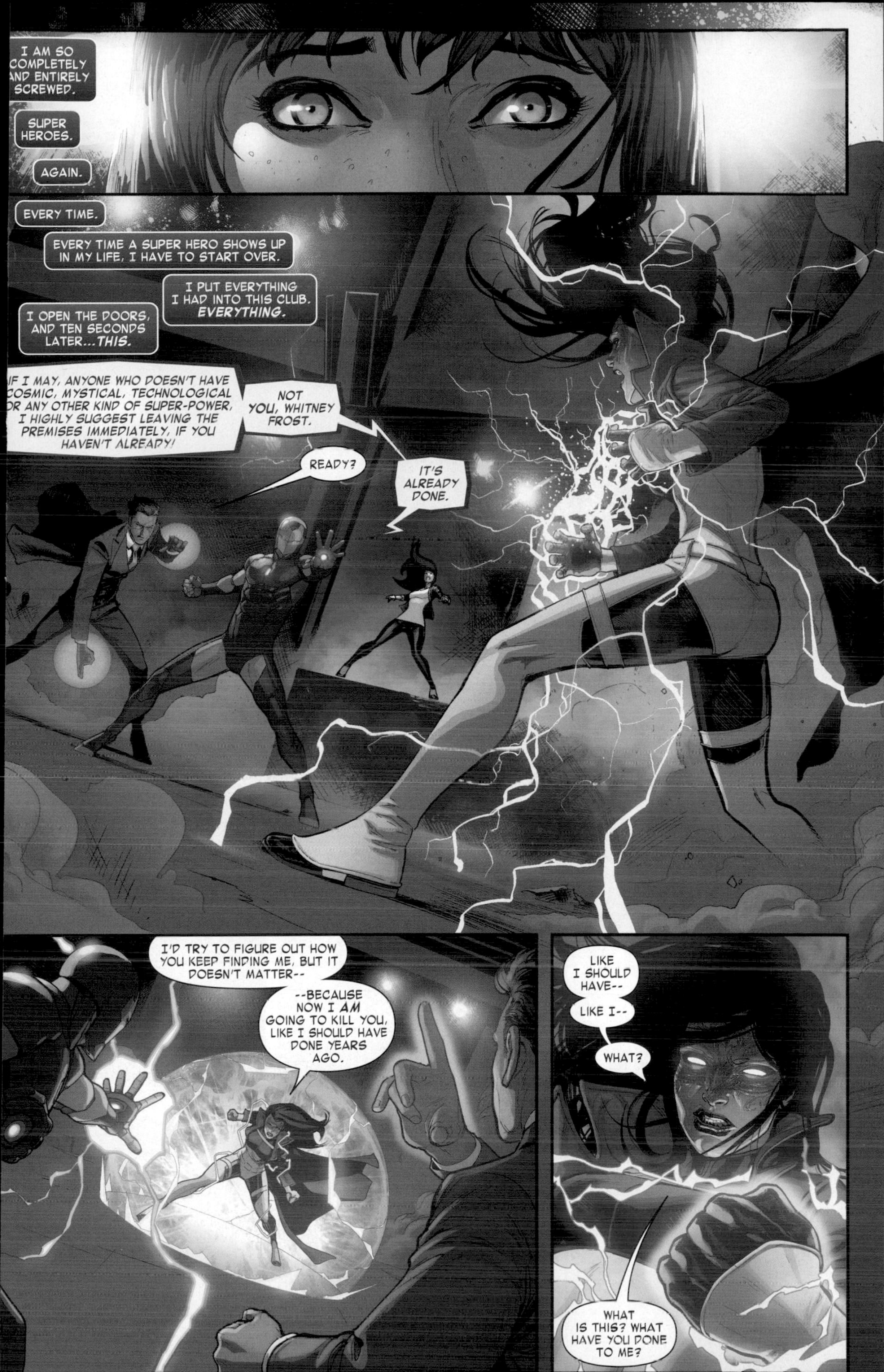

I AM SO COMPLETELY AND ENTIRELY SCREWED.
SUPER HEROES.
AGAIN.
EVERY TIME.
EVERY TIME A SUPER HERO SHOWS UP IN MY LIFE, I HAVE TO START OVER.
I PUT EVERYTHING I HAD INTO THIS CLUB. EVERYTHING.
I OPEN THE DOORS, AND TEN SECONDS LATER...THIS.
IF I MAY, ANYONE WHO DOESN'T HAVE COSMIC, MYSTICAL, TECHNOLOGICAL OR ANY OTHER KIND OF SUPER-POWER, I HIGHLY SUGGEST LEAVING THE PREMISES IMMEDIATELY, IF YOU HAVEN'T ALREADY!
NOT YOU, WHITNEY FROST.
READY?
IT'S ALREADY DONE.
I'D TRY TO FIGURE OUT HOW YOU KEEP FINDING ME, BUT IT DOESN'T MATTER--
--BECAUSE NOW I AM GOING TO KILL YOU, LIKE I SHOULD HAVE DONE YEARS AGO.
LIKE I SHOULD HAVE--
LIKE I--
WHAT?
WHAT IS THIS? WHAT HAVE YOU DONE TO ME?

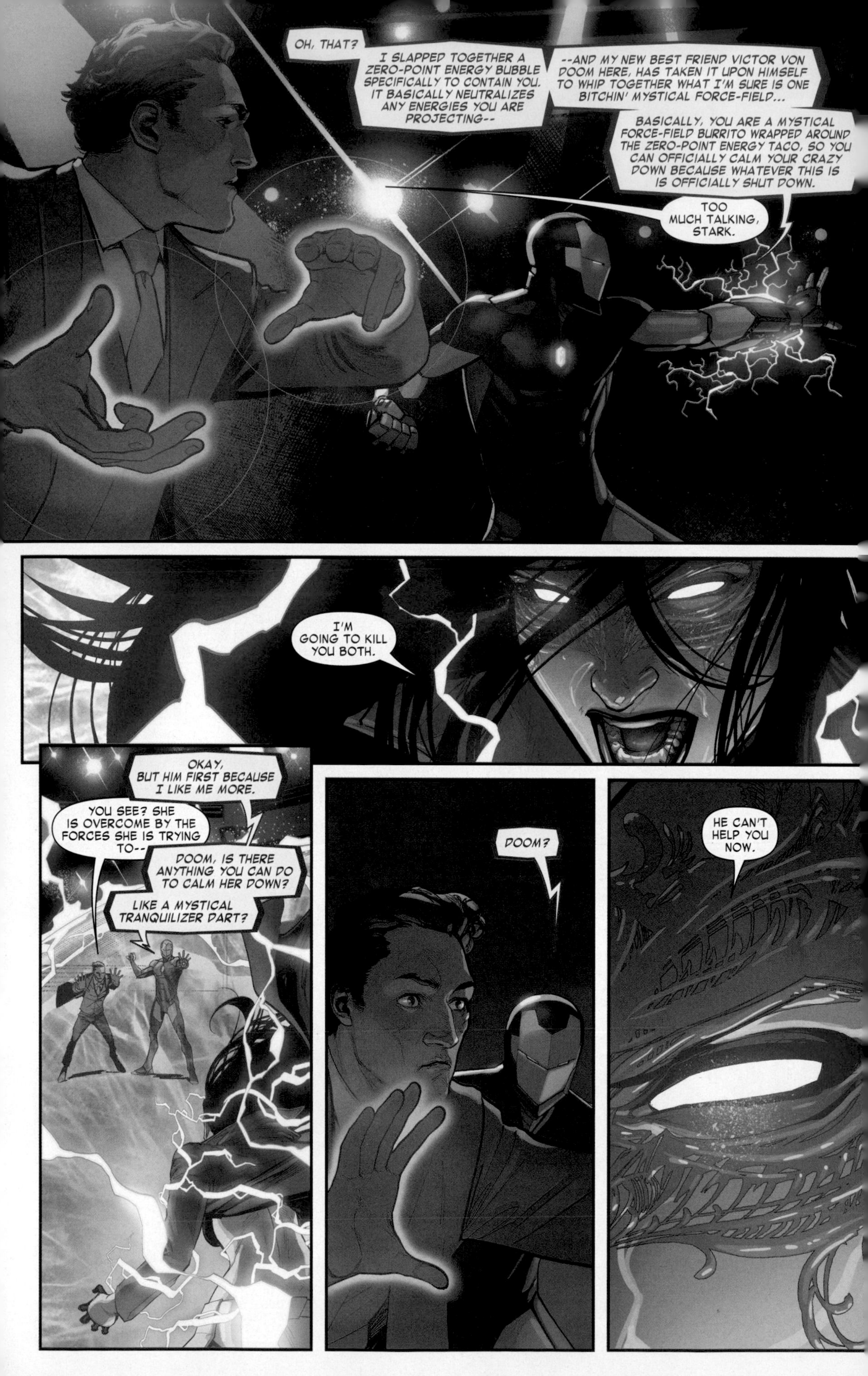
OH, THAT?
I SLAPPED TOGETHER A ZERO-POINT ENERGY BUBBLE SPECIFICALLY TO CONTAIN YOU. IT BASICALLY NEUTRALIZES ANY ENERGIES YOU ARE PROJECTING--
--AND MY NEW BEST FRIEND VICTOR VON DOOM HERE, HAS TAKEN IT UPON HIMSELF TO WHIP TOGETHER WHAT I'M SURE IS ONE BITCHIN' MYSTICAL FORCE-FIELD...
BASICALLY, YOU ARE A MYSTICAL FORCE-FIELD BURRITO WRAPPED AROUND THE ZERO-POINT ENERGY TACO, SO YOU CAN OFFICIALLY CALM YOUR CRAZY DOWN BECAUSE WHATEVER THIS IS IS OFFICIALLY SHUT DOWN.
TOO MUCH TALKING, STARK.
I'M GOING TO KILL YOU BOTH.
OKAY, BUT HIM FIRST BECAUSE I LIKE ME MORE.
YOU SEE? SHE IS OVERCOME BY THE FORCES SHE IS TRYING TO--
DOOM, IS THERE ANYTHING YOU CAN DO TO CALM HER DOWN?
LIKE A MYSTICAL TRANQUILIZER DART?
DOOM?
HE CAN'T HELP YOU NOW.

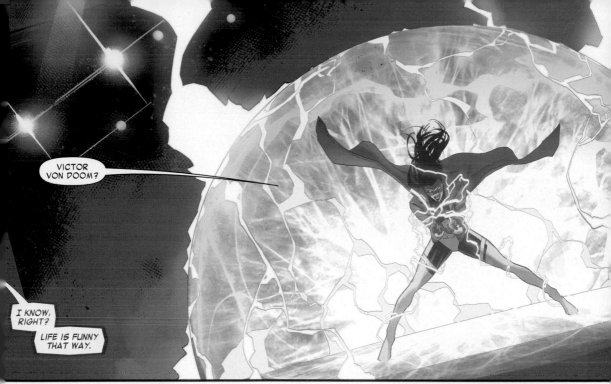

VICTOR VON DOOM?

I KNOW, RIGHT?

LIFE IS FUNNY THAT WAY.

SHE IS ATTEMPTING TO BREACH THE ARMOR WITH AN ENERGY MATRIX THAT I AM UNFAMILIAR WITH...

...WHICH MEANS IT IS MOST PROBABLY MYSTICAL IN NATURE.

YES, FRIDAY, I--

WE HAVE TO ASSUME THAT SHE HAS TAKEN HOLD OF DOCTOR DOOM AND IS ATTEMPTING TO DO THE SAME TO YOU.

YEAH...

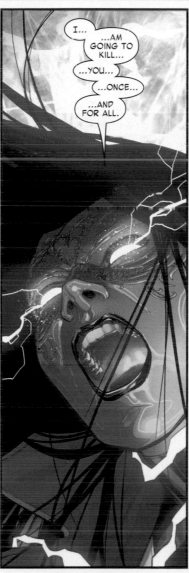

I...

...AM GOING TO KILL...

...YOU...

...ONCE...

...AND FOR ALL.

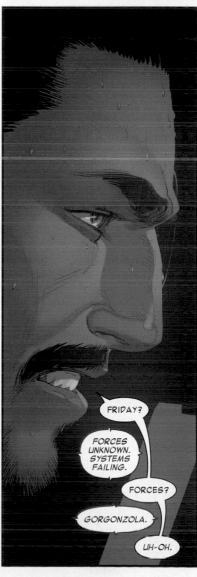

FRIDAY?

FORCES UNKNOWN. SYSTEMS FAILING.

FORCES?

GORGONZOLA.

UH-OH.

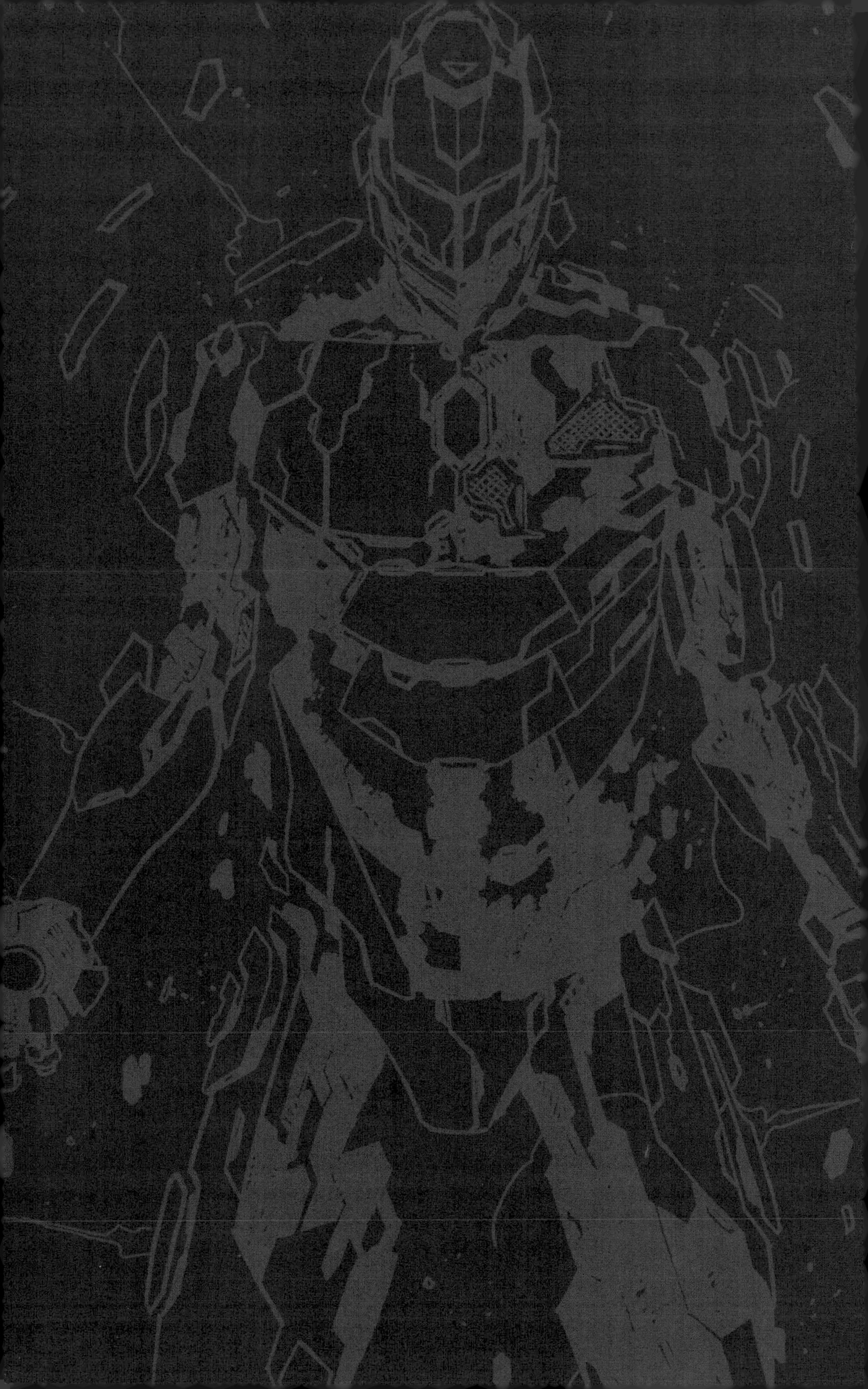

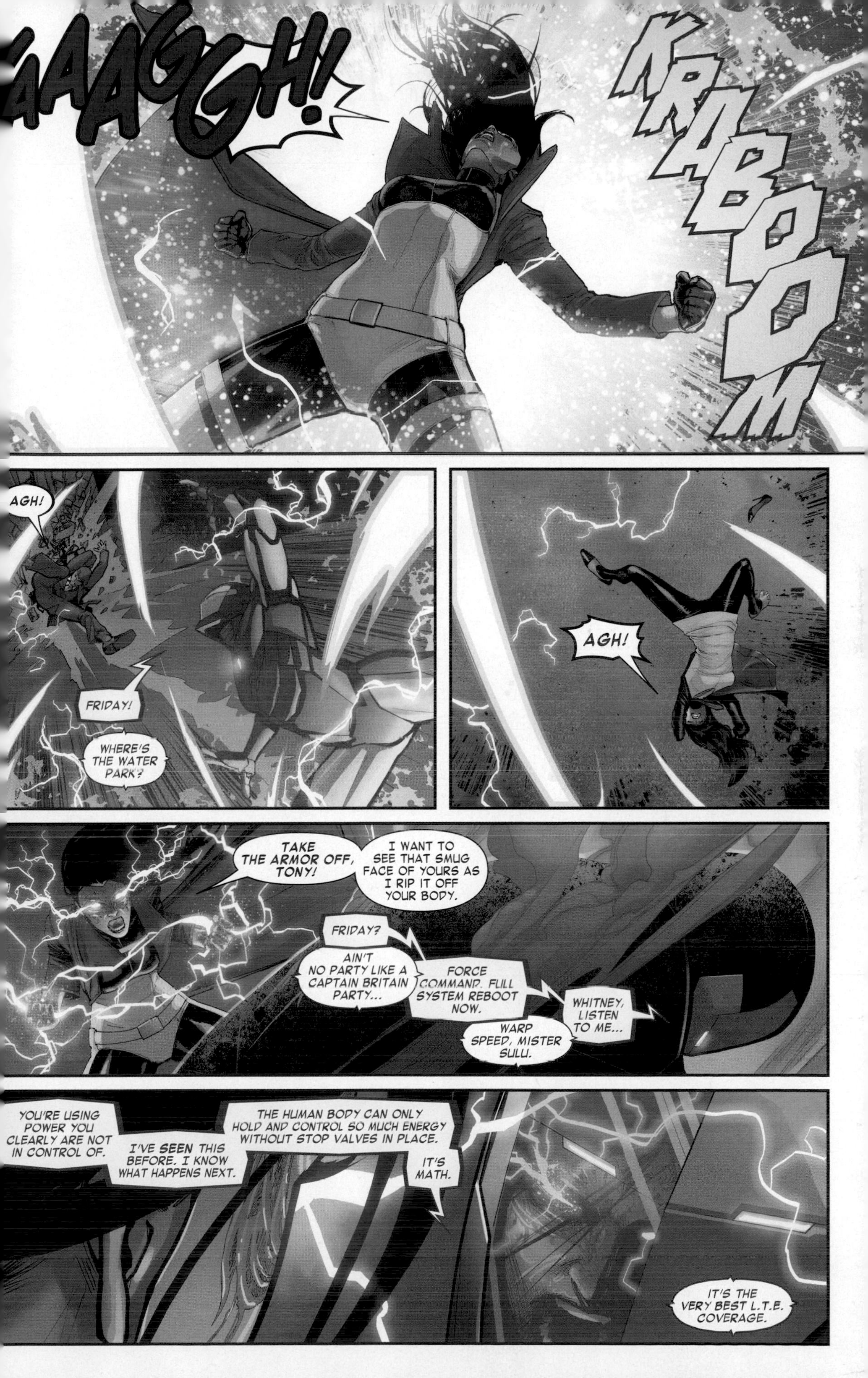
AAAGGH!
KRABOOM
AGH!
FRIDAY!
WHERE'S THE WATER PARK?
AGH!
TAKE THE ARMOR OFF, TONY!
I WANT TO SEE THAT SMUG FACE OF YOURS AS I RIP IT OFF YOUR BODY.
FRIDAY?
AIN'T NO PARTY LIKE A CAPTAIN BRITAIN PARTY...
FORCE COMMAND. FULL SYSTEM REBOOT NOW.
WHITNEY, LISTEN TO ME...
WARP SPEED, MISTER SULU.
YOU'RE USING POWER YOU CLEARLY ARE NOT IN CONTROL OF.
I'VE SEEN THIS BEFORE. I KNOW WHAT HAPPENS NEXT.
THE HUMAN BODY CAN ONLY HOLD AND CONTROL SO MUCH ENERGY WITHOUT STOP VALVES IN PLACE.
IT'S MATH.
IT'S THE VERY BEST L.T.E. COVERAGE.

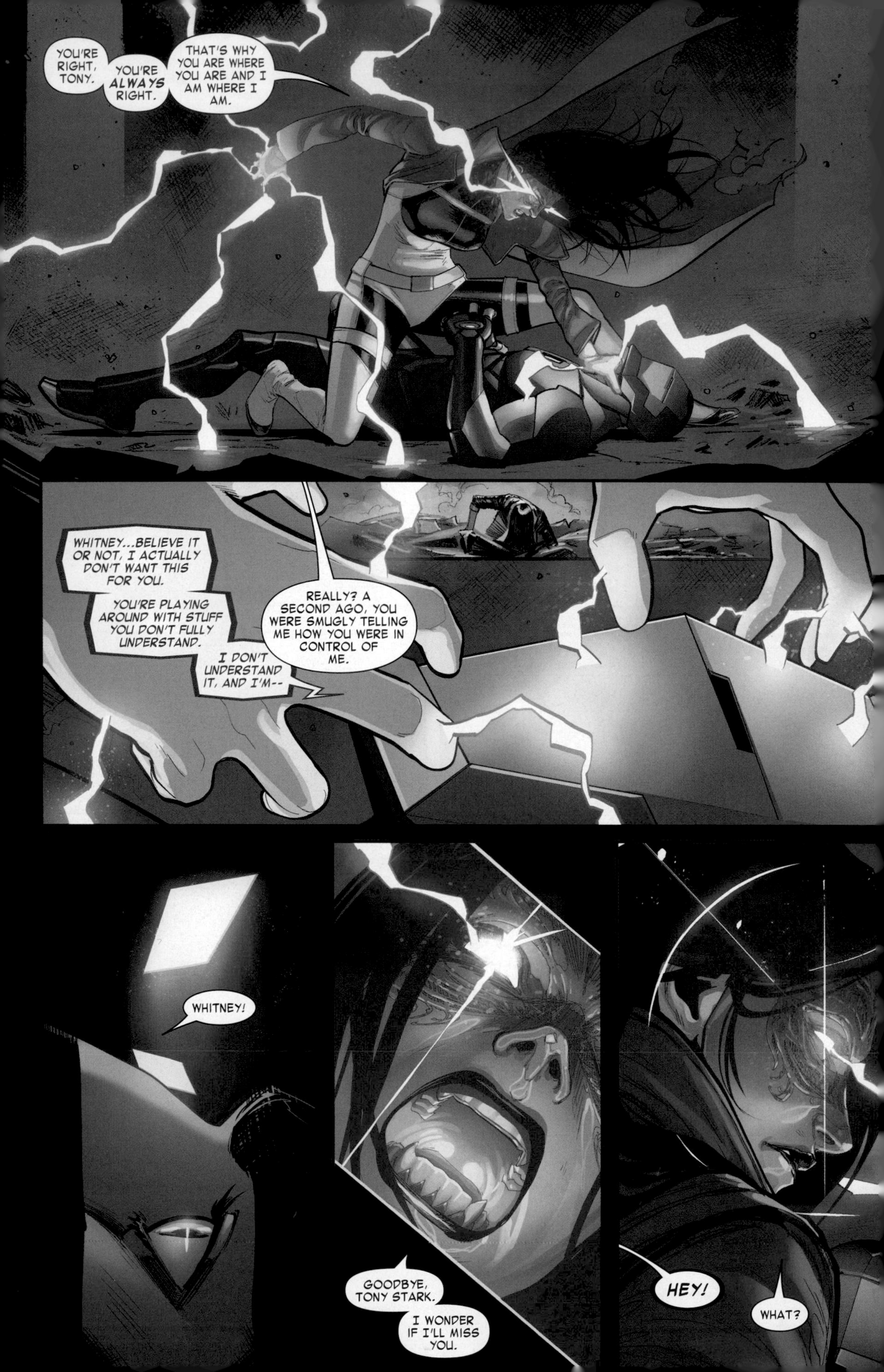
YOU'RE RIGHT, TONY.
YOU'RE ALWAYS RIGHT.
THAT'S WHY YOU ARE WHERE YOU ARE AND I AM WHERE I AM.
WHITNEY...BELIEVE IT OR NOT, I ACTUALLY DON'T WANT THIS FOR YOU.
YOU'RE PLAYING AROUND WITH STUFF YOU DON'T FULLY UNDERSTAND.
I DON'T UNDERSTAND IT, AND I'M--
REALLY? A SECOND AGO, YOU WERE SMUGLY TELLING ME HOW YOU WERE IN CONTROL OF ME.
WHITNEY!
GOODBYE, TONY STARK.
I WONDER IF I'LL MISS YOU.
HEY!
WHAT?

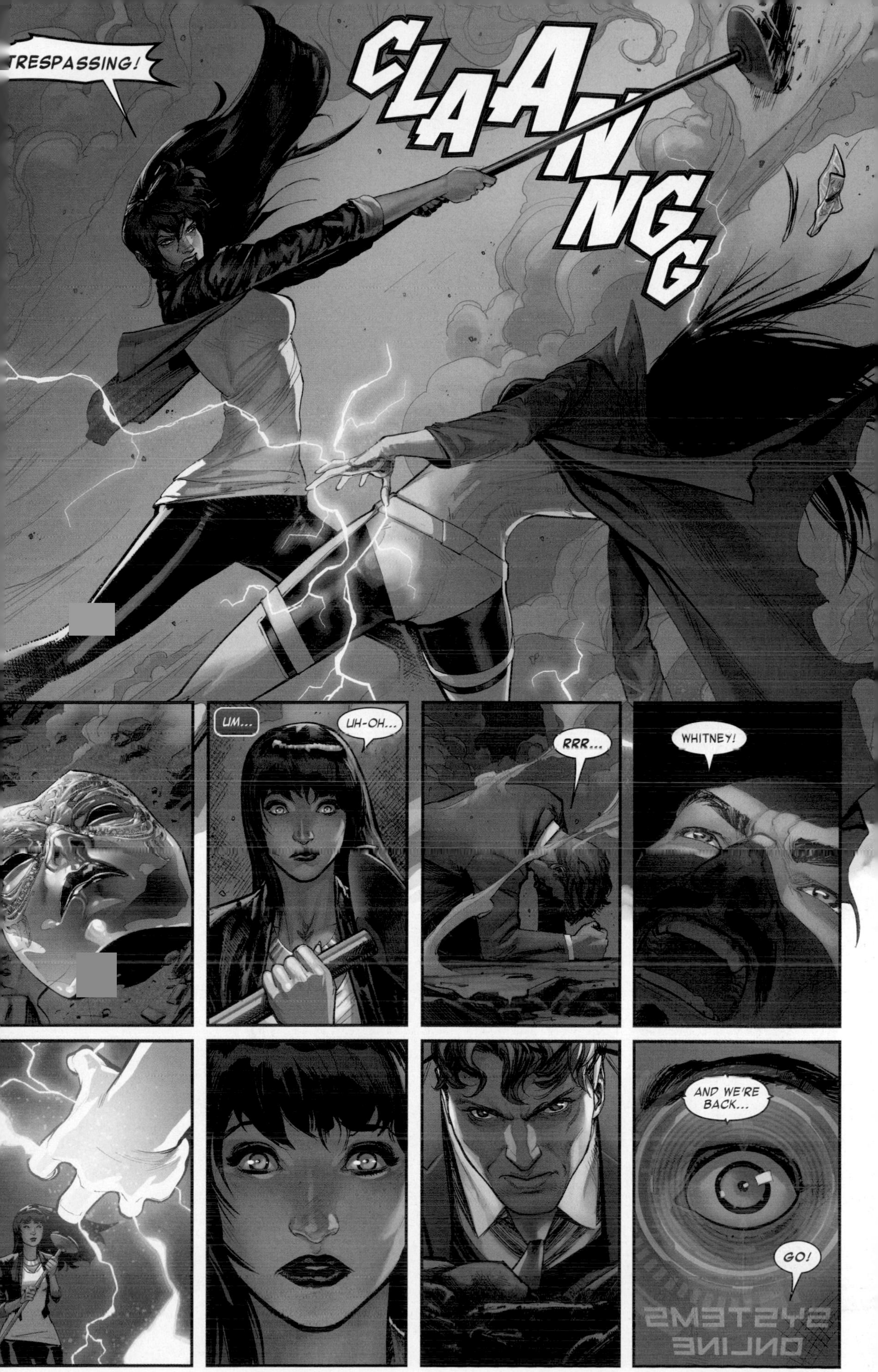
TRESPASSING!
CLAANNGG
UM...
UH-OH...
RRR...
WHITNEY!
AND WE'RE BACK...
GO!

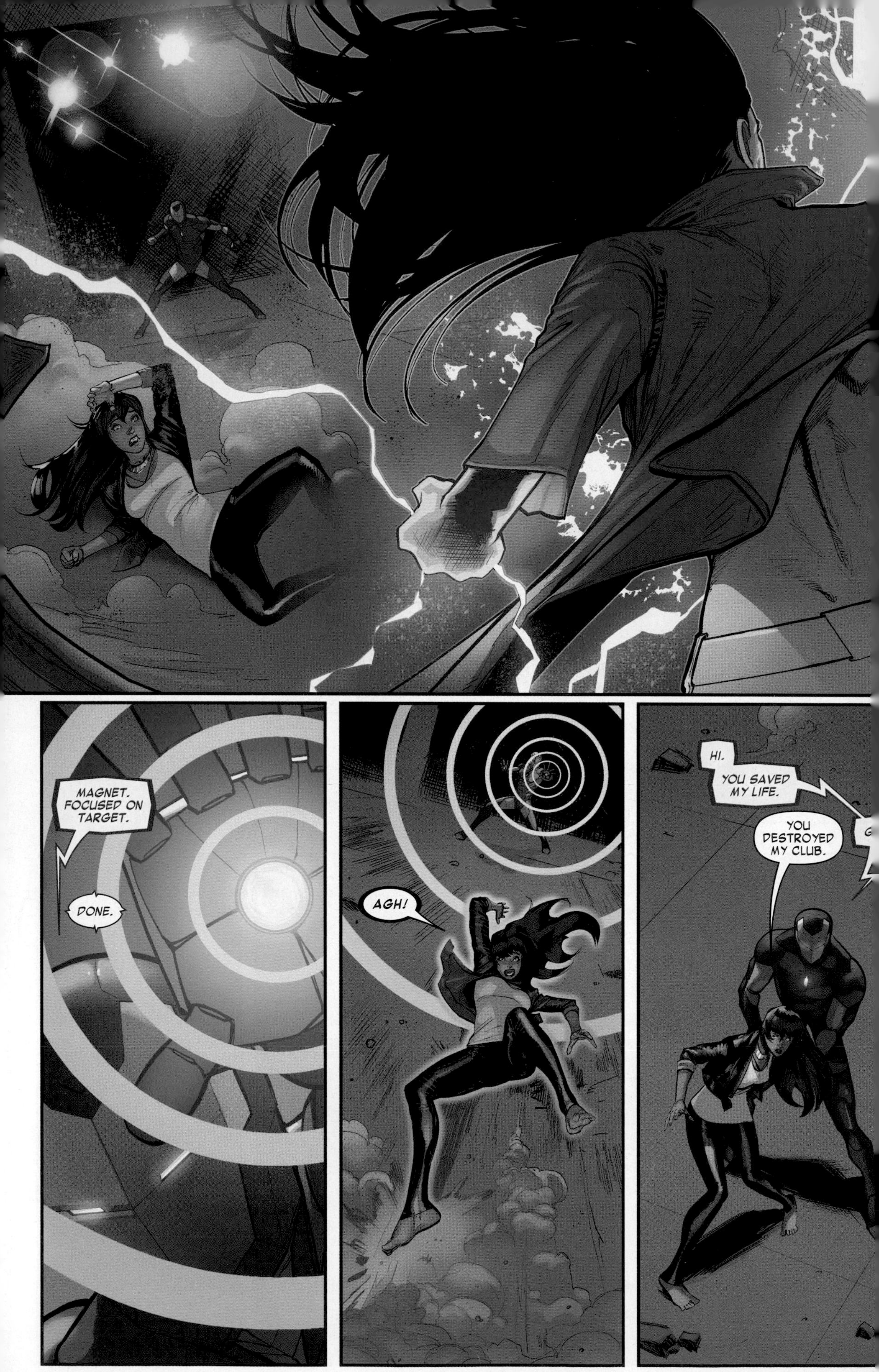
MAGNET. FOCUSED ON TARGET.
DONE.
AGH!
HI.
YOU SAVED MY LIFE.
YOU DESTROYED MY CLUB.

SHE LOOKED FAMILIAR.

MARY JANE WATSON. SUPERMODEL.

COOL.

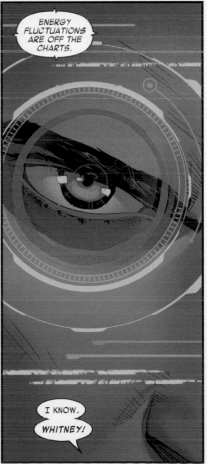

ENERGY FLUCTUATIONS ARE OFF THE CHARTS.

I KNOW.

WHITNEY!

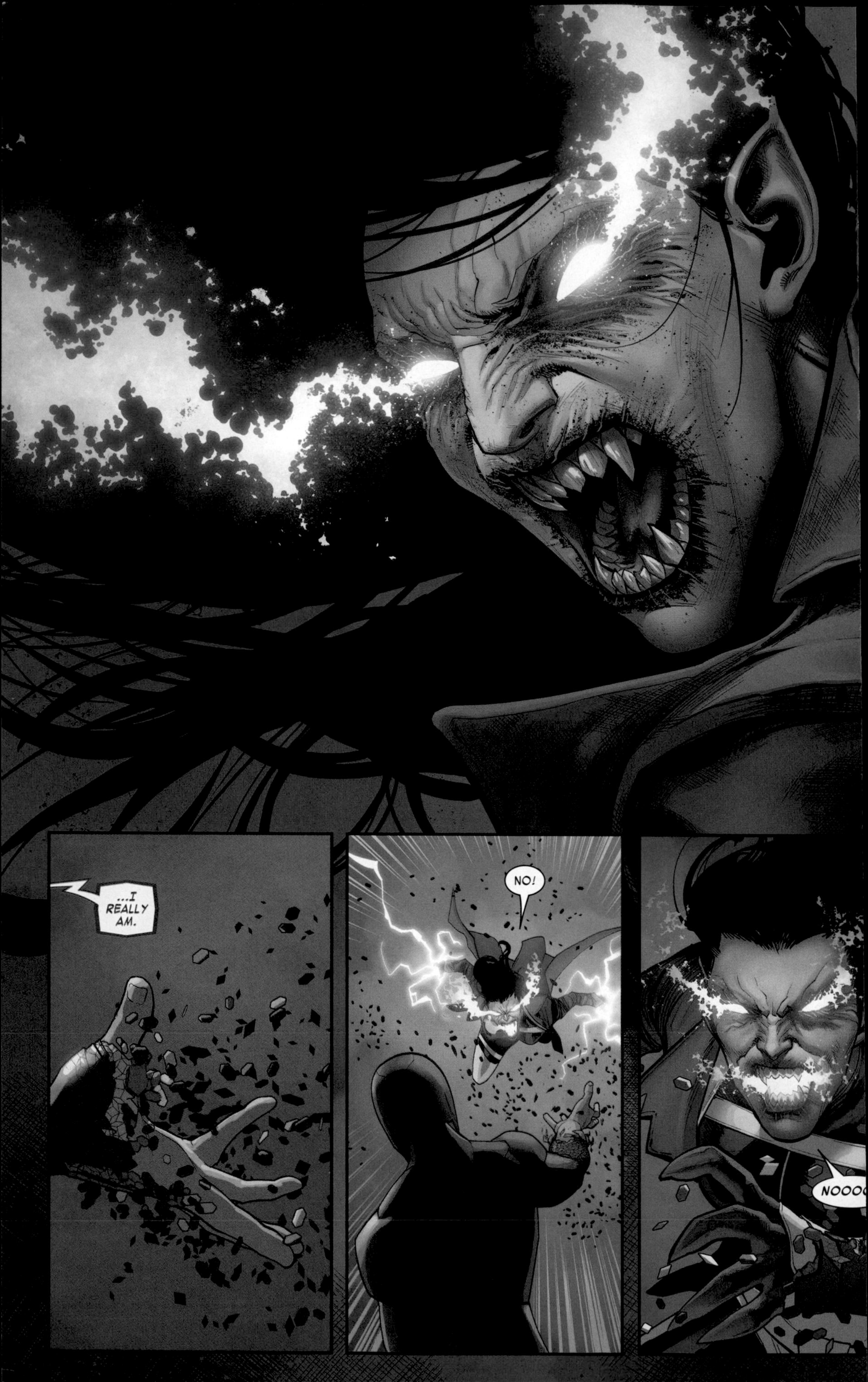
...I REALLY AM.
NO!
NOOO

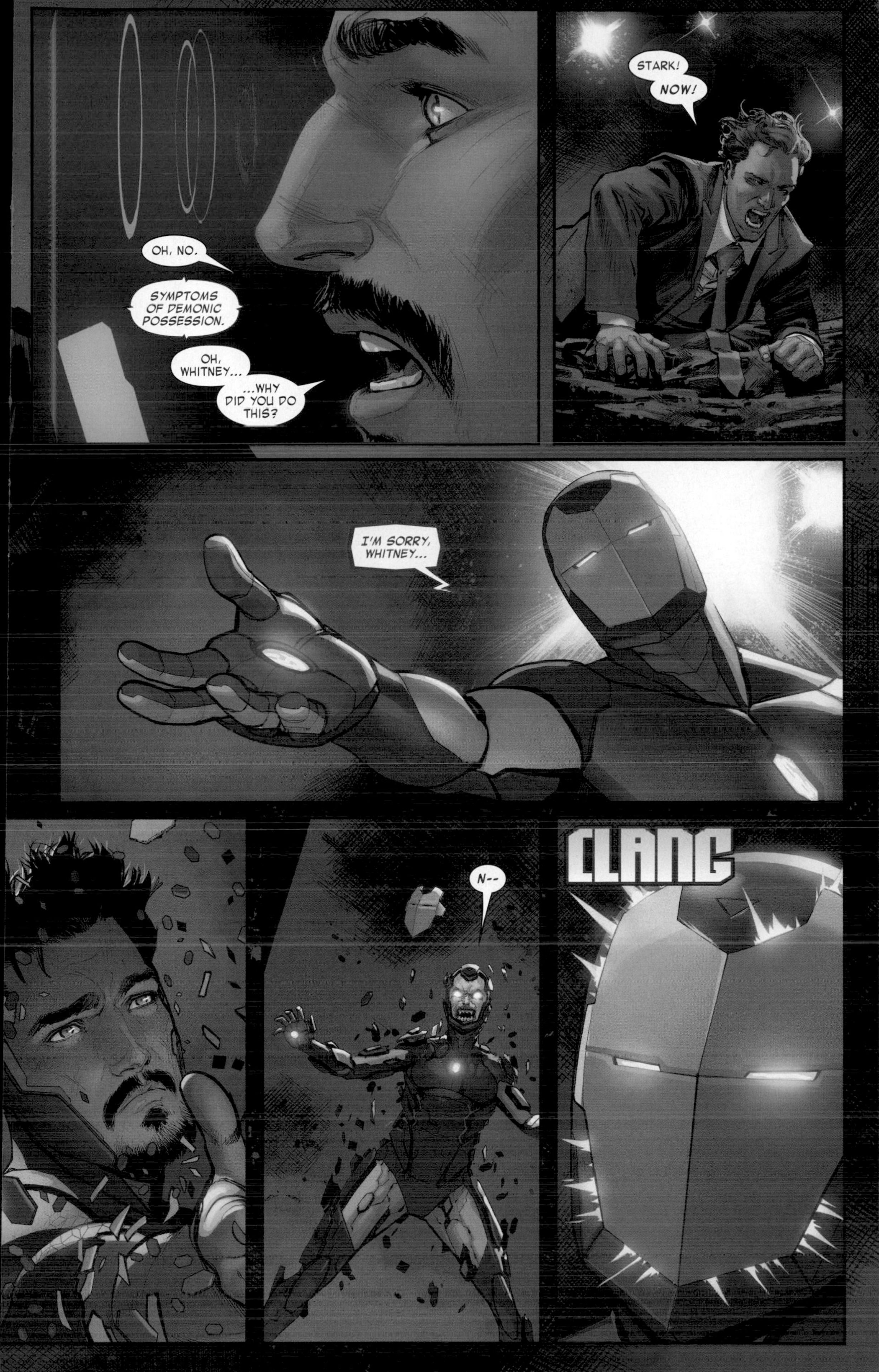
OH, NO.
SYMPTOMS OF DEMONIC POSSESSION.
OH, WHITNEY...
...WHY DID YOU DO THIS?
STARK! NOW!
I'M SORRY, WHITNEY...
N--
CLANG

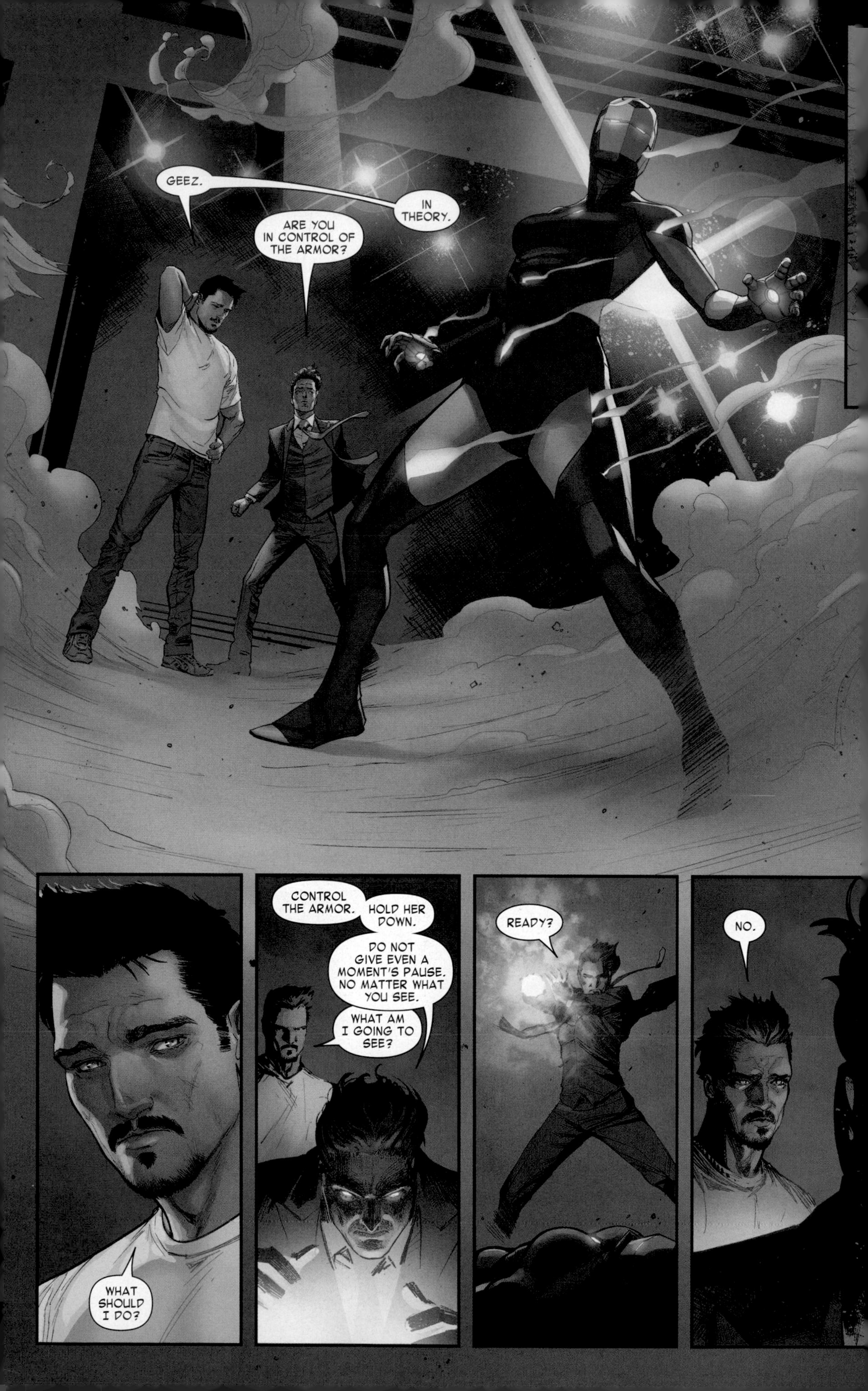
GEEZ.
ARE YOU IN CONTROL OF THE ARMOR?
IN THEORY.
WHAT SHOULD I DO?
CONTROL THE ARMOR.
HOLD HER DOWN.
DO NOT GIVE EVEN A MOMENT'S PAUSE. NO MATTER WHAT YOU SEE.
WHAT AM I GOING TO SEE?
READY?
NO.

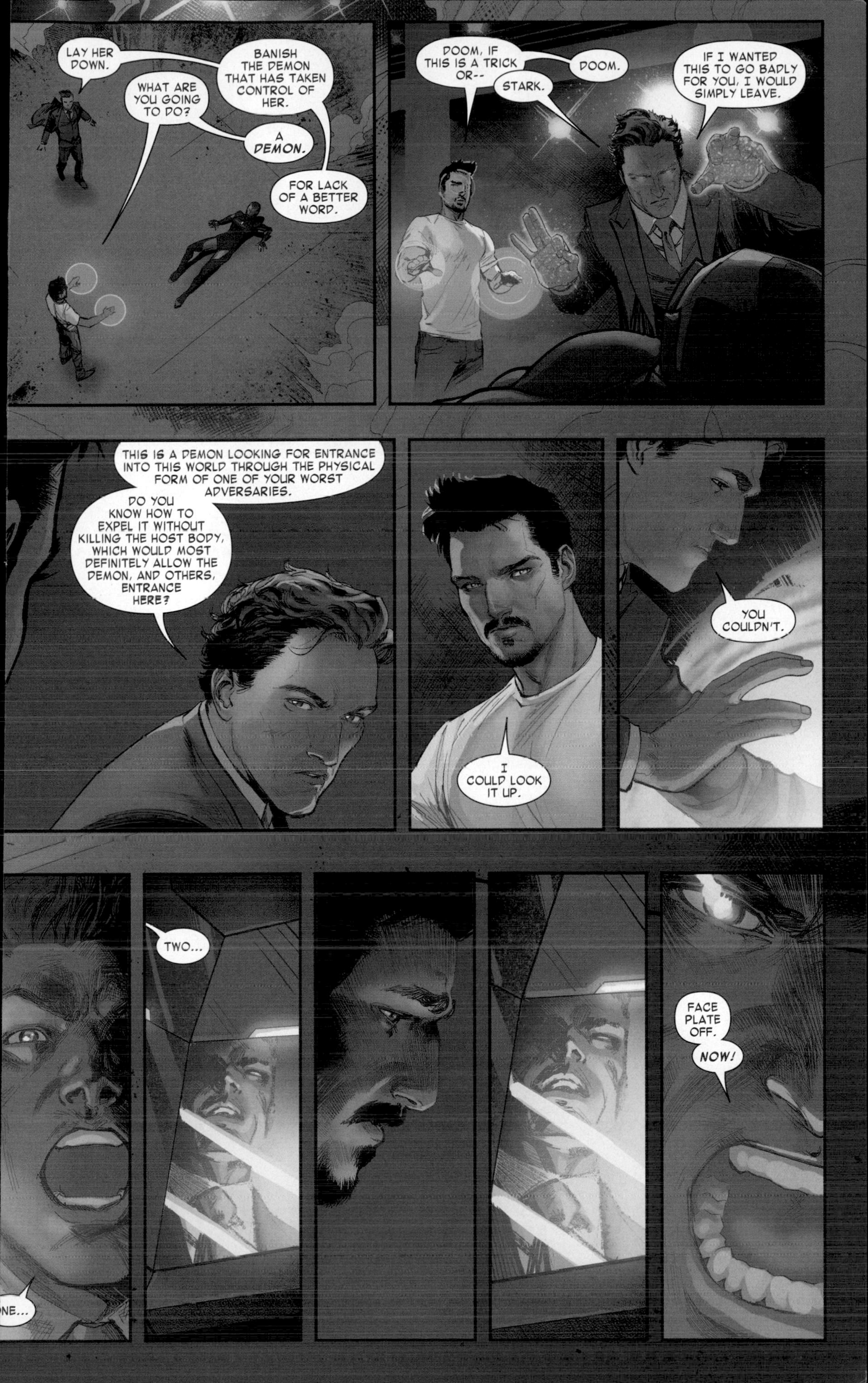
LAY HER DOWN.
WHAT ARE YOU GOING TO DO?
BANISH THE DEMON THAT HAS TAKEN CONTROL OF HER.
A *DEMON.*
FOR LACK OF A BETTER WORD.
DOOM, IF THIS IS A TRICK OR--
STARK.
DOOM.
IF I WANTED THIS TO GO BADLY FOR YOU, I WOULD SIMPLY LEAVE.
THIS IS A DEMON LOOKING FOR ENTRANCE INTO THIS WORLD THROUGH THE PHYSICAL FORM OF ONE OF YOUR WORST ADVERSARIES.
DO YOU KNOW HOW TO EXPEL IT WITHOUT KILLING THE HOST BODY, WHICH WOULD MOST DEFINITELY ALLOW THE DEMON, AND OTHERS, ENTRANCE HERE?
I COULD LOOK IT UP.
YOU COULDN'T.
ONE...
TWO...
FACE PLATE OFF.
NOW!

BACK TO WHERE YOU CAME!

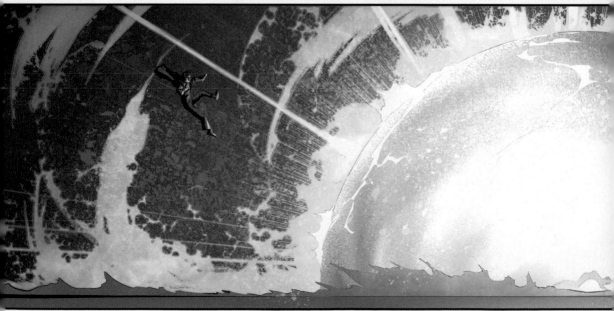

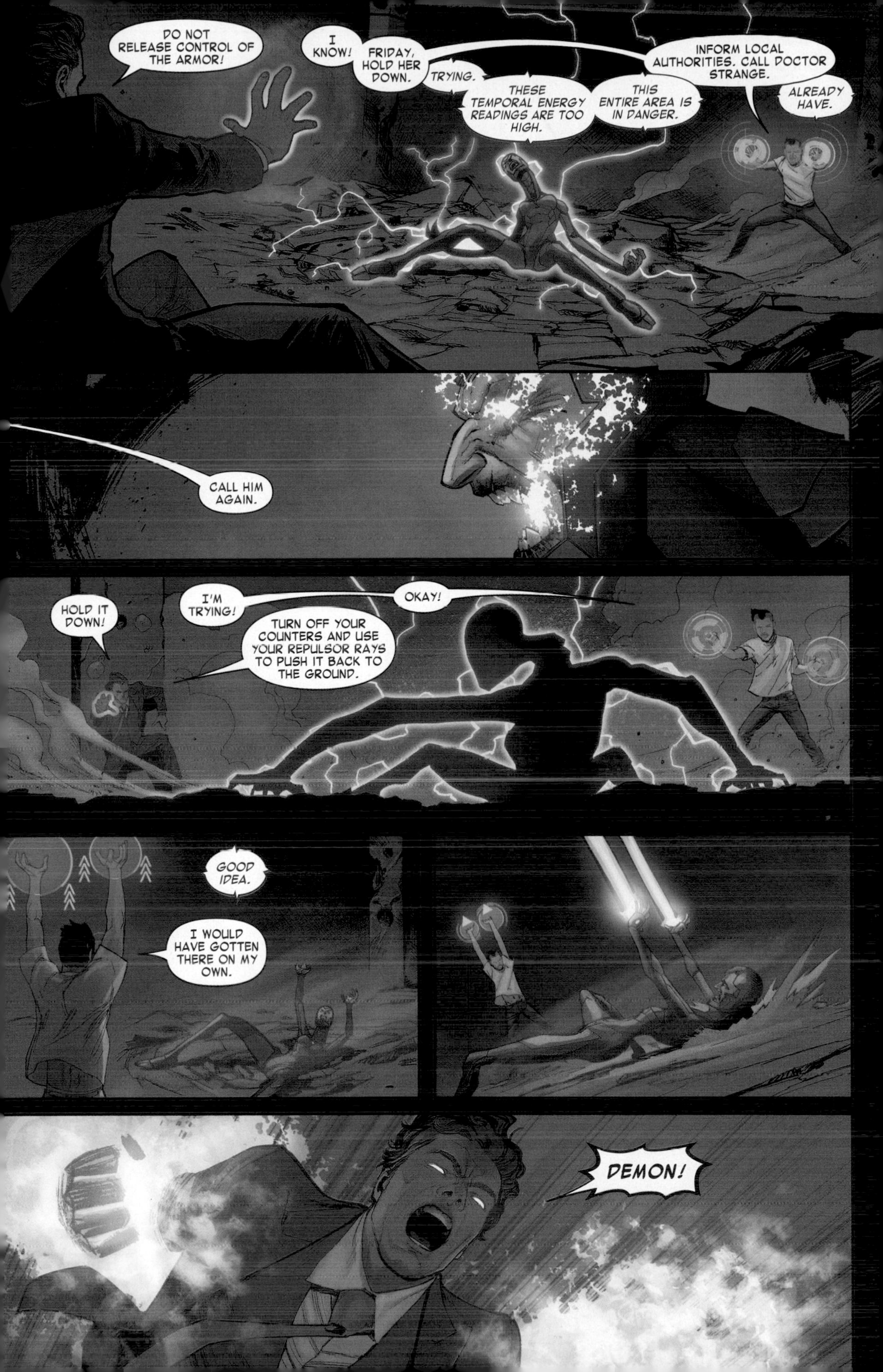
DO NOT RELEASE CONTROL OF THE ARMOR!
I KNOW!
FRIDAY, HOLD HER DOWN.
TRYING.
THESE TEMPORAL ENERGY READINGS ARE TOO HIGH.
THIS ENTIRE AREA IS IN DANGER.
INFORM LOCAL AUTHORITIES. CALL DOCTOR STRANGE.
ALREADY HAVE.
CALL HIM AGAIN.
HOLD IT DOWN!
I'M TRYING!
OKAY!
TURN OFF YOUR COUNTERS AND USE YOUR REPULSOR RAYS TO PUSH IT BACK TO THE GROUND.
GOOD IDEA.
I WOULD HAVE GOTTEN THERE ON MY OWN.
DEMON!

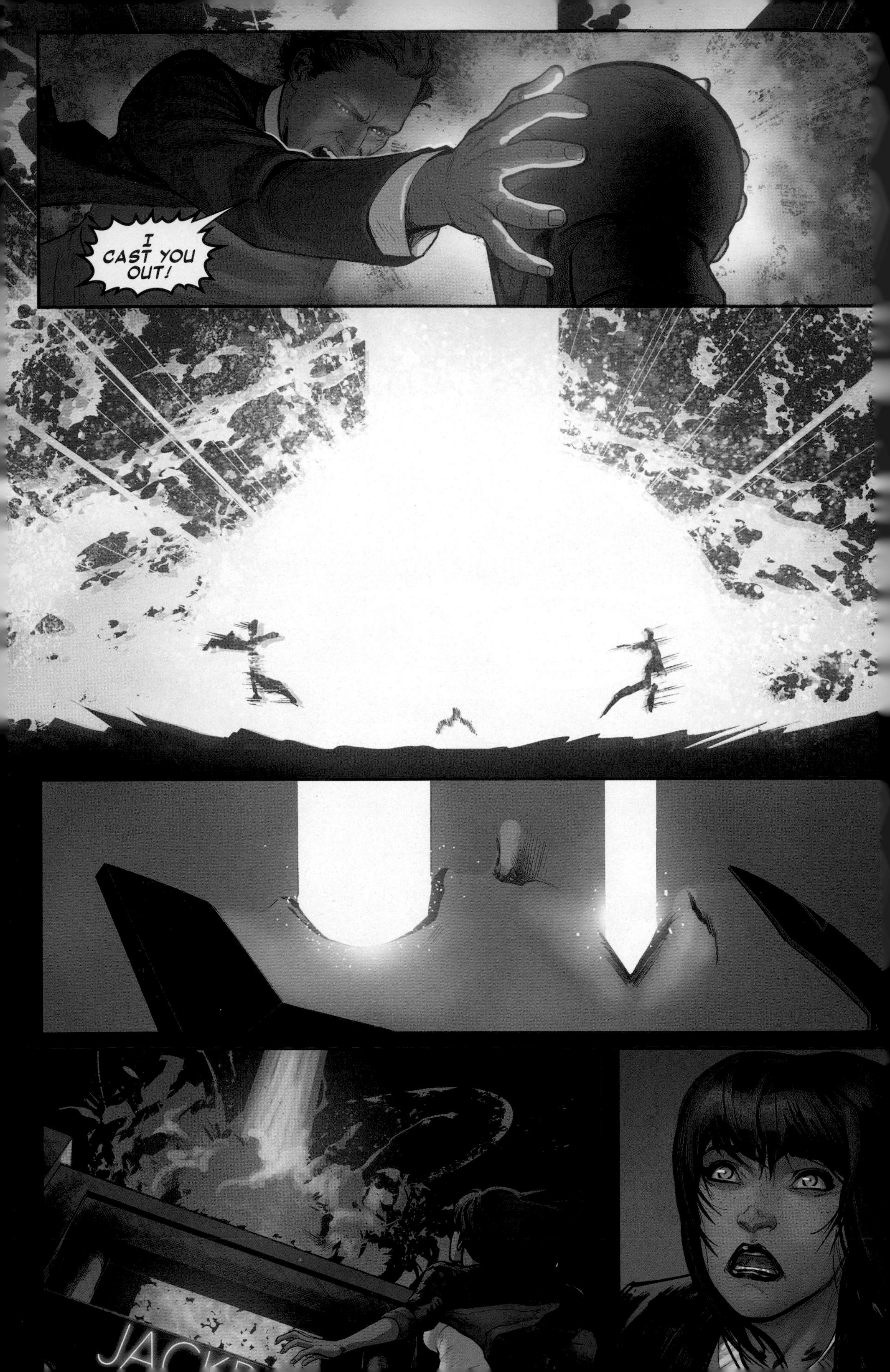
I CAST YOU OUT!

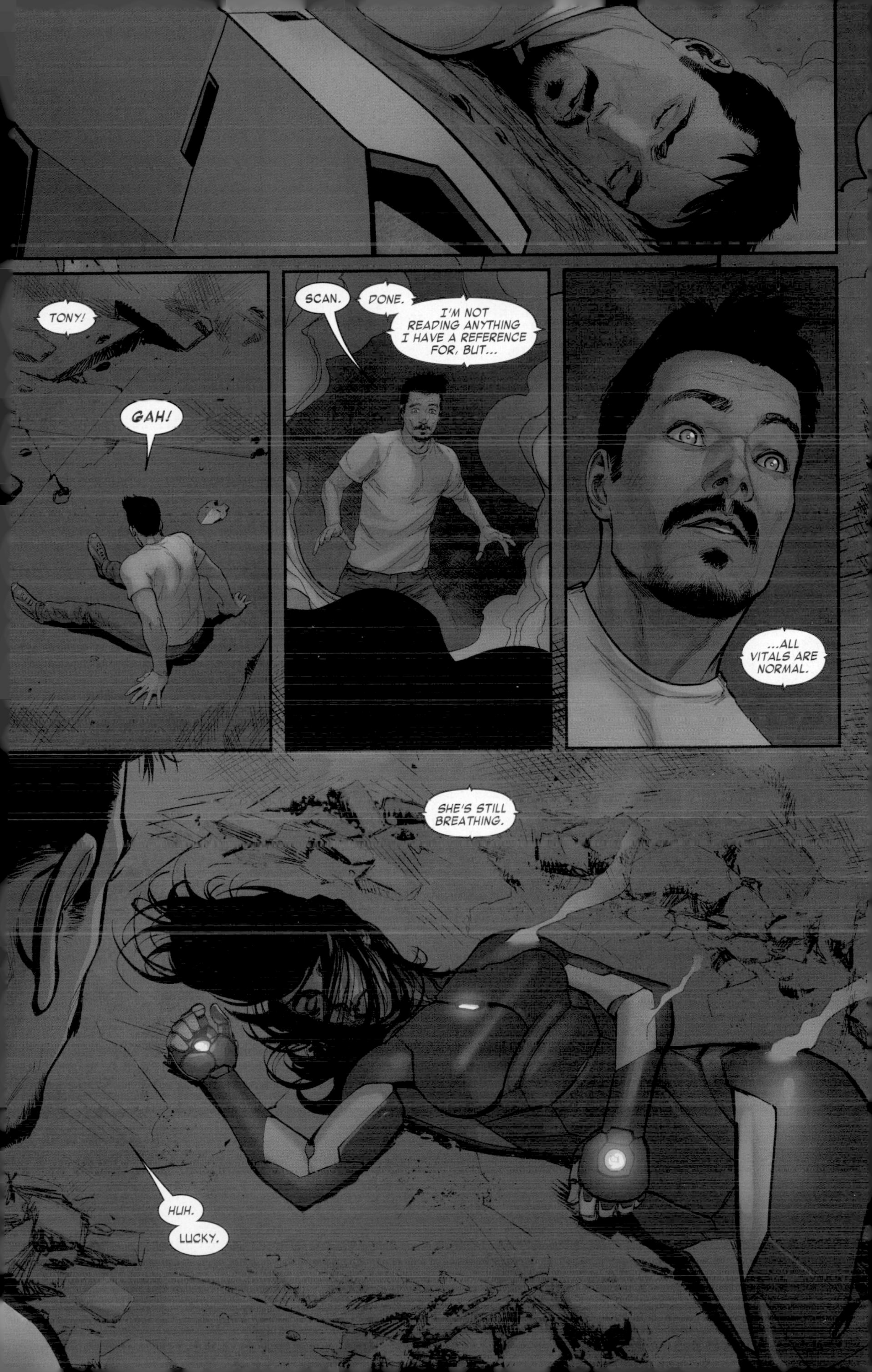
TONY!
GAH!
SCAN.
DONE.
I'M NOT READING ANYTHING I HAVE A REFERENCE FOR, BUT...
...ALL VITALS ARE NORMAL.
SHE'S STILL BREATHING.
HUH.
LUCKY.

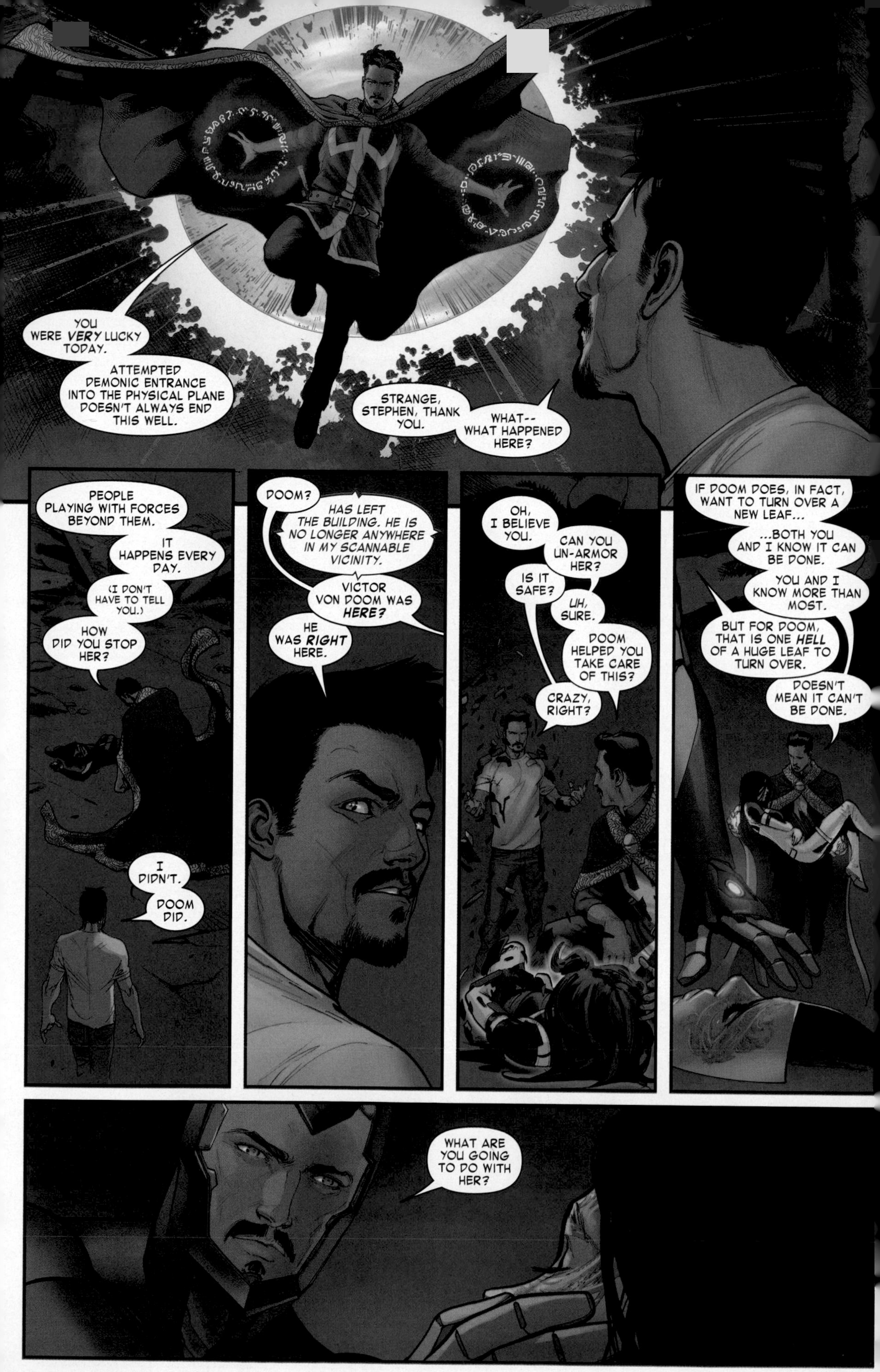
YOU WERE *VERY* LUCKY TODAY.
ATTEMPTED DEMONIC ENTRANCE INTO THE PHYSICAL PLANE DOESN'T ALWAYS END THIS WELL.
STRANGE, STEPHEN, THANK YOU.
WHAT-- WHAT HAPPENED HERE?
PEOPLE PLAYING WITH FORCES BEYOND THEM.
IT HAPPENS EVERY DAY.
(I DON'T HAVE TO TELL YOU.)
HOW DID YOU STOP HER?
I DIDN'T.
DOOM DID.
DOOM?
HAS LEFT THE BUILDING. HE IS NO LONGER ANYWHERE IN MY SCANNABLE VICINITY.
VICTOR VON DOOM WAS *HERE?*
HE WAS *RIGHT* HERE.
OH, I BELIEVE YOU.
CAN YOU UN-ARMOR HER?
IS IT SAFE?
UH, SURE.
DOOM HELPED YOU TAKE CARE OF THIS?
CRAZY, RIGHT?
IF DOOM DOES, IN FACT, WANT TO TURN OVER A NEW LEAF...
...BOTH YOU AND I KNOW IT CAN BE DONE.
YOU AND I KNOW MORE THAN MOST.
BUT FOR DOOM, THAT IS ONE *HELL* OF A HUGE LEAF TO TURN OVER.
DOESN'T MEAN IT CAN'T BE DONE.
WHAT ARE YOU GOING TO DO WITH HER?

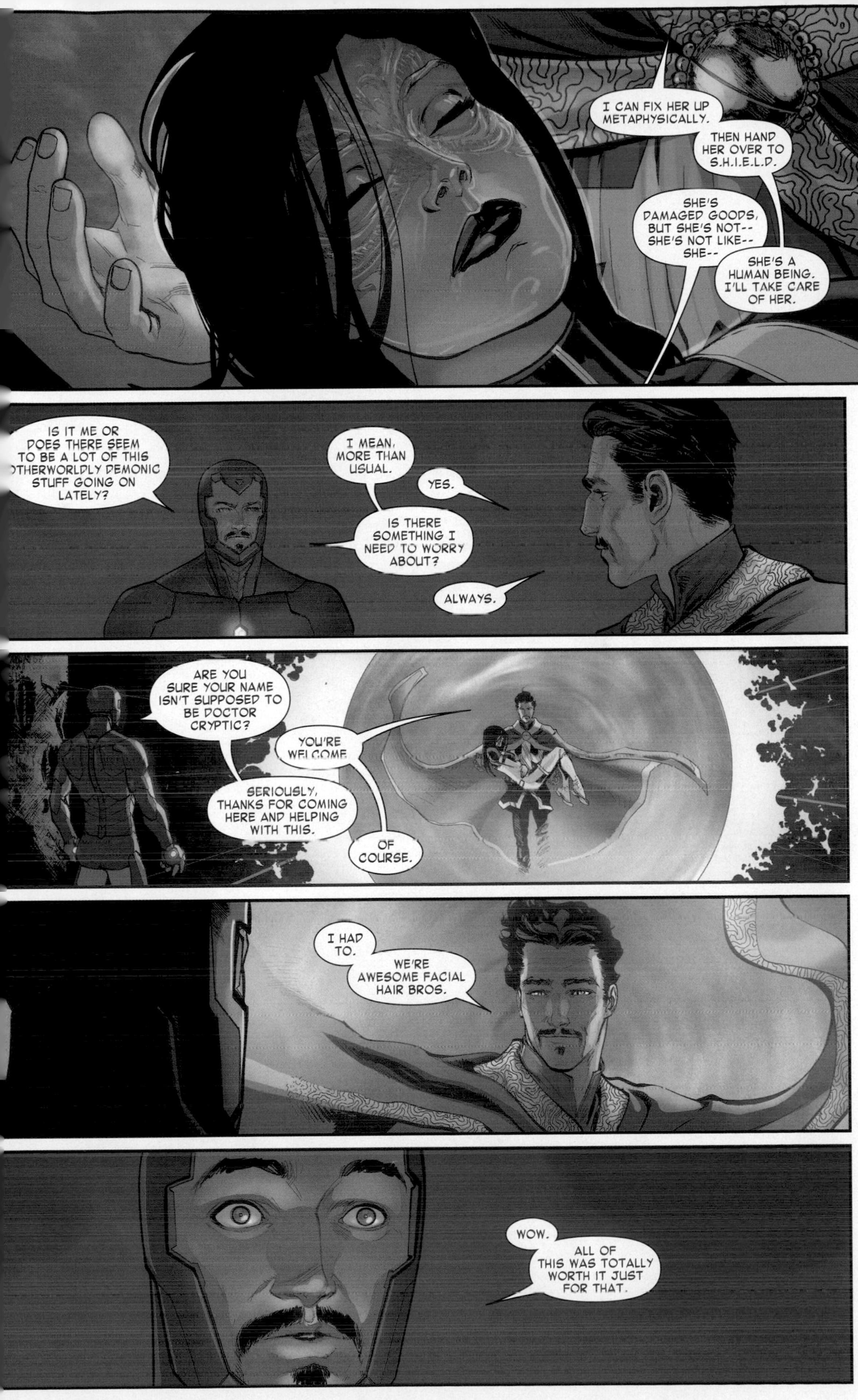

I CAN FIX HER UP METAPHYSICALLY.
THEN HAND HER OVER TO S.H.I.E.L.D.
SHE'S DAMAGED GOODS, BUT SHE'S NOT-- SHE'S NOT LIKE-- SHE--
SHE'S A HUMAN BEING. I'LL TAKE CARE OF HER.
IS IT ME OR DOES THERE SEEM TO BE A LOT OF THIS OTHERWORLDLY DEMONIC STUFF GOING ON LATELY?
YES.
I MEAN, MORE THAN USUAL.
IS THERE SOMETHING I NEED TO WORRY ABOUT?
ALWAYS.
ARE YOU SURE YOUR NAME ISN'T SUPPOSED TO BE DOCTOR CRYPTIC?
YOU'RE WELCOME.
SERIOUSLY, THANKS FOR COMING HERE AND HELPING WITH THIS.
OF COURSE.
I HAD TO.
WE'RE AWESOME FACIAL HAIR BROS.
WOW.
ALL OF THIS WAS TOTALLY WORTH IT JUST FOR THAT.

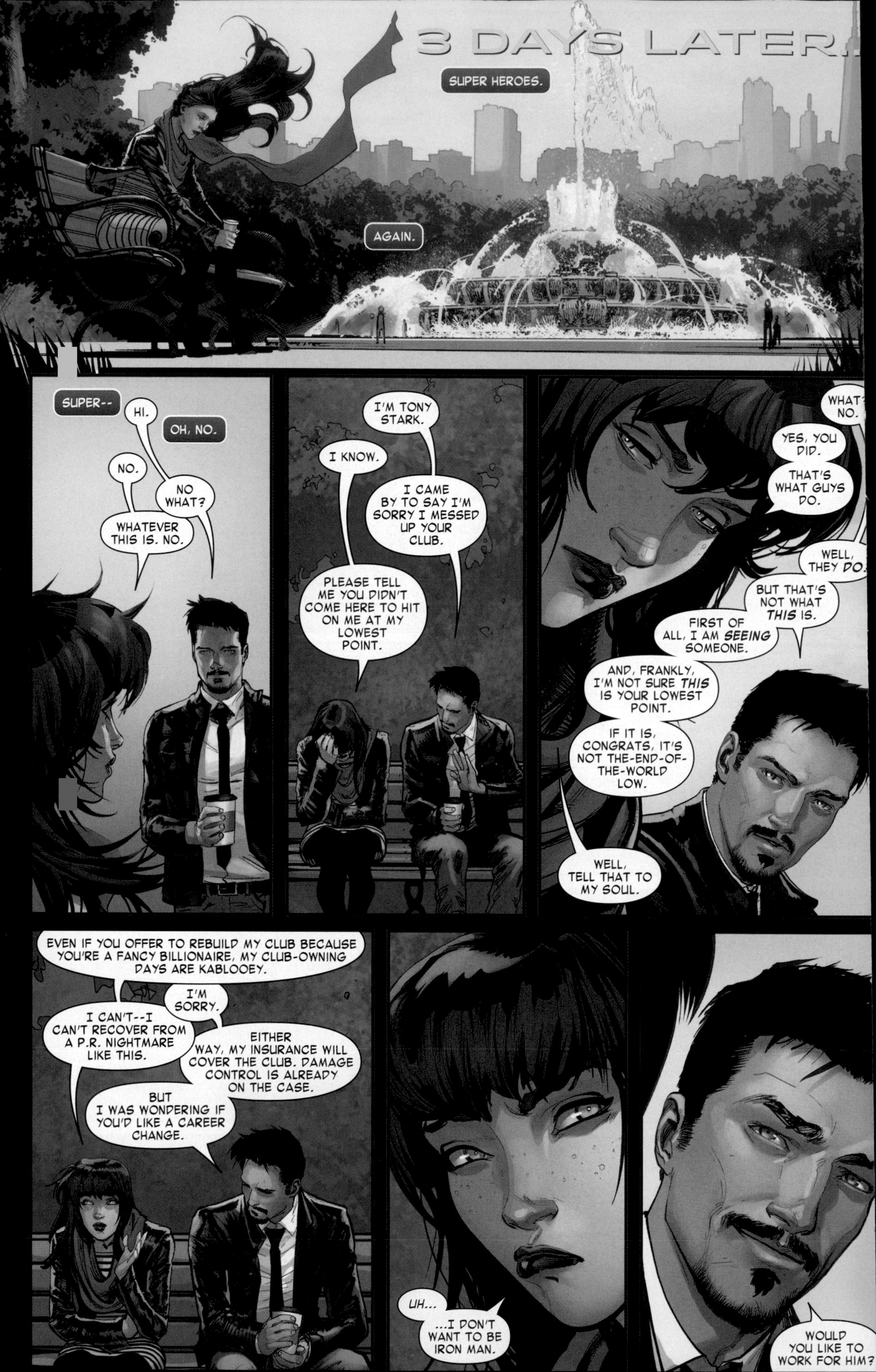
3 DAYS LATER...
SUPER HEROES.
AGAIN.
SUPER--
HI.
OH, NO.
NO.
NO WHAT?
WHATEVER THIS IS. NO.
I'M TONY STARK.
I KNOW.
I CAME BY TO SAY I'M SORRY I MESSED UP YOUR CLUB.
PLEASE TELL ME YOU DIDN'T COME HERE TO HIT ON ME AT MY LOWEST POINT.
WHAT? NO.
YES, YOU DID.
THAT'S WHAT GUYS DO.
WELL, THEY DO.
BUT THAT'S NOT WHAT THIS IS.
FIRST OF ALL, I AM SEEING SOMEONE.
AND, FRANKLY, I'M NOT SURE THIS IS YOUR LOWEST POINT.
IF IT IS, CONGRATS, IT'S NOT THE-END-OF-THE-WORLD LOW.
WELL, TELL THAT TO MY SOUL.
EVEN IF YOU OFFER TO REBUILD MY CLUB BECAUSE YOU'RE A FANCY BILLIONAIRE, MY CLUB-OWNING DAYS ARE KABLOOEY.
I'M SORRY.
I CAN'T--I CAN'T RECOVER FROM A P.R. NIGHTMARE LIKE THIS.
EITHER WAY, MY INSURANCE WILL COVER THE CLUB. DAMAGE CONTROL IS ALREADY ON THE CASE.
BUT I WAS WONDERING IF YOU'D LIKE A CAREER CHANGE.
UH...
...I DON'T WANT TO BE IRON MAN.
WOULD YOU LIKE TO WORK FOR HIM?

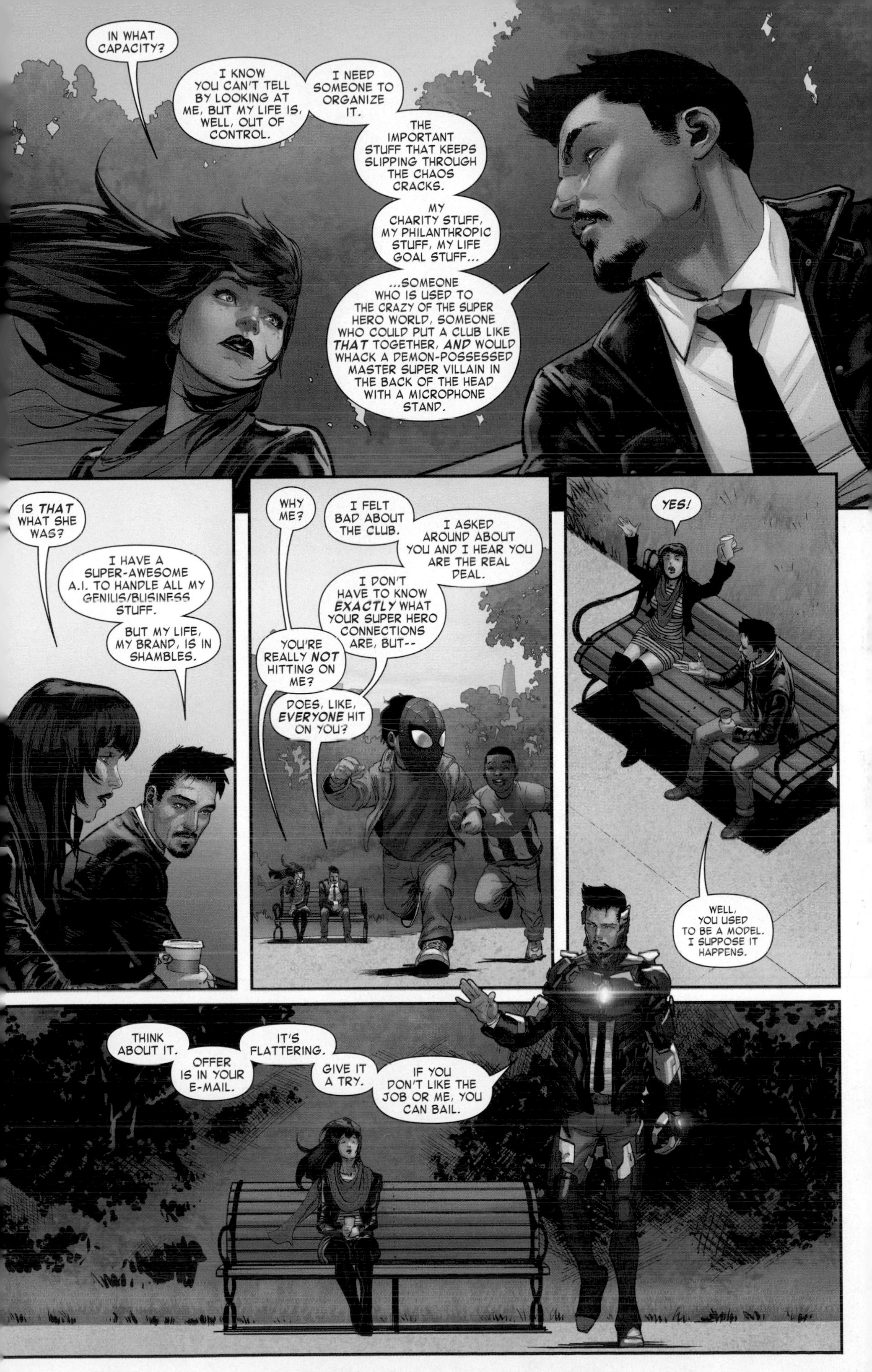
IN WHAT CAPACITY?
I KNOW YOU CAN'T TELL BY LOOKING AT ME, BUT MY LIFE IS, WELL, OUT OF CONTROL.
I NEED SOMEONE TO ORGANIZE IT.
THE IMPORTANT STUFF THAT KEEPS SLIPPING THROUGH THE CHAOS CRACKS.
MY CHARITY STUFF, MY PHILANTHROPIC STUFF, MY LIFE GOAL STUFF...
...SOMEONE WHO IS USED TO THE CRAZY OF THE SUPER HERO WORLD, SOMEONE WHO COULD PUT A CLUB LIKE *THAT* TOGETHER, *AND* WOULD WHACK A DEMON-POSSESSED MASTER SUPER VILLAIN IN THE BACK OF THE HEAD WITH A MICROPHONE STAND.
IS *THAT* WHAT SHE WAS?
I HAVE A SUPER-AWESOME A.I. TO HANDLE ALL MY GENIUS/BUSINESS STUFF.
BUT MY LIFE, MY BRAND, IS IN SHAMBLES.
WHY ME?
I FELT BAD ABOUT THE CLUB.
I ASKED AROUND ABOUT YOU AND I HEAR YOU ARE THE REAL DEAL.
I DON'T HAVE TO KNOW *EXACTLY* WHAT YOUR SUPER HERO CONNECTIONS ARE, BUT--
YOU'RE REALLY *NOT* HITTING ON ME?
DOES, LIKE, *EVERYONE* HIT ON YOU?
YES!
WELL, YOU USED TO BE A MODEL. I SUPPOSE IT HAPPENS.
THINK ABOUT IT.
OFFER IS IN YOUR E-MAIL.
IT'S FLATTERING.
GIVE IT A TRY.
IF YOU DON'T LIKE THE JOB OR ME, YOU CAN BAIL.

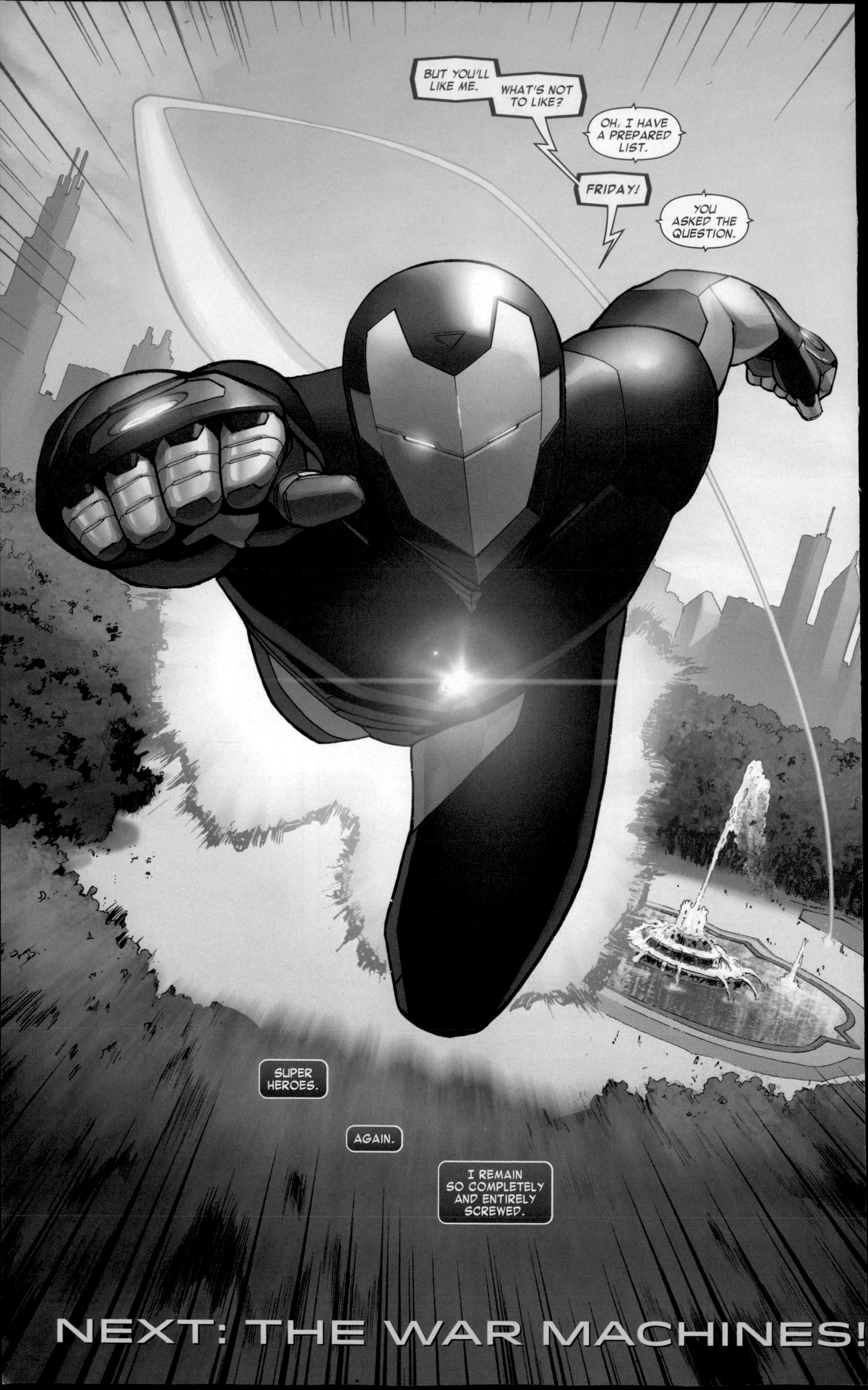
BUT YOU'LL LIKE ME.
WHAT'S NOT TO LIKE?
OH, I HAVE A PREPARED LIST.
FRIDAY!
YOU ASKED THE QUESTION.
SUPER HEROES.
AGAIN.
I REMAIN SO COMPLETELY AND ENTIRELY SCREWED.
NEXT: THE WAR MACHINES!

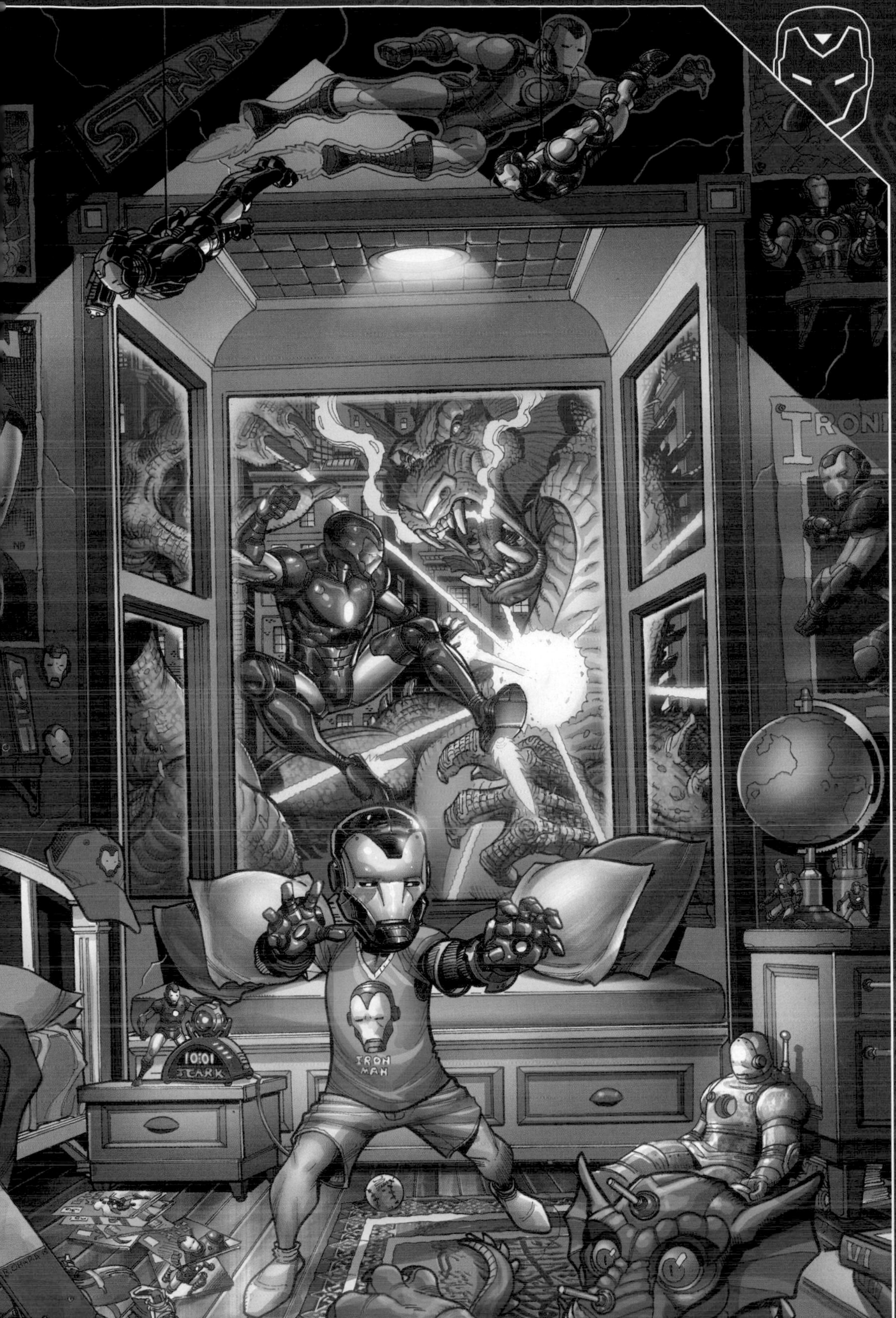
STARK
IRON
10:01
STARK
IRON MAN

#1 YOUNG GUNS VARIANT BY NICK BRADSHAW & PAUL MOUNTS

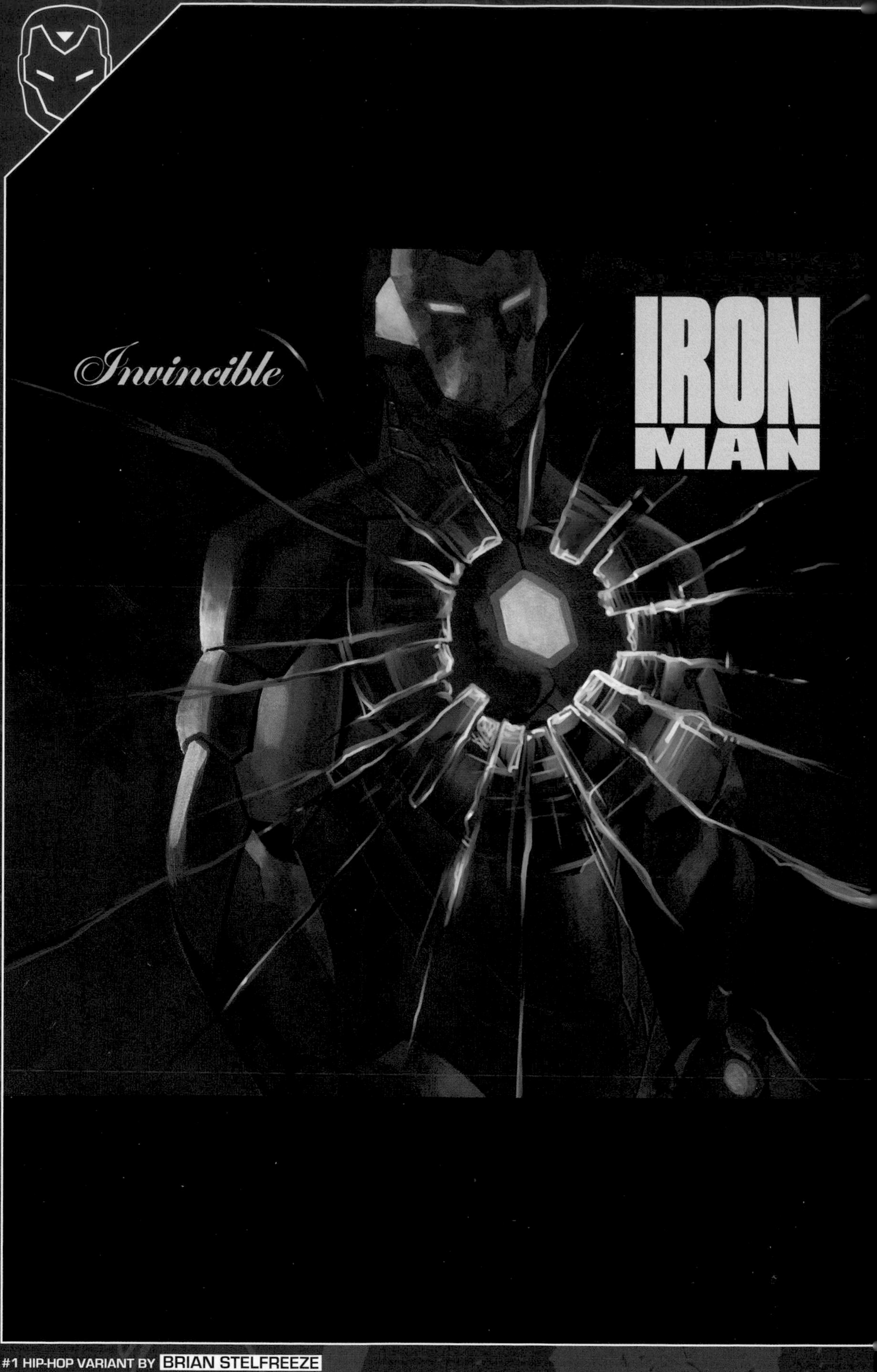
Invincible
IRON
MAN

#1 HIP-HOP VARIANT BY BRIAN STELFREEZE

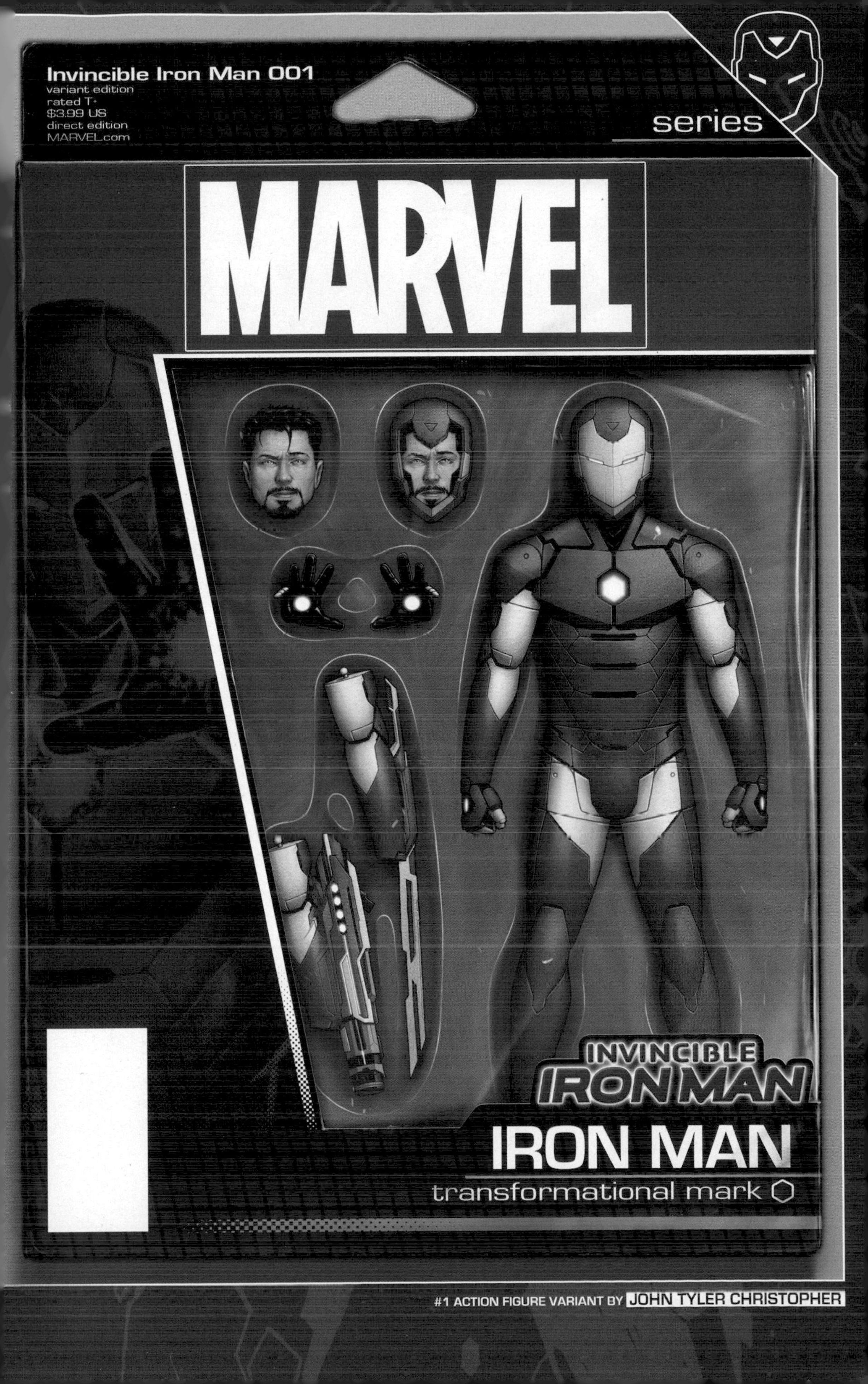
Invincible Iron Man 001
variant edition
rated T+
$3.99 US
direct edition
MARVEL.com
series
MARVEL
INVINCIBLE
IRON MAN
IRON MAN
transformational mark
#1 ACTION FIGURE VARIANT BY JOHN TYLER CHRISTOPHER

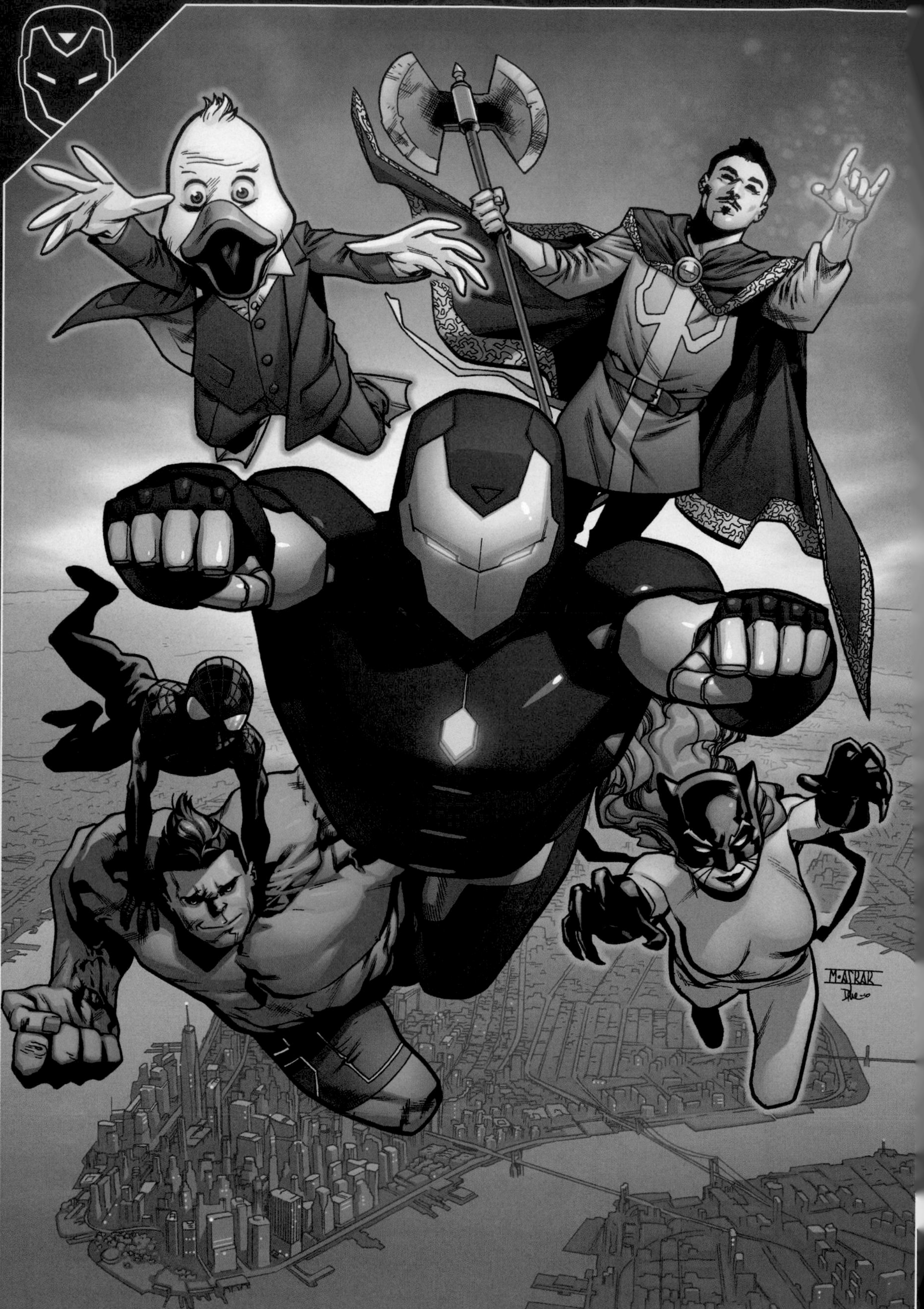
M. ASRAR

#1 NYCC VARIANT BY MAHMUD ASRAR & DAVE MCCAIG

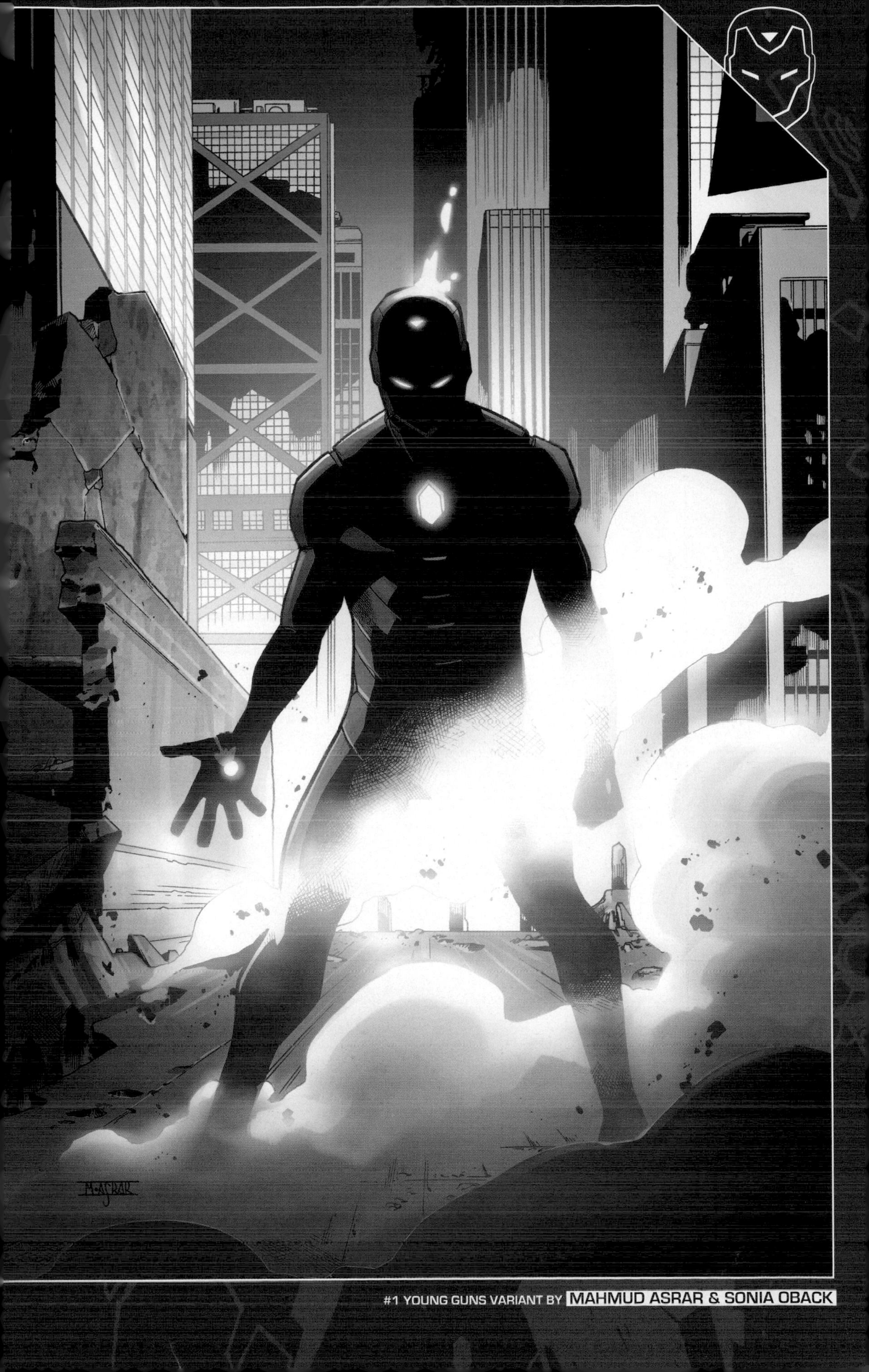

#1 YOUNG GUNS VARIANT BY MAHMUD ASRAR & SONIA OBACK

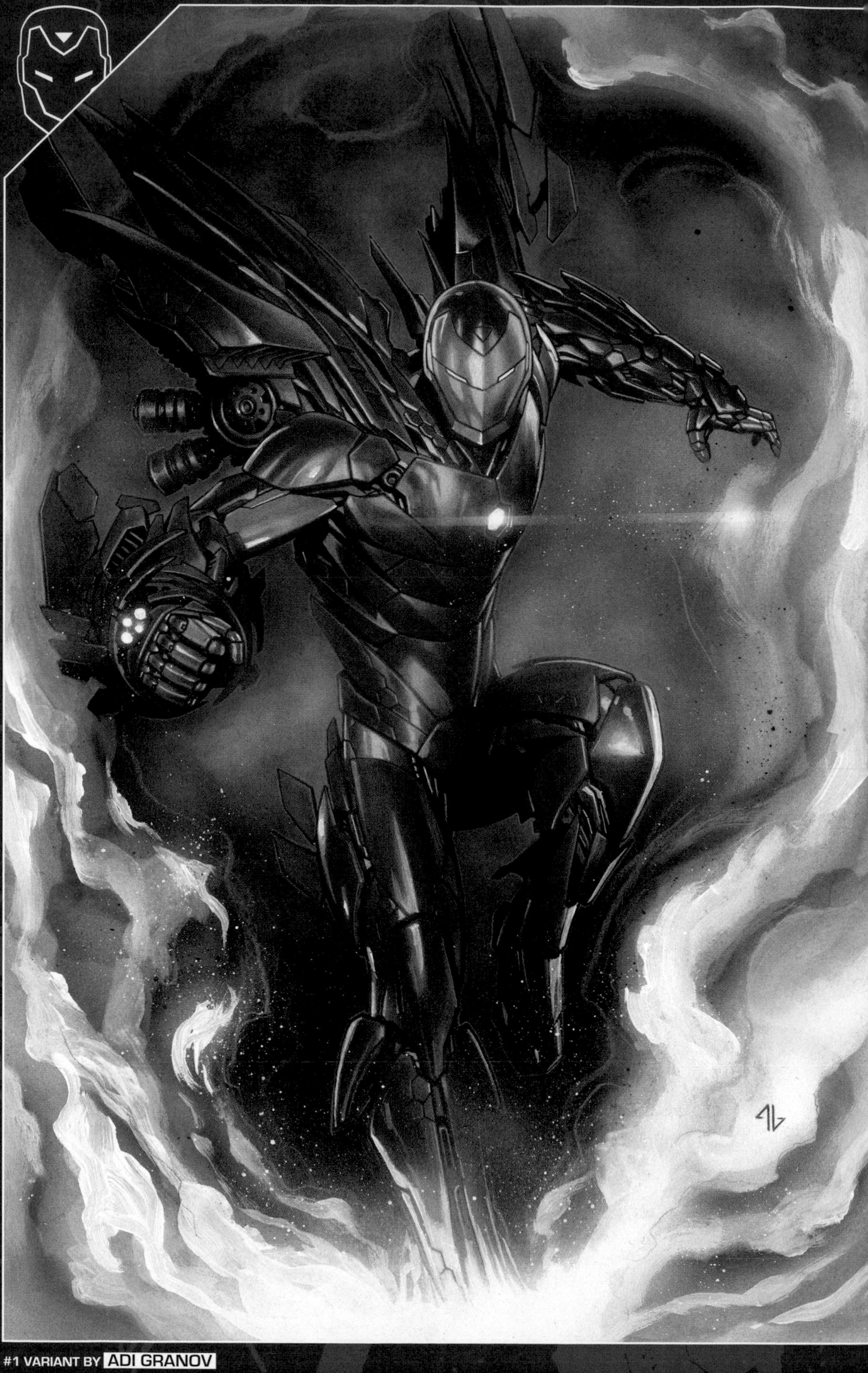

#1 VARIANT BY ADI GRANOV

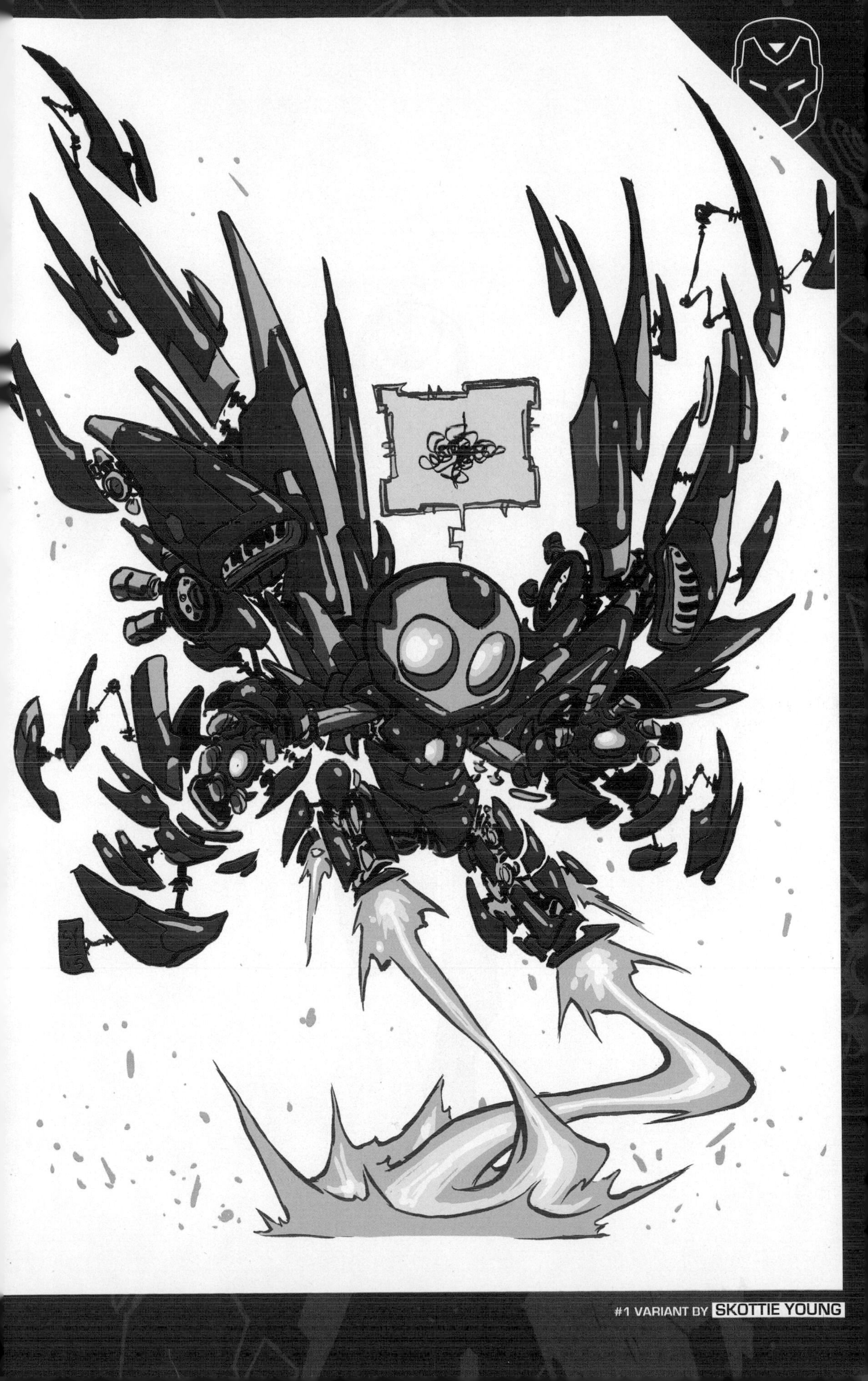

#1 VARIANT BY SKOTTIE YOUNG

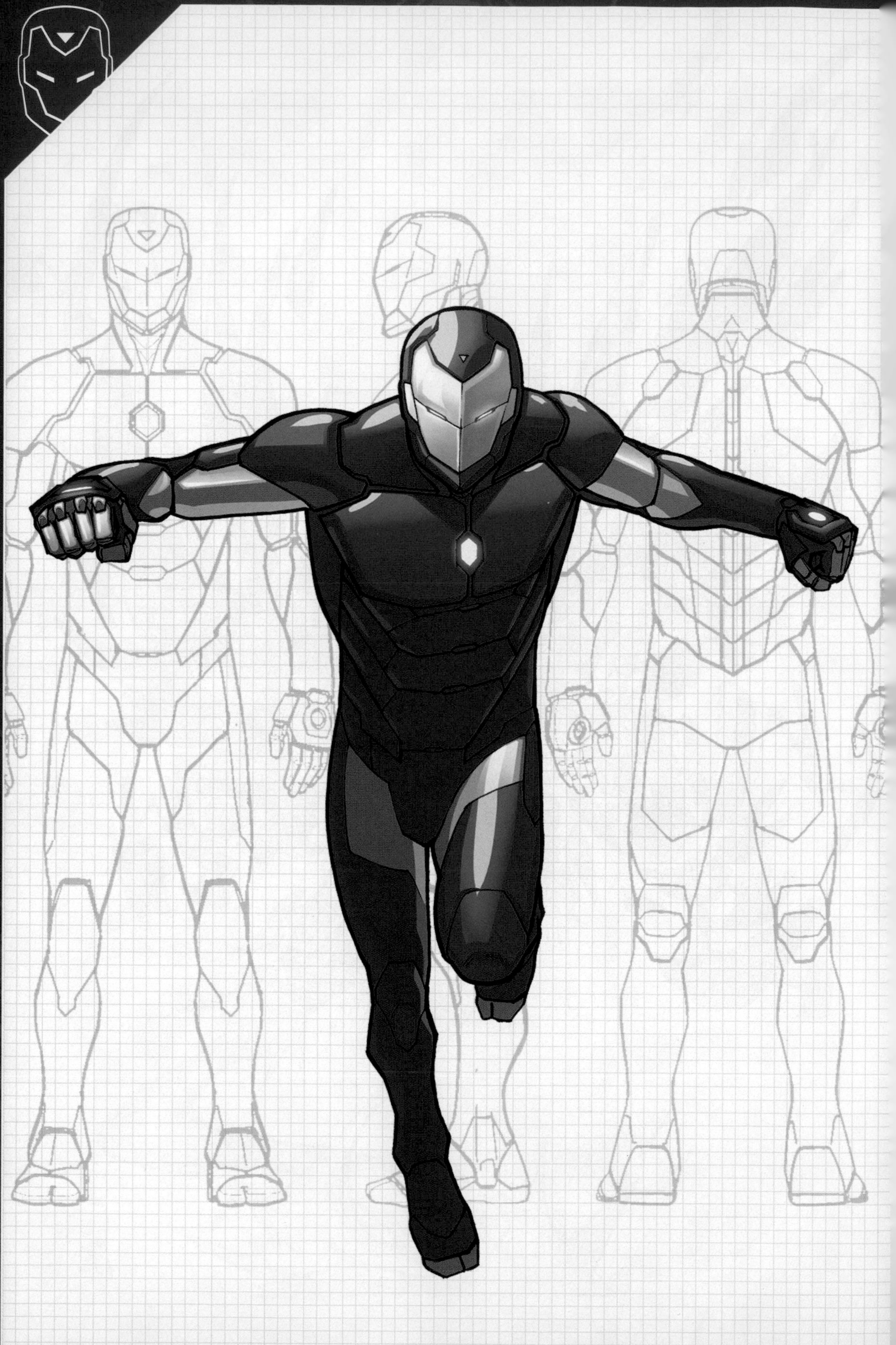

#1 YOUNG GUNS VARIANT BY DAVID MARQUEZ & MATTHEW WILSON

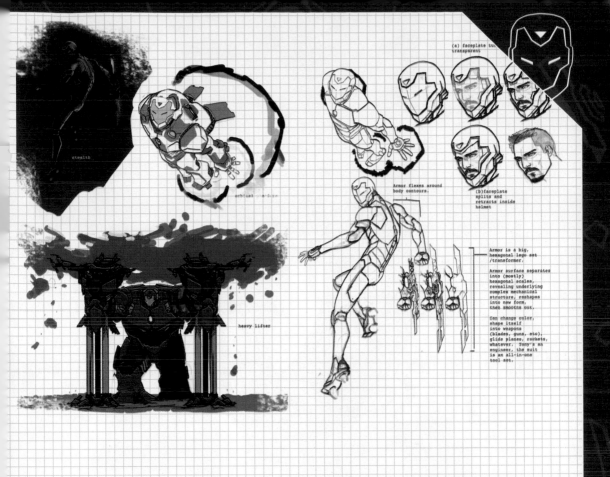

stealth

orbital strike

heavy lifter

(a) faceplate turns transparent

(b) faceplate splits and retracts inside helmet

Armor flexes around body contours.

Armor is a big, hexagonal lego set /transformer.

Armor surface separates into (mostly) hexagonal scales, revealing underlying complex mechanical structure, reshapes into new form, then smooths out.

Can change color, shape itself into weapons (blades, guns, etc), glide planes, rockets, whatever. Tony's an engineer, the suit is an all-in-one tool set.

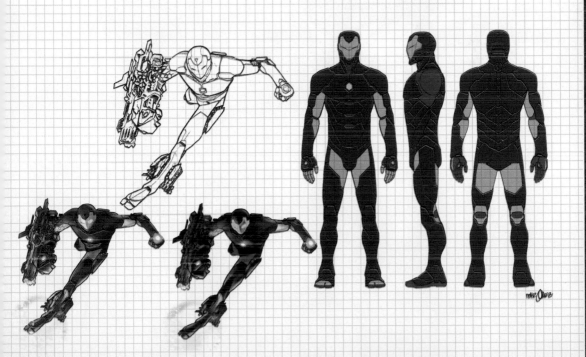

#1 DESIGN VARIANT BY DAVID MARQUEZ

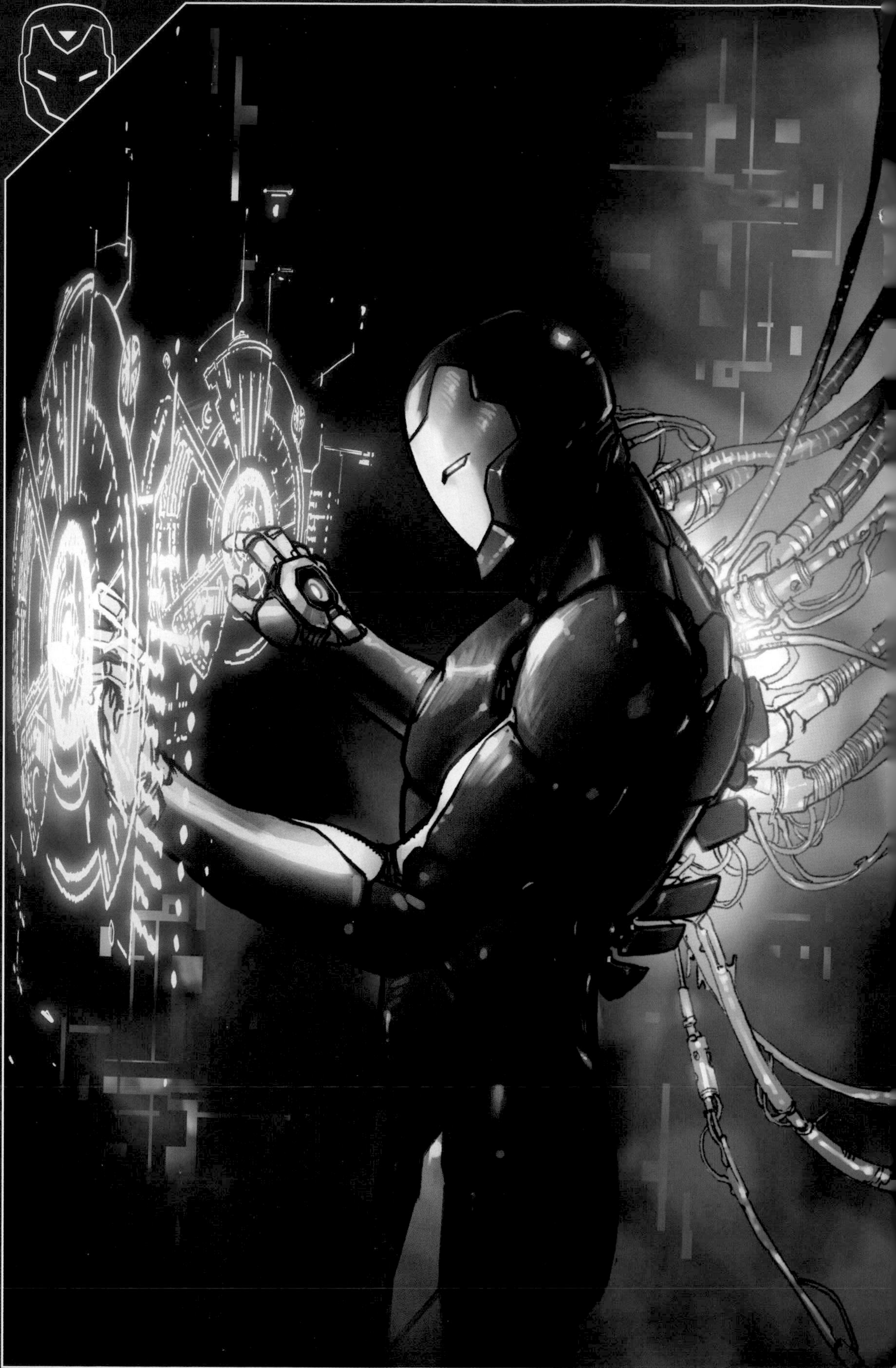

#1 YOUNG GUNS VARIANT BY SARA PICHELLI & JASON KEITH

WHO?
WHO?
WHO?

#1 PARTY VARIANT BY YASMINE PUTRI

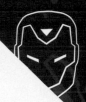

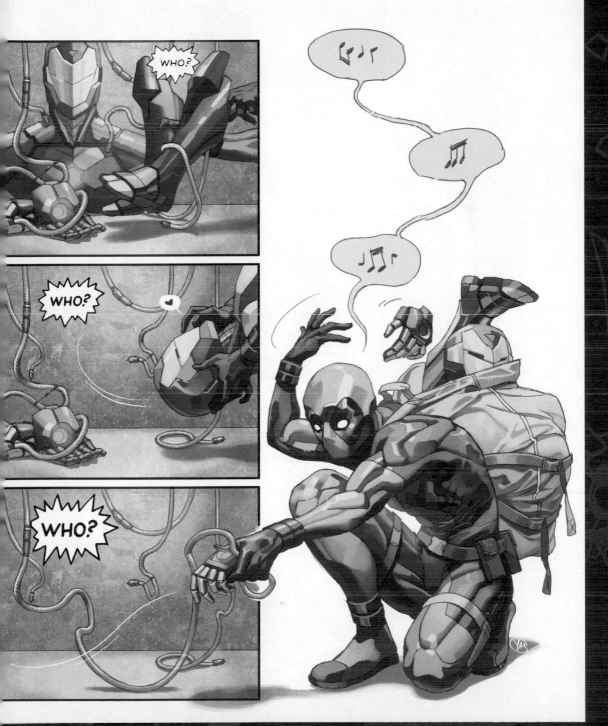

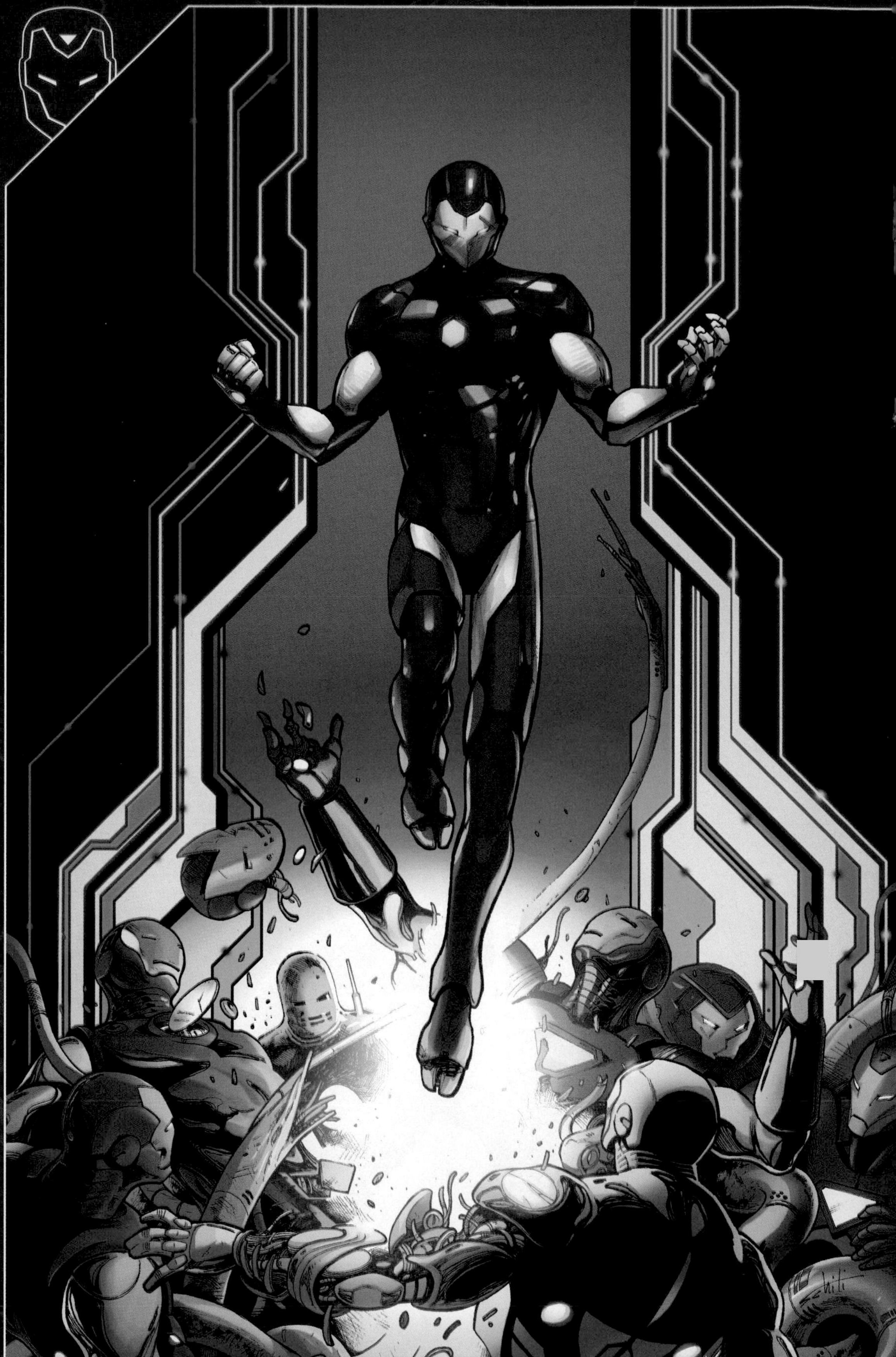

#1 YOUNG GUNS VARIANT BY VALERIO SCHITI & JASON KEITH

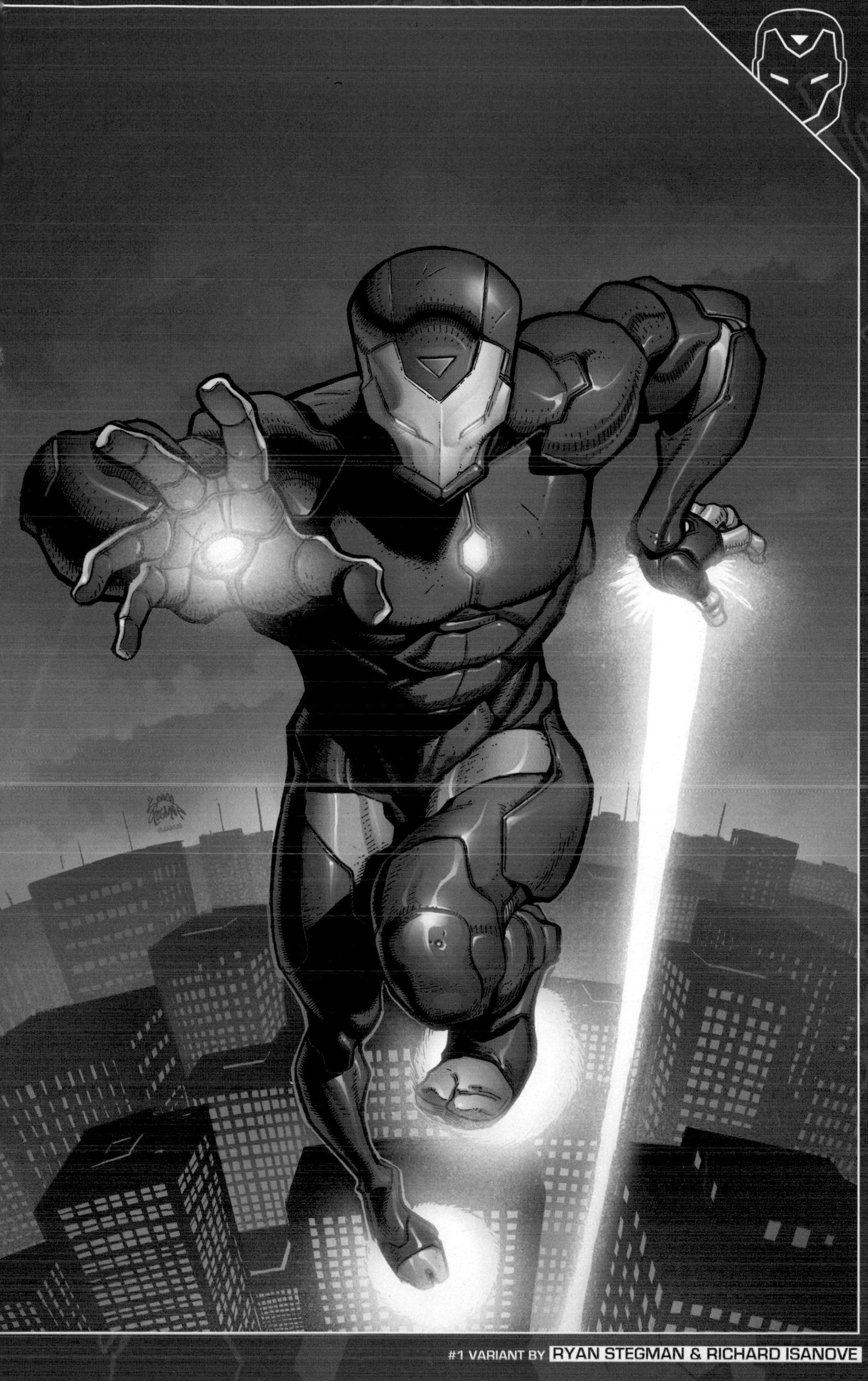

#1 VARIANT BY RYAN STEGMAN & RICHARD ISANOVE

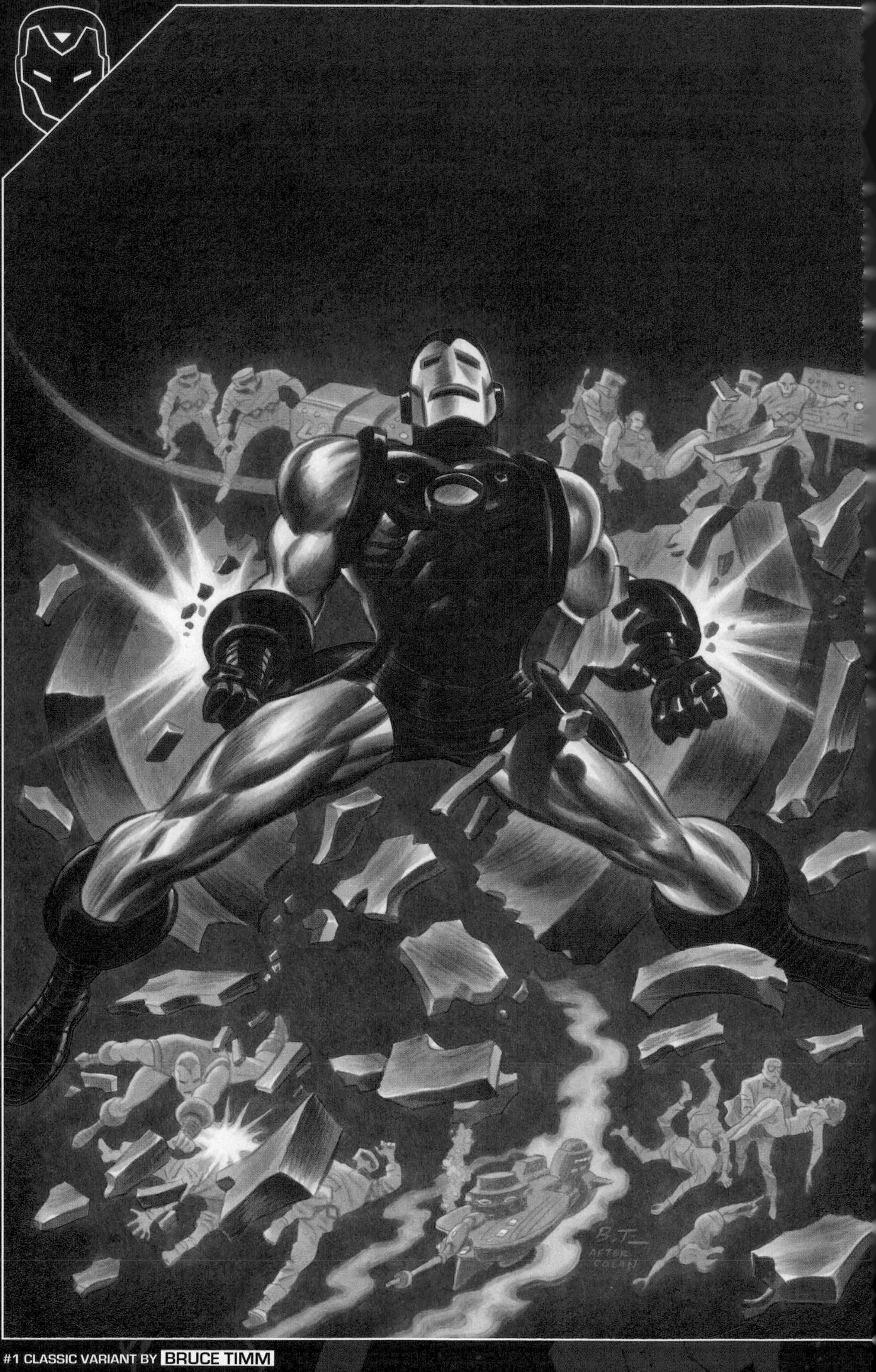
B.T. AFTER COLAN

#1 CLASSIC VARIANT BY **BRUCE TIMM**

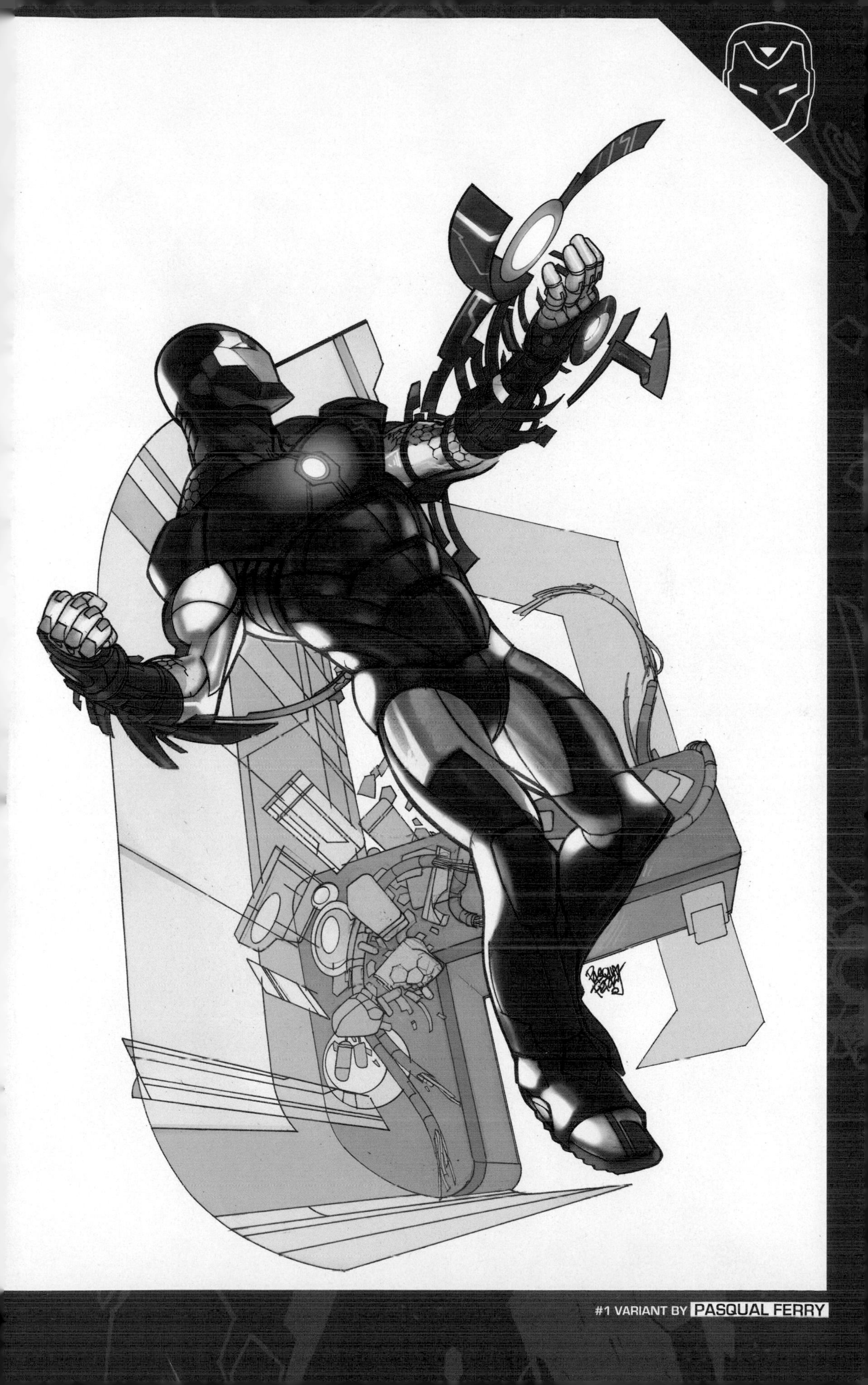

#1 VARIANT BY PASQUAL FERRY

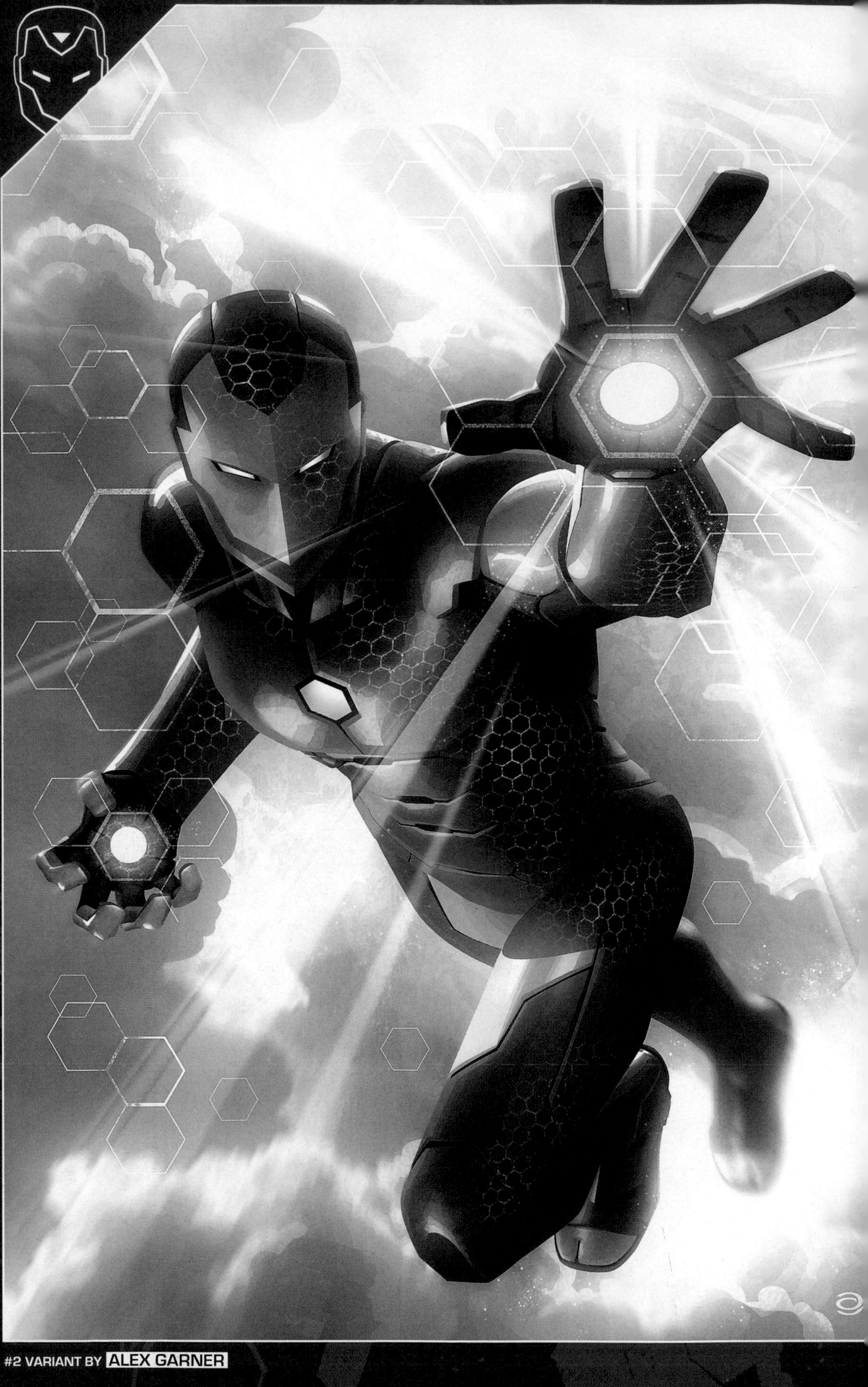

#2 VARIANT BY ALEX GARNER

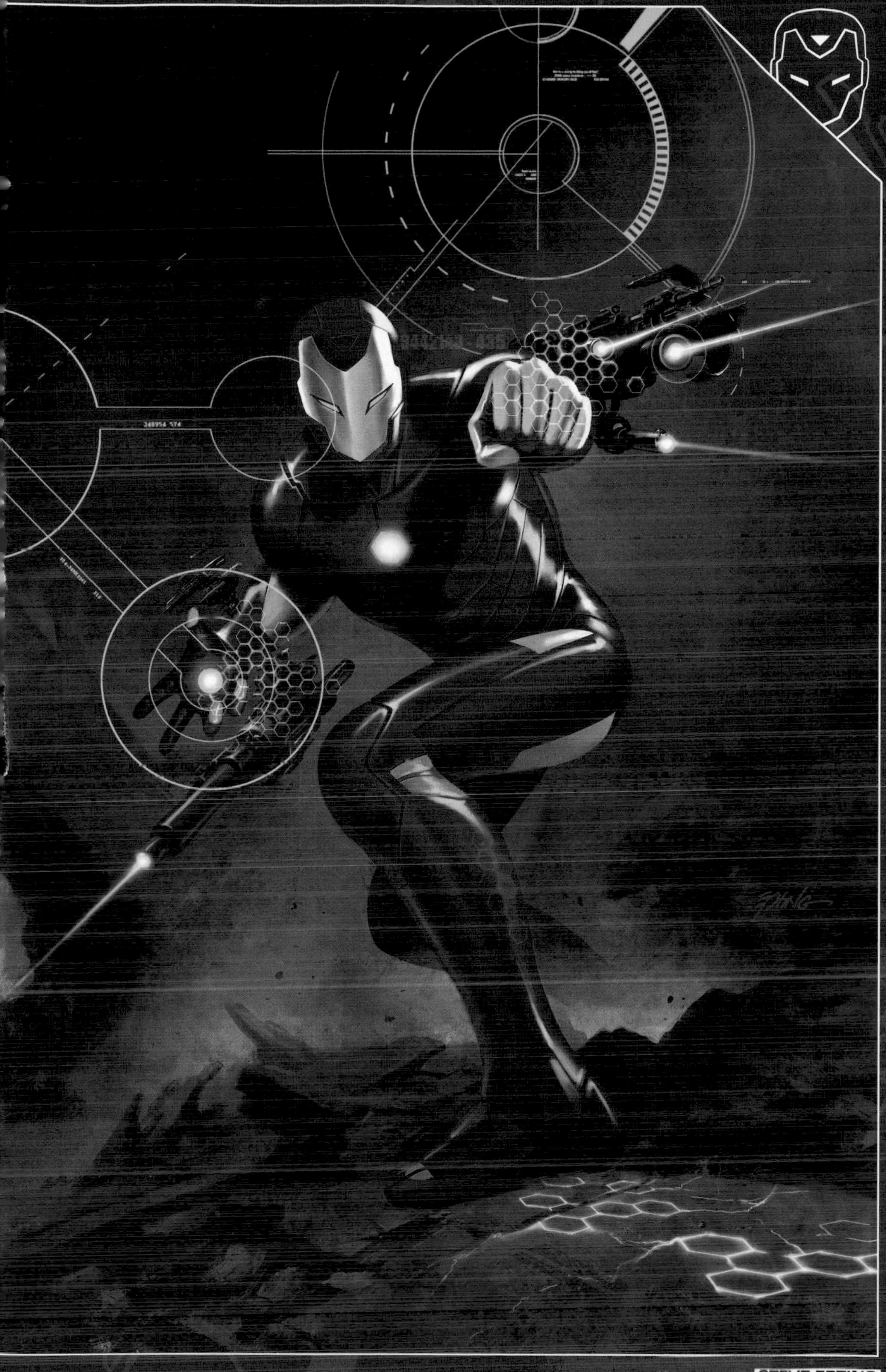

#3 VARIANT BY STEVE EPTING

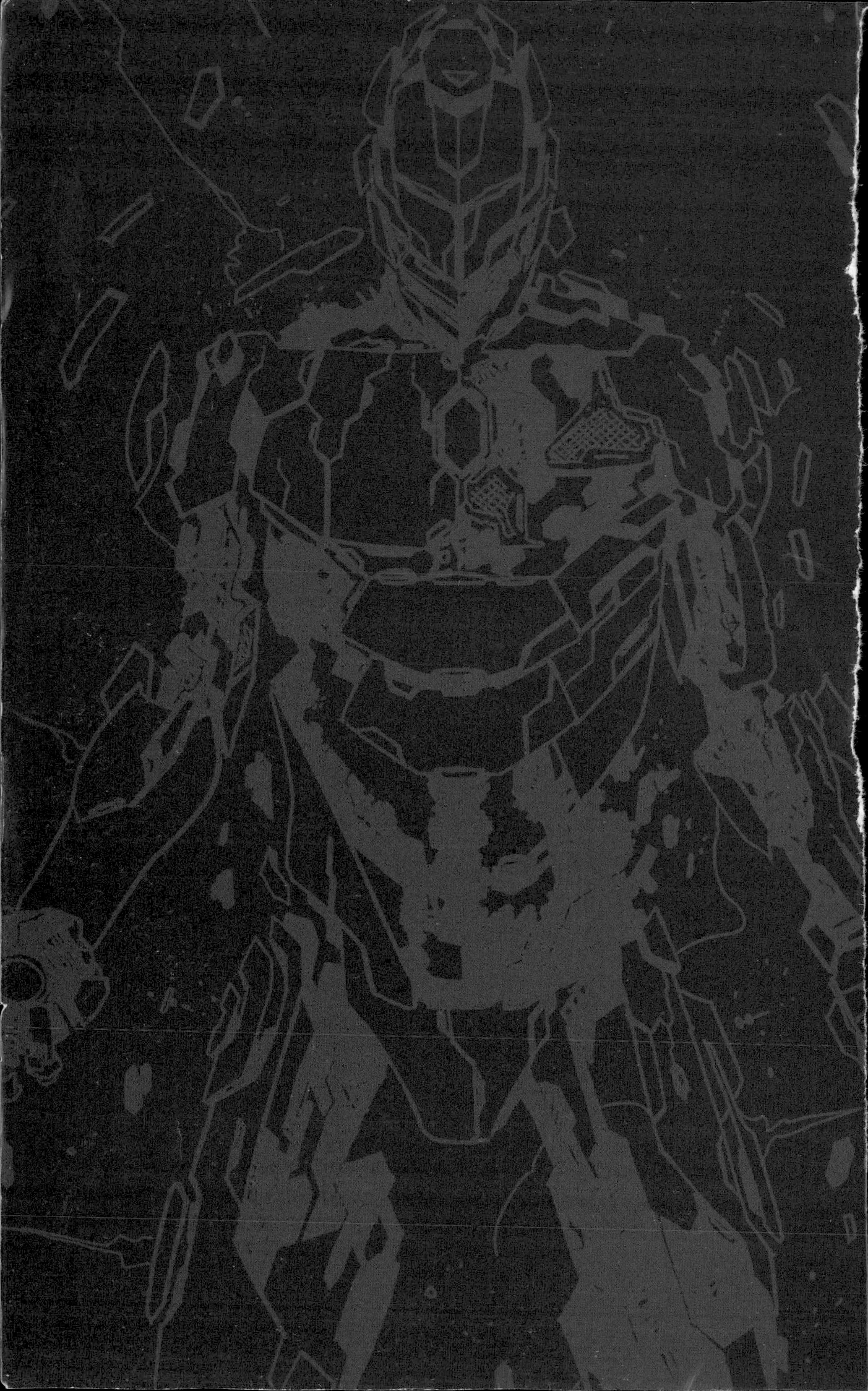